A Woman in the Crossfire

A Woman in the Crossfire

Diaries of the Syrian Revolution

Samar Yazbek

Translated from the Arabic by Max Weiss

This book has been translated with the assistance of the Sharjah International Book Fair Translation Grant Fund

Haus Publishing
London

First published in 2012 by
Haus Publishing Ltd
70 Cadogan Place
London SW1X 9AH
www.hauspublishing.com

A CIP catalogue record for this book is available from the British Library

ISBN 978-1-908323-12-5
eISBN 978-1-908323-14-9

Typeset in Warnock by MacGuru Ltd
Printed and bound by CPI Group (UK) Ltd, Croydon, CR0 4YY

This book has been selected to receive financial assistance from English
PEN's Writers in Translation programme supported by Bloomberg.
English PEN exists to promote literature and its understanding, uphold
writers' freedoms around the world, campaign against the persecution and
imprisonment of writers for stating their views, and promote the friendly
co-operation of writers and free exchange of ideas.

cross-ˈfire, n.
where an individual or a political or military group is within
range of two or more lines of fire, from both enemy and ally alike.
Also *fig.*

FOREWORD

by Rafik Schami

Sometimes reality is more fantastic than a story created by the imagination could hope to be. A talented documentary filmmaker can, with the help of a good cameraman, turn an occurrence into an outstanding film, which surpasses any movie. To make a non-fiction account sound poetic yet real is much harder, since the author only has words as creative tools. Few have this gift. Samar Yazbek is one of them.

For one hundred days, the Syrian writer and filmmaker documented the revolution in her country – up close and personal. Not only that: she actively took part in it. And whenever the situation allowed it she wrote down what she had experienced in the hours and days before, what she felt and thought; all in impressive, powerful language. Powerful because despite the brutal murders, all the dead and dying around her, despite the fear for her own safety and that of her daughter, the tears and the interrogations by the security forces, she writes poetically. It is this poetic phrasing, which allows readers to truly experience the *intifada* in the company of Samar Yazbek, without feeling crushed by it, or struggling to breathe.

As mentioned, Samar Yazbek was an active witness. And while

she was risking her life, she helped wounded demonstrators and comforted children whose parents had been detained. But even more impressive than her courage was her attitude towards her clan, the Alawites, Syria's ruling minority. It is the stand she took against them that endangered her life. In her hometown she was branded a traitor – the green light for the regimes's murderous thugs, known as the *shabbiha*, to go after her. The *shabbiha* are killers, criminals, mercenaries who do the regime's dirty work for little pay. They kill without batting an eyelid. Samar Yazbek had to proceed with utmost caution; she knew every step she took in the street could have been her last.

Where does this extraordinary woman find the courage to abandon all the securities of a well-to-do Alawite family and to declare her solidarity with Syria's oppressed? The disappointment of her family is palpable on every page. Samar Yazbek was born into a respected Alawite family in Jableh in 1970, the very year that Assad's father toppled his own associates in a coup and established an unprecedented dictatorship based on clan and religious affiliation. Syria, once a lively and vibrant country, was turned into a kind of Assad family farm. Samar Yazbek, in other words, belongs to a generation that has known no system other than the current one. She wrote short stories and TV screenplays (even for the state TV station) and produced documentaries and she became famous for her novels, in which she crosses boundaries and ignores rules; writing about forbidden love, corrupt politicians and the claustrophobia and hypocrisy of living within her clan. Syria's professional moral guardians did not hold back their criticism of her books. But she was privileged and hence not punished.

Samar Yazbek is a feminist and cultural activist. Her family, and the connections they afforded her, allowed her a degree of freedom not enjoyed by others but she was not blinded by it. Long before the outbreak of the revolution on 15 March 2011, she acted with great courage. Her sensitive solidarity with the weak and disenfranchised in Syria led to a direct confrontation with Assad. Samar Yazbek quickly joined the protest movement.

The Assad regime was happy to overlook an author illicitly inserting erotic passages into her novels; the ruling clan were never overtly religious. When the Alawite President prayed in the Umayyad Mosque, the Great Mosque of Damascus, with the Sunni Mufti, it was nothing more than hypocrisy. No Alawite bought that show, as the Umayyahs were deadly enemies of Ali, the Prophet Muhammad's son-in-law, from whom the Alawites derive their name. The situation became much more serious when the intellectuals began to take action. The regime was being directly threatened, and if these intellectuals belong to the Alawite minority, they are doubly threatening; the criticism is coming from within. When an Alawite professes their opposition to the regime rather than declaring their loyalty, they can expect to be more severely punished. Samar Yazbek lost all her privileges and was branded a traitor.

To properly appreciate Samar Yazbek's position one has to look more closely at the Syrian dictatorship. The Assad clan keeps twenty million Syrians locked-up and its head, Bashar al-Assad, is himself is a prisoner of his own system. He lies when he speaks of reforms; not for fun, mind you, but because he cannot do anything else. Because the first step on the road to reform would require the disbandment of all fifteen secret service divisions, the release of 100,000 political prisoners and the punishment of the murderers of over 4,000 innocent people. Until that happens it is absurd to talk about raising wages and improvements to the health service. But the dissolution of the secret service would mean the immediate toppling of the regime.

Assad has promised several times to withdraw the army and their snipers from towns and cities. Aware that an hour after this command was given these towns and cities would be controlled by revolutionaries, he did not keep his word. That is why there are no fewer tanks, and the snipers are still in position. He had eleven years to instigate reform, but the injustice created by his father has not changed a single iota. How can he now implement reforms in a matter of weeks? Impossible!

Arab dictators believe they are born heroes. They worship and glorify their mother and father for bringing them into the world. They believe themselves destined to rule forever. And when they die, even if from illness, as was the case with Assad's father, or in a car crash, as with his brother, Bassel, they die as saints.

Assad, Saddam Hussein, Gaddafi and the Yemeni Ali Saleh all overcame the abject poverty of their childhoods and poor education. They made a pact with the Devil to come to power. They destroyed the state and in its place built something which, viewed from a distance, looked remarkably similar: a Mafia-like network of power, which allowed them to subdue their countrymen. All positions of power were assigned to brothers, cousins, brothers-in-law or sons-in-law. If the clan was not numerous enough, friendly clans, neighbours or childhood friends were roped-in. This is how these corrupt pyramids of power were built, layer upon layer. At the very bottom are the people. The longer such a regime remains in power, the heavier the burden of oppression on the people becomes, the better equipped it is to resist attack. The Assad regime's bloody rule has lasted for 40 years – the first generation is now old and grey and has been succeeded by second and third generations of the clan.

Bashar al-Assad's father, however, was much too clever to overlook the fact that the Alawites could not rule alone forever. That is why he gave the Sunnis a stake in society, allowing them enough influence to become economic beneficiaries, but not enough to politically empower them. So it does not make sense for Islamists to curse only the Alawites. The system remains hierarchical; a Sunni or Christian general fears an Alawite corporal. This is not the law of the military, but of the Mafia.

In such a system, loyalty is the only means of accessing power. It is not surprising, therefore, that only yes-men reach the top of government, those who learnt quickest that the president wanted to hear nothing but approval. His portraits and monuments became bigger and bigger, all-important innovations were named after him; a reservoir on the Euphrates and the National Library. Books were written about his imaginary heroic deeds and hymns were composed to praise him. The media knelt down in front of him and from that lowly perspective he became a giant. How could Gaddafi, Saddam Hussein and al-Assad (the father and the son) doubt their own genius?

All this demonstrates a particular characteristic of all Arab dictatorships. Dictators from Ben Ali to Bashar ruled from the isolated peak of a pyramid of power. They could not and would not believe that this army of slaves, whom they called 'insects' or 'rats', could ever rise up against them. Bashar al-Assad cannot comprehend something as moving as a peaceful revolution and therefore blames the West. By doing so, he inadvertently reveals the remnants of a colonial mindset. In his sick mind, Syrians are too primitive to organise something so perfect, so beautiful, so brilliantly orchestrated. If they do, despite the fifteen secret service divisions and a quarter of a million regime informers, then it has to have been instigated by Europeans. They are the superior beings. That is what the colonial powers beat into his parents. He is simply reciting that belief.

I had no idea of the grumblings of the people until 15 March 2011. Nobody had. The dictator had no clue, nor did the secret service; the opposition had no inkling, neither had the exiles. Whoever claims to have known is simply lying. On that day, the first letters of a completely new, unprecedented and peaceful revolution were written. It all started in Dar'a, a dusty, poor city in the South. The town's youth innocently sprayed words on walls, expressing what we were all thinking: "Down with corruption!"

The chief of Dar'a municipal secret service, Atef Najib, a cousin of the president, who is known both for his corruptibility and his sadistic predisposition to humiliating high-ranking Sunni officers, had the youths detained and brutally tortured. When parents asked after their children, they were tortured further. That was the straw that broke the camel's back. In a peaceful demonstration they voiced their grievances. They did not demonstrate against Assad, but against a great injustice for which Atef Najib was responsible, and against the corruption in their town, of which he was the principal exponent. Instead of seeing reason, the secret service fired on the gathered crowd.

And the president? He sent troops, who shot protestors and encircled the city. Assad is commander-in-chief of all secret service divisions and therefore personally culpable for each of these murders. The first funerals became the starting point for the demonstrations, but soon people gathered every day.

Word spread to other towns. People flooded into the streets to show their solidarity with the people of Dar'a. Some had never heard of the town before. Syrians soon learned the geography of their country as open rebellion erupted in hundreds of towns simultaneously, towns whose names nobody had known but now could not be forgotten.

Samar Yazbek stayed close to these events, all the time fearing for herself and for her daughter. She went underground while criss-crossing the country, meeting activists, listening to their stories and recording all she could. She has rendered her story in *A Woman in the Crossfire* in straightforward language; it was not the time for exuberant words or small talk. The result is a poetic précis.

The long arm of the regime hit out harder and harder. Samar Yazbek was interrogated, beaten and detained. The regime did not shy away from using dirty tricks to discredit her. Leaflets accused her of treason, spread defamatory rumours, openly invited a lynch mob to take action against her. But that made Samar Yazbek even more determined to continue.

This is the miracle of the revolution: the individual becomes the whole, and the whole is embodied by each revolutionary, in the same way Samar Yazbek turned from media personality to passive opponent, and finally to active underground resistance fighter, branded a criminal by the regime and the president, the Syrian people became ever more radical and determined, the more the regime tried to suppress them.

When Samar Yazbek eventually felt the noose tightening, she fled. She saved herself, her daughter and the diaries of the revolution. Through this record a wider public will find out first-hand what happened in Damascus and other cities. They will find out that wonderful people risked their lives and took to the streets, despite the heavy secret service and military presence that made the city of Damascus such a dangerous place for resistance fighters. Samar Yazbek describes in minute detail how the secret service roamed the streets looking for troublemakers. Orwell's *1984* and Ray Bradbury's *Fahrenheit 451* have left the realm of fiction.

On 15 March 2011, the Syrians invented a new kind of revolution, a courageous, but peaceful uprising. And Samar Yazbek is the chronicler of that revolution.

Rafik Schami
Spring 2012

These diaries are not a literal documentation of the first four months of the Syrian uprising. They are simply pages I relied upon during those days in order to confront fear and panic as well as to generate some hope. But they are true, real, and have no connection whatsoever to the imagination.

Unfortunately, significant events in the popular mobilization that took place in cities such as Dayr al-Zur and al-Qamishli are absent either because I was unable to travel to them, or because I did not have the good fortune of recording the testimonies of activists in Damascus about the contributions people there made to the uprising.

I refer to activists who are still alive by the first letters of their names, and for the most part I intentionally use pseudonyms.

I have chosen to keep the names of the doctors entirely secret, even though some of them have been martyred, some are still missing and uncertainty shrouds the fate of others.

Samar Yazbek
Spring 2012

25 March 2011

....

It's not true that death, when it comes, will have your eyes!

It's not true at all that the desire for love is anything like the desire for death, not in that moment itself. Perhaps they are comparable in their nothingness, though, as they both drown in oblivion. In love: communion with another person. In death: communion with being itself and metamorphosis from tangible matter into an idea. Human beings have always thought death nobler than existence: why else would they venerate the dead? Even those who were still with us just a few moments ago, as soon as they disappear they are turned into radiance!

I would not say I am calm right now, but I am silent. I can hear my heart thumping like the sound of a distant explosion, clearer than the sounds of gunfire, than the screaming children and wailing mothers. Clearer than the trembling of my mother's voice as she implores me not to go out into the street.

There are killers everywhere.

Death is everywhere.

In the village.

In the city.

On the coast.

Killers take over, terrorizing the people, fanning out around our neighbours' houses, telling them how we are going to kill them, only to then come back at us, shouting the same thing in reverse: They're going to kill all of you!

I am an incidental visitor here. I am incidental to life. I don't belong in the environment where I live. Like a wild animal I've been drifting through the void. I flail around, empty except for the liberty of my very existence. I have been here ever since the protest movement began, looking out of my window and watching. My voice doesn't come out. I just want this to be over soon. Buried under this deluge of detail, I never knew that apathy could turn me into such a grim and fragile woman. Or that I could cling to life with this much fear: Fear of what, though? What are people so afraid of here? Without realizing it, people subsist on fear, which has become as automatic as breathing. Ever since my daughter and I moved to the capital fifteen years ago, I have a knife I never take out of my bag; I carry it wherever I go. A small, sharp switchblade to be used in self-defence. For years now I have said I'll plunge it into the body of anyone who tries to insult me for being a single woman living alone. I didn't use it very often, flashing it a few times in the face of stunned men, but lately I have begun saying that I'll plunge this knife into my own heart before I let them insult my dignity.

What's the point of everything I am saying now amidst this carnival of death? Simply going out into the street means the possibility of dying; this thought hit me, that walking down the street you feel someone might kill you at any moment. A crazy idea, but it's strange, you go out with your friends to demonstrate, knowing that there are snipers from general security who could shoot you at any time. The same security forces who have stamped on people's necks for decades, calling them whores and traitors, locking them up, killing them, and then continuing to saunter down the street in cold blood.

How does the human body get turned into a lethal killing machine? Hands, eyes, hair, brain – all these organs that resemble your own, how are they transformed into giant probes and long fangs? In the blink of an eye, reality becomes fantasy. But reality is more brutal. They say writing a novel requires imagination, but I would say it takes reality: nothing more, nothing less. What we write in novels is less brutal than what occurs in real life.

Bouthaina Shaaban appears on television. My mother tells us all to listen up, "She's talking about traitors and sectarian strife! Oh, the horror! Shut the windows!" Images of the tortured children and dead little boys return. The face of the little boy I held in al-Merjeh Square, as he watched his family getting beaten and arrested. I hear a man on television talking about the blood of the martyrs in Dar'a, calling for revenge, "We won't respond to this woman [he means Bouthaina Shaaban], we don't respond to women. They expect us to listen to a woman?!" Nothing that is happening seems anything like me: my family cheering for this lady, my friends cheering for the blood of the martyrs. I am ashamed of the blood of the martyrs.

Oh Lord in Heaven, if there is human sin, and it turns out You are sitting up there, unwilling to come down and witness what is happening, then I will reach up and drag You down from your seven heavens, so that You may hear and see.

As I step out onto the balcony, the lemon trees revive me. This place is calm for a few moments, then gunfire breaks out. Everybody knows that the city's calm before was not a natural calm, since nobody could challenge the power of the security apparatus. Agents are always in the street. Suddenly the streets are transformed into a carnival of horror. Chaos is everywhere. Security forces watch the people: some flee, others get arbitrarily eliminated. The gangs sprouted out of the ground just like everything here, out of thin air, without any rhyme or reason. How could armed men suddenly appear and start killing people? How did all this happen? I have been exiled from the city, from the village and even from the sea air itself. Everyone glares harshly at me, from all directions. I understand both sides. I know the other aspects of life in Damascus, where the city was transformed into another kind of village.

What am I doing here?

Waiting around to die?

As the debates start up once again – the saboteurs, the infiltrators – I cower inside myself. Now I am an infiltrator among my own family, an infiltrator in my own bed. Now I infiltrate everything and I am nothing. I am a lump of flesh curled up under the blankets, infiltrating below the asphalt on the street. I infiltrate the sorrow of every Syrian who passes before my eyes. I hear the sounds of gunfire and prayer. I am a mass of flesh, trudging each morning from house to house, trying to find one last document for salvation, claiming to be doing something adequate to my belief in the value of working for justice: but what does that even mean anymore? Nothing. All the slogans, all the pain, all the murder-inciting hatred and all the death have become meaningless in the face of this reality: empty streets, a ghost town. Military convoys are dispatched every which way, but there's no army presence. Where has the army gone? Who can believe such a farce now? The army lets these gangs kill people and intimidate them; it won't intervene. In the face of these gangs, the security forces that once terrorized the people are suddenly transformed into the downtrodden.

What is this madness?

Death is a mobile creature that now walks on two legs. I hear its voice, I can stare right at it. I am the one who knows what it tastes like, who knows the taste of a knife against your throat, the taste of boots on your neck. I have known it for a long time, ever since I first escaped that narrow world, then a second time, then a third. I am the crime of treason against my society and my sect, but I am no longer afraid, not because I am brave – indeed, I am quite fragile – but you get used to it.

Today, on the Friday of Dignity, the Syrian cities come out to demonstrate. More than two hundred thousand demonstrators mourn their dead in Dar'a. Entire villages outside Dar'a march toward the southern cemetery. Fifteen people are killed. In Homs three are killed. People are killed and wounded in Latakia. In the heart of the capital, Damascus, in the al-Maydan district, demonstrators come out; some are wounded and then moved to al-Mujtahid hospital. Army forces surround Dar'a and open fire on any creature that moves. In al-Sanamayn the military security commits a massacre, killing twenty people.

I am no longer afraid of death. We breathe it in. I wait for it, calm with my cigarette and coffee. I imagine I could stare into the eye of a sniper on a rooftop, stare at him without blinking. As I head out into the street, I walk confidently, peering up at the rooftops. Crossing the sidewalks and passing through a square, I wonder where the snipers might be now. I think of writing a novel about a sniper who watches a woman as she walks confidently down the street. I imagine them as two solitary heroes in a ghost town: like the street scenes in Saramago's *Blindness*.

I return to the capital, and I know this place will never be the same again. Fear no longer seems as automatic as breathing. Once and for all, and all at once, life here has changed.

I return to the capital, knowing I will not despair from tirelessly fighting for justice, even if death rips open my chest. Like I said: You get used to it. Nothing more, nothing less. I am waiting for death to arrive, though I will not carry flowers to my own grave.

....

I will infiltrate the sleep of those murderers and ask them, "Did you look into the eyes of the dead as the bullets hit their chests? Did you even notice the bullet holes?" Perhaps they glance for a moment at the red holes left behind in foreheads and stomachs, the same place where our eyes always come to rest.

Here in Damascus the murderers will soon fall asleep, and we'll remain the guardians of anxiety. Death is no longer a question. Death is a window we open up to our questions.

Damascus is just like any other city. It becomes more beautiful at night, like a woman after making love.

Who kills from the rooftops? Is it a cowardly killer? It most certainly is – how could he be deemed courageous when he has already been stripped of his morality?

From my house I head out in the direction of the squares and the mosques. In the middle of the afternoon, I need to see the city streets, street by street, square by square. I don't believe anything but my own eyes. The squares are empty, possibly because today's a holiday. Everyone is holed up inside their fear.

Security patrols roam dense in the streets; everywhere I go cars are coming and going, fast and slow; giant buses are jam-packed with security forces; men wearing helmets and military uniforms fan out in the markets and the squares, in the broad intersections and anywhere else demonstrations might break out.

Men in plain clothes congregate here and there, but the size of their presence gives them away. How did I learn to distinguish between a security agent and an ordinary man on the street in Damascus? The truth of the matter is that it's hard to pinpoint exactly when this game I play actually started, when my acumen became more reliable than any question or conversation. I know them by their eyes, by the drape of their clothes, by their shoes. Today more security forces than ordinary people are on the streets, in the alleyways, beside the kiosks, in the squares, outside the schools: security forces everywhere I go.

Patrols are deployed near the entrance to the Souk al-Hamidi-yyeh, and near Bab Touma they stop some men for questioning, grabbing their IDs. I can't wait around long enough to find out whether they kept their IDs in the end; I must keep moving. I glance at them out of the corner of my eye as I pass them, and then turn into a crowded alley. Here, almost, is human life. The security presence is heavy all around the Umayyad Mosque, and hordes of people are holding up flags and portraits of the president.

The mosque is closed, they won't let me in, they claim there are people inside praying, but before leaving I sit down outside to smoke a cigarette and calmly watch the situation.

Suddenly I start to notice strange figures I haven't ever seen before materializing in the street. Oversized men with broad and puffed-out chests, their heads shaved, wearing black short-sleeved shirts that reveal giant muscles covered in tattoos, seething at everything that moves. Glaring as they walk, their hands swinging at their sides, figures that sow terror wherever they go, thickening the air all around them: Why have I never noticed them in the city before? Where do they live? And why have they appeared today?

I walk back through the Souk al-Hamidiyyeh, nearly empty except for a few street vendors. The shops are all closed. Nothing but security forces scattered all around while at the end of the market even more buses sit packed with armed men. I can now appreciate the meaning of the phrase 'tense calm'. I have heard this expression before, thinking it more a figure of speech than an actual description. These days in Damascus I can understand 'tense calm' by people's eyes and movements. I walk out of al-Hamidiyyeh towards al-Merjeh Square despite having resolved not to go there any more after what happened one day a few weeks ago outside the Interior Ministry.

Al-Merjeh Square is empty except for security forces who are lined up in significant numbers, spread throughout the square. Not too far off there is a bus filled with men and weapons. With its wretched hotels Al-Merjeh Square seems more distinctive when all the people have disappeared and its shops are closed.

It looks nothing like it did on 16 March, when dozens of prisoners' families assembled outside the Ministry. *Nearly* assembled, they did not actually succeed. Standing there in silence, they looked odd, almost elegant, holding pictures of their loved ones who had been imprisoned for their political opinions. I stood with them, beside the husband and two sons of a female prisoner. Suddenly the earth split open with security forces and *shabbiha*, who started beating people. The small group started to panic, and I, staring right at those men, screamed, "Anyone who kills his own people is a traitor!" The people didn't fight back, they took all the blows and the insults and then started disappearing one after the other. They were taken away by men who had emerged just then out of the street, men with huge rings and inflated muscles and gaunt eyes and cracked skin – they created a human wall as they flung themselves upon the demonstrators and beat them, throwing them down on the ground and stamping on them. Other men captured people and hauled them away, made them disappear. I saw them open up a shop, throw a woman inside and shut the iron door behind her before heading after some other woman.

The group, while trying to stand together, got broken up. The husband beside me vanished, leaving his small four-year-old son behind. Several men grabbed the father along with his ten-year-old son. I stood there, like a defiled statue. I pulled the little one in close to my chest, as if I was in a movie scene. Is there really any difference between reality and fiction? Where is the line that separates the two? I was shivering. Suddenly I noticed the little boy gaping at his father and his brother as they were beaten, watching as the two of them were stuffed inside a bus. The face of the ten-year-old was frozen, as if he had just been administered an electric shock, and a powerful fist came flying at his little head: THUMP. His head went limp, and after a second, they kicked him along with his father inside the bus. I recoiled and turned the little boy's head away so he wouldn't be able to see what was happening, slung him over my shoulder and ran. Just then a friend of mine appeared nearby in the square, and three men pounced on her. I grabbed for her arm, screaming, "Leave her alone!" They threw me aside, along with the little boy who was by now weeping in my arms, and took her away. I kept running, stopping outside a store where the owner shouted at me, "Get out of here! Can't you see we're trying to make a living?" As I ran away, one of the demonstrators ran up alongside me to help carry the boy. We then continued briskly walking. Why had I run? The little boy asked me to stay with him; he was going to wait for his father, saying how scared he was now that his father and brother had left him, and that he was going to hit the policeman who had struck his brother. When he asked me whether they had been taken to prison just like his mother had been, I was silent, unable to respond, until I simply told him, "You're coming with me now."

Actually it wasn't the police who beat up his father, the police just watched while people got punched and kicked and insulted and arrested; they just stood there, silent. Then a group came out chanting slogans and carrying flags and pictures of the president, including some of the very same people who had carried out the beatings in the first place, as well as others who had appeared suddenly. They, too, started beating people with their flags, and the people who had almost managed to assemble there dispersed, bewilderment all over their faces. That night the news reported that infiltrators among the demonstrators had picked a fight, and that the Minister of the Interior had received complaints from the prisoners' families. I heard all this on Syrian state television, still haunted by the eyes of that little boy I had carried away, imagining him instead lost beneath the stampeding feet, wandering the city streets alone in search of his father and his brother.

Crossing al-Merjeh Square weeks after the incident, I see those phantasms, behind sliding metal prison bars. Then I hop in a taxi and head toward a mosque I hear remains under siege. There is no crowd there. I think there has to have been some mistake or some kind of media distortion. Through the car window I observe the city between al-Merjeh Square and the Kafr Sousseh roundabout. I don't want to rely on anything but myself and what I can see with my own two eyes. Scanning the internet on my mobile phone, I find reports that the mosque has been surrounded, but the radio broadcast says the entire city is calm.

Security has been deployed at the Kafr Sousseh roundabout, patrols the Syrian people know all too well. Foreigners would never imagine there could be so many cars in the squares. They prevent me from entering: the road is closed. We pass through the square and turn down a side street. Elsewhere the situation seems calm; there are places far removed from what is going on, especially wealthy neighbourhoods. I get out of the taxi and head towards the mosque, but it is hard to get close. Motorcycles. Shouting and chanting. High-ranking security officers. Crowds holding flags and pictures of the president. I ask what's going on. Everyone says there is a deadly silence inside and advises me to get out of there. There are no other women present, and one of them scornfully asks me, "What are you doing here?" I turn my back on him as the chanting rises up alongside the flags and the pictures. Security forces surround the mosque; it truly is under siege. I don't know if I can get inside; the only way would be to infiltrate those who are holding pictures and flags.

It's not easy to find yourself among men in civilian clothes who appear all of a sudden and beat up a young man, throw him to the ground and take away his phone. Some of them climb up onto the buildings overlooking the mosque. I overhear them say they want to make sure nobody is filming, but I can't confirm anything except the fact that the whole place is surrounded by security forces, police and military officers – and by the flag and picture carriers who are really no different than security forces, alternating between beating up demonstrators and holding their pictures of the president. People outside the mosque are talking about negotiations under way inside between an imam and the security forces so that everyone can come out peacefully, without violence or bloodshed. I would later discover that when the young demonstrators finally came out of the mosque they were taken straight to prison.

My heart shudders. I can hear it beating like someone addressing me, warning me of danger. My heart is a better guide than my head. I spot an angry-eyed man with a picture of the president walking towards me. I dash for the car. The man follows me, pointing menacingly. I ask the driver to step on it. The man rejoins the flag-bearers.

"Sister," the driver asks, "why are you getting involved in all this? They don't treat women any better than men!"

I keep silent. My eyes cloud over. The image of the besieged place terrifies me. What is going to happen? I hear news of killing in Douma, news that my friends have been detained, news of injured people and hospitals overcrowding with demonstrators after the army opened fire on them. Lots of news comes from all directions. I ask the driver to take me to see the situation in Douma, but he nearly jumps out of his seat, shouting, "My God, you can't go there!"

I am armed with nothing but my conscience. It doesn't matter to me whether the coming period brings moderate Islam and all they say comes with it. The faces of the murderers don't matter to me, and neither does all the talk nor all the lies. All that matters now to me is to break my demonic silence, as people speak only the language of blood. What matters to me is that with my own two eyes I have seen unarmed, peaceful people getting beaten up and locked away and killed for no other reason than that they were demonstrating. I have seen the children of my people fall one by one like unripe peaches from a tree.

The driver turns into a guardian and a preacher, saying, "The road to Douma's closed. It's forbidden to enter."

"Is Douma under siege as well?"

"Don't talk like that, sister. What have I got to do with all of this?"

"So who told you, then?"

"The army's there, there's gunfire," he says.

"What do you think, uncle? What's going on?"

"What have I got to do with it? I can barely make ends meet."

"But people are dying," I reply.

"God have mercy upon them, but we're all going to die someday."

"What would you do," I ask him, "if it were one of your children who was killed?"

He is silent for a moment, then shakes his head and says, "The world wouldn't be big enough to contain me!"

"I heard," I say, "that they put a young man in Dar'a into a refrigerator. While he was still alive. And when they pulled out his corpse, they found he had written with his own blood: *When they put me in here I was still alive send my love to my mother*."

He shakes his head in silence.

"I hope it's not true," I say.

He remains silent, his ears turning red.

Today there is a demonstration at the Damascus University Faculty of Letters; they detain all the students and confiscate their cell phones. The town of Talbiseh is still under siege, and all lines of communication are cut; they receive their children's dead bodies from the security forces. In al-Ma'damiya, near Damascus, the people tear down a giant picture of President Bashar al-Assad, and a young man is killed. In Latakia eight prisoners are burned to death in the central prison.

In a moment we are about to reach my house.

I am trembling. I can see that bloodshed only begets more bloodshed. I can see gaping holes in life, holes bigger than existence. I notice them in the chests of the martyrs, not in the faces of the killers. Back at home I think about how I will infiltrate the sleep of the killers and ask them whether they ever noticed the holes of life as they took aim at the bare chests of their unarmed victims.

8 April 2011

. . . .

This is Damascus: a phrase we all used to hear on the radio when we were children. Every Syrian knows the timbre of that phrase. Obviously this is Damascus. But ever since Syrians started to migrate from their small cities and villages and deserts, Damascus has become a transfer station, like the humdrum chore of a woman making dinner for her husband without a trace of love.

But still: This *is* Damascus!

Today is Friday. A soft drizzle stops long enough for people to go out into the streets and demonstrate in the squares and the mosques.

Who even remembers that every demonstrator is marked for death?

Death is a game whose rules are unclear. These diaries turn death into a canvas for painting, a darkened mysterious canvas that appears before me upon the chests of unarmed young men going out to die. How will the gently rocking mothers ever forgive those murderers? How can all these Don Quixotes tilt at justice amidst those hordes and so much injustice, when working for justice only rarely amounts to anything at all? But heroism isn't the glory of a crown of laurels; that's a Greek illusion. Heroism is to stand on the side of the weak until they are strong, for me to spin the world on my fragile fingers and rewrite it with a few gauzy words. Shall I do as Rimbaud wrote in his *A Season in Hell*: 'To the devil, I said, with martyr's crowns, the beams of art, the pride of inventors, the ardour of plunderers; I returned to the Orient and to the first and eternal wisdom.'

The drizzle stops. A miserly sun shines through until the rain returns to roll down my cheek once again. I drink a few droplets before getting into a taxi and heading to Douma. I conceive of these diaries as deliverance or an exclamation, but in the end they are just words. People around me may think them courageous, but they are wrong, because as soon as the car sets off in the direction of the demonstration, my knees become weak, my throat dries up and I can hear my fear pounding.

Fear is a human condition that humanity has never given its due, a mysterious commentary on meaning or love. Fear means you are still human amidst the rubble.

We approach Harasta, the suburb we have to get through in order to reach Douma. My driver is a young man in his mid-twenties, taciturn; I would later discover he is also courageous.

"Road's closed," he tells me.

I snap out of my reverie and notice the long line of cars. Utter silence. It was the first time I have ever seen a place that crowded with people yet so quiet. I get out and walk past a few parked cars in order to see what is going on. Several green public buses with yellow seats are stopped, blocking the flow of traffic. Young men are jammed inside the buses, standing up, sitting down, one on top of the other. When they step off they are deployed on both sides of the street. The hordes pour out in silence. The marching young men are led by others wearing navy and grey uniforms. The young men's faces are severe, exhausted; most have shaved heads and poverty seems to be written all over them. I approach one of the men directing them all and ask, "What's going on?" He frowns and ignores my question. There are almost no women in the street, just one I can make out from afar, draped in a black *niqab* and dragging a child behind her as she runs in panic. The man in the car sticks out his head and says, "Get back in, sister. Those guys are security agents."

"And the guys coming out of the buses, what are they for?" I ask.

Although he doesn't respond, I can guess. There are hundreds of them, maybe more. We wait there for half an hour, until they all get out and deploy up and down both sides of the street, forming a small army, while people retreat from the sidewalks and disappear, with horror all over their faces.

There is a military checkpoint outside Douma. Legions of security forces inspect trucks and check IDs, as scores of cars turn

around and return the way they had come. Young men are standing off to the side as groups of security forces question them. I
am unaware that, at that very moment, Douma is surrounded, and
there is a military chokehold around Damascus and its suburbs.

Beyond the security forces, a lot of men dressed in military
uniform, replete with helmets, stand at the ready on both sides
of the street. They stop the car, and one man asks me brusquely,
"Where to?" When I tell him I have a meeting, he looks at me with
the same brusqueness and orders me to get out of the car. After I
do that, he curiously scrutinizes me. He is short, and perhaps it
infuriates him that I am taller than he is, so he backs away a little
bit and demands my identification. After turning over my ID, he
says, "Madame, there are thugs around here, I must ask you not to
go any further."

"But I have an appointment at the seamstress. It will only take
ten minutes," I say.

Luckily I know a seamstress there. I give him her name and say,
"Call her, if you want."

He opens the car door for me and asks the driver to move along.
I take a breath, and then naively ask, "What's happening here?"

"Oh, nothing at all, there's nothing happening here."

"So why are they so many soldiers, why all this security?"

"It's nothing, I swear to God, it's nothing," he adds.

I take comfort in the fact that I have perfectly played my
favourite role, pretending not to know anything in order to learn
everything, remaining silent in front of others who love to talk, and
the most important thing of all: observing.

The car starts to move. I have just turned to face forward when I
see both a military and a security checkpoint. What's this? Between
one checkpoint and another checkpoint there's a checkpoint? I tell
the driver, "We've got to take one of the side streets."

"Let's just go back," he says. "Seriously, I'm worried about you."

The second checkpoint is a big one. Soldiers line up next to each
other, forming a roadblock, and in front of them there is another
roadblock made up of security men. I feel like I am in a movie
about an occupied Palestinian town. What a terrifying vision. In
fact, it isn't just visual, because my knees start to tingle and shake.

When the officer opens the car door and says in a gruff voice, "Get out," my knees crack as I stand up. He watches me suspiciously as he takes my ID. He is dressed in civilian clothes, and beside him there is a man who I know by his accent comes from the Jazira region. The man checking my passport is from the coast. What is this? The security and the army are all either from the Syrian Jazira region or from the coastal region. Maybe this is just a coincidence today, because I have had my share of run-ins with the security forces, – in this I am no different from every other Syrian – but the unifying feature is that they are all minorities.

The Jazrawi man looks at me and asks, "Are you a journalist?"

"No," I reply.

He scrutinizes me, and suddenly reaches out his hand to grab my sunglasses, pulling me hard by the hand, and demands, "What are you doing here?"

Then a second man jumps in, "A journalist? Oh yeah, I know your name. I've seen you on TV."

Growing despondent, I tell him, "You're mistaken. I have an appointment with the seamstress." Feeling a little bit emboldened, my voice gets louder, "And you, sirs, are scaring people, can't you see? What's going on here, anyway?"

The coastal man says, "You used to host a show called *Ladies First*, I know you. My wife used to watch that show."

He jumps to his feet and shouts to the other guy, "Sir, she's from Orient TV," and within seconds the world turns upside down. Surrounded by scores of armed men, civilians too, I become like a dot at the centre of a bull's eye. I cannot see anything any more and the odours suffocate me.

"Sir, I'm a writer," I insist. "It's true that two years ago, for about three months, I hosted a program on *Orient*, and before that I used to host a cultural program on the Syrian satellite network. But please, let me just be on my way."

"Sir," one of them asks, "won't she leak information to those dogs at *Orient*?"

He draws in closer to me, and grabs me by the shoulder.

"Please, sir, I don't have anything to do with any channel, and if you do know me, you should be respectful and just let me go. You work for the security services, and it's your job to protect me, not intimidate me. Besides, won't you at least tell me what's going on here?"

They all come back in a single voice, "Nothing's going on, nothing."

"Then what are all these soldiers and security personnel doing?" I ask.

"Nothing," they repeat, "it's nothing."

To the man who appeared to be the most senior, I say, "All right then, then let me just get out of here."

He is silent for a while, nodding his head, and I am about to suffocate from how close they are to me as my hand edges closer to the knife in my bag. These are long moments, but finally he barks at me, "Get the hell out of here!" They all scatter but before I get back in the car he says in a Bedouin accent, "I swear to God, if you ever come back to here, I'll use your skin to make a hand drum."

I close my eyes and squeeze them shut so he cannot see my tears, as I imagine human skin turned into a drum and beaten in order to make hips shake. We cross the second checkpoint. Why are there all these soldiers and security forces? Where are all the people who live here? Is it now a ghost town? I try to call my friend and tell her I am in Douma, but there is no service. So the town is blockaded from without and from within. There are two more identical military checkpoints, and beyond the second one I see the same giant government buses, from which even more young men are streaming out. Are they the same young men I saw in Harasta? I assume the entire security apparatus has been called up today, because the effort is clear and their heavy presence indicates they must have come from multiple branches. I pity those starving men stuffed into the buses, a tiny monster lurking inside each one of them. I promise the officer at the fourth checkpoint that I will leave Douma. But at the end of the broad street where the town ends, I ask the driver to turn off, and we drive down the alleys. A ten-year-old boy riding a bicycle helps us, and we follow him as he shows us the way to the municipal square near the Great Mosque. We loop around agricultural land with olive trees, which pains me, because a few days ago I heard a Palestinian from Lyd on television talking about how the Israelis had forced him to demolish his own house. "They asked me, who's your master?" he said, crying. "Then," he said, sitting down under an olive tree outside his demolished house, "The olive trees are my master."

An expanse of small houses, cattle pens, goats and the stench of poverty.

Most of the men have long beards, and the women are wrapped in black, they're entirely in black, nothing showing but their eyes. I find out later that scores of people are also assembling in adjacent neighbourhoods in order to join the demonstrators in the square. That must be why there are military and security checkpoints set up all over the place: to prevent the demonstrators from reaching the square. There are even checkpoints in the alleyways. Always the same script.

"Pretend you're lost," I tell the driver. "We're trying to get out of here, but we got lost, that's what we'll tell the security and the soldiers."

I repeat these words to the military checkpoints and to the security men. "We got lost trying to find our way out of here. But what's going on here?"

They each respond with the same answer, "Nothing."

Once I get past I see some residents and ask them where the town square is. At least we reach it, and the car parks beside a Red Cross vehicle. The square is surrounded with security agents, who don't approach the demonstrators, at least not before 3 p.m., which is when I am there until. There are no more than two thousand demonstrators, but soldiers and security forces are everywhere, and the demonstrators hold up Syrian flags and banners with slogans like *God, Syria, Freedom, That's It!* and *No Sunnis, No Alawites, No Druze, No Isma'ilis, We are all Syria*. Some hold olive branches. Apparently the olive trees are their masters too. No women are present, and as I try to get closer three men approach, taking me by the hand and whispering, "What do you want?"

"I'm just watching. I got lost." I answer, playing dumb. "Why, what's going on?"

"Nothing, it's nothing." The two men let me go, and one of them commands, "*Yalla*, get out of here at once."

On my way back, I ask people what happened. They are reticent and sad, but they tell me how they went out to demonstrate peacefully, and how gunfire came raining down on their heads, how they were forced to set fire to the building across the square in order to bring down the snipers who had climbed up onto the rooftops and were killing the young men. As the men talk about the virtuous martyrs they refuse to look me in the face. Even a woman I speak to stares back at me in fear. When I approach someone else to ask about it, he evasively replies with the oath, "I seek refuge in God from the accursed devil." I understand now what my presence as an unveiled woman means: an agitator. Since I am trapped, I find a way to ignore whatever they say to me and keep walking. I am truly lost now, not just pretending, and I want to get out of here. Checkpoint upon checkpoint, so many security agents and soldiers. By the last one, I am exhausted and starting to get annoyed. I take one last look back at Douma, an occupied city. I am armed only with stories.

On my way home, passing through Harasta, I think to myself: *A day without bloodshed? That would be wonderful.* I don't know how much blood is actually being spilled in Dar'a, that there are more than 40 martyrs on this Friday and that every Syrian city is witnessing a comparable protest movement. Even inside Damascus there are protests and beatings and bullets. In Homs, on top of the beating and the arrests, I hear about the story of an officer killed by the security forces. They shot him twice in the head for refusing to order his troops to fire on the demonstrators. I also don't know that this particular Friday, which the demonstrators have dubbed the Friday of Steadfastness, is going to become a turning point in the history of Syria. This Friday constitutes the largest and most broadly based protest campaign the cities have seen, with the largest number of martyrs, and the Kurds participating alongside the Arabs despite their newly granted citizenship. This Friday proves, in all simplicity, that everything the president has said about reforms only means one thing to them: that he refuses to make any reforms.

What I also don't know until the very moment that we pass back through Harasta and leave Douma behind is that soon I will, for the first time in my life, see a dead man's face and a murderer's shadow.

On the way back from Harasta I notice the young men have got out of the buses, and the men directing them have disappeared. The security forces remain spread out all over the place, and become the only ones I see. I hear that more have been brought and that they are cracking down on the demonstrators. Someone later tells me those guys call themselves supporters. As I try to get closer, I see men holding up the sticks they use to beat people, the sounds of gunfire grow louder, and I run to stand outside a shop, where I see those young faces that had got off the buses attacking people. The eyes of the attackers are all white, or maybe I just imagine that as the illusive sun occasionally peeks through to illuminate their features, but to me their eyes seem empty and white, and that's when I notice all the blood. I have no idea how it happened. I crouch down among all the feet, trying to get away. I am surrounded, and suddenly I find myself down on the ground. I see a sleeping face, eyes half-closed: my grandmother used to call this the 'Gazelle's Sleep.' People are pushing and shoving all around the sleeping face. I call it sleep, because death is like sleep. The only difference between sleep and death is that we disintegrate after death. In sleep, we prepare for another kind of disintegration – a subtle distinction. Will this young face disintegrate after a while? How will his mother kiss his forehead before it is swallowed up by the dirt? My skin turns to stone.

I run away from the surging waves of people, and a hot wallop catches me across the back. I wheel around to look behind me, and all of a sudden I see a leather strap in the hands of the security forces. I have no idea where the blow came from. Pain sears my lower back, moving down to the soles of my feet. Terrifying eyes stare at me. I start running as soon as I can stand, catching sight of the dead man's face a second time, with the faces of murderers all around him. Who is opening fire? Where are the shots coming from? Maybe there are snipers, maybe my head is a target. A young man shouts and points to a man up on top of a building. Two young men grab me and pull me out of the group, screaming, "Please get out of here, sister!"

Everyone here calls women "sister". Most women wear *niqab*s and the rest are veiled. I think of Saadallah al-Jabiri, the Syrian Prime Minister in 1944 when Shukri al-Quwwatli was president. During that era some Damascene families allowed their daughters to go unveiled, and mixed associations with both men and women were formed, but then the clerics made a fuss and demanded their dissolution. They went to see al-Jabiri and there were altercations and gunfire. Then he asked them to form a delegation in order to discuss the matter calmly with him. He addressed them at the Orient Palace Hotel in Damascus, responding to their demand to dissolve the associations by asking them, first of all, to stop their practices against unveiled girls, which was to throw acid in their faces, telling the *shaykhs*, "Listen, *shaykh*, if you want to cover your daughter, nobody's going to tell you no. But it's none of your business whether another person wants his daughter to go unveiled. Now go in peace."

I try to find one woman, someone to speak with more easily, but there are no women in the street. When I hear women screaming and the distant sounds of gunfire I head back to the car. By the end of the day, I am going home with documents. Documents of flesh and blood, of wailing and bullets and the faces of murderers who don't know where they're going.

Feeling the need for a cigarette, I roll down the window and inhale smoke into my lungs. Harasta and Douma are behind me, my back hurts, the wailing and blood fill my head, the eyes of the young man sleeping like a gazelle. Suddenly I hear a groan and look up at the driver in the mirror, the day's final surprise: the young man, tears pouring from his face, silent, unable to speak. In that moment I hear nothing but the grinding of my own teeth.

....

Oh spinning world, if my little heart, as small as a lump of coal, is wider than your borders, I know how narrow you are!

As the car rattles along I think about how narrow the world is. My chest is pounding. I can hardly breathe. The images that appear on television today of men taken from their homes in the village of al-Baida, which is still besieged by army forces and security personnel, those men who are gathered together in the square, with their stomachs on the ground, their hands tied together with thin plastic twist-ties that become knives digging into their skin, their heads buried in the asphalt and their backs to the sky – those images haven't left my mind. The scene reminds me of the film *Kafr Qasim* by Burhan Alaouie.

Those men are forbidden from lifting their heads, they are kicked and stamped on and beaten mercilessly, they are forced to repeat slogans in support of the president before being taken away to the trucks, which drive them to some unknown location where they disappear.

State television news reports that they are traitors, that they have weapons in their possession, but when a video clip surfaces they say the images are fabricated. A few days later my friend from Baniyas would tell me that what really happened wasn't anything like what they said, but that some men had gone out to demonstrate, chanting peacefully about freedom without any sectarian slogans, when some groups showed up and started shooting, killing a number of them even as the rest were carted off to prison and the whole town was surrounded.

I cannot get into Baniyas in order to see what is actually going on today. I try a number of roads to get there, but it is impossible. Even when we try to pass through a few buildings in order to enter

the city and the old *souq*, there are checkpoints that kept us out –
for our own safety, of course. I rely on stories from people I meet
and from my friends, on the pictures I took. Here is one of them:
Men on their stomachs in handcuffs, humiliated and insulted. That
is the title of a Dostoevsky novel. I approach these stories like an
investigator. They are my unrivalled passion. This isn't the only way
men get arrested, though. Houses are broken into and scores of
children are taken off to prison. The army and the security forces
are combing al-Baida, there hasn't been any electricity for days, no
supplies, entry and exit is forbidden. Men and children have been
arrested, and I am later able to confirm that women and children
staged a sit-in along the international road demanding the release
of their men. Yes, this much is certain, and state television cannot
falsify it, because I go to confirm it myself.

Scores of trucks block the road. There is news about ambulances being disabled. Women shout alongside their children. One
woman appears on television the next day, screaming at the top of
her lungs, *We are the people of Baniyas and we are the people of
freedom!* as women behind her shout, *Freedom, Freedom!* All the
women were veiled. When I ask someone from the army what is
going on, he responds confidently but without any explanation; he
seems distracted, preoccupied by something. A man in his forties
approaches me at the checkpoint connecting the city of Baniyas
with the mountain villages, where the international road splits off.
After a while he tells me he is a police officer – he really is wearing
a black police uniform – adding that the people are scared of the
armed fighters. He makes no comment when I tell him, "I doubt
that the men of al-Baida have any weapons." Then I add, "Wasn't
arresting and killing them a barbaric thing to do?" He doesn't reply,
just motions for me to move along. The car is close, so he opens the
door and says with the utmost propriety, "I beg you, ma'am, please
get out of here." He turns his back. Anger is obviously written all
over his face; I can tell because I am angry too. A man sitting not
too far away tells us that the officer's brother had been killed in the
bus the army targeted two days before, in which a group of officers
and soldiers were also killed.

"But some people say the ones who killed the army and the

people and some of the security forces were operating like gangs. Do people in Baniyas know who they are?"

"Yes," he says. "But who's saying that?"

I tell him I read it somewhere. He is tall, thin, and has a scruffy beard, and adds, "Everybody knows who they are, but everyone is afraid."

"Of what?" I ask.

He says the Alawites are afraid of the rumours being spread amongst them. "My house is in an Alawite neighbourhood and I'm afraid to go home. There are some neighbourhoods where Alawites and Sunnis live together, but things could explode at any moment."

"Someone is terrorizing people and stirring up sectarian strife," I say.

"Yes, there are some who are frightening people. The problem is they've succeeded." He mentions a few family names of people who are taking up arms and frightening people, who work for one of the president's relatives. I had already read some of their names on the net, seen their pictures too, and he adds two more names. "Everybody knows who they are," he says, "but who would dare to expose them?"

Even though I find it strange for him to be so bold with me, I know why: he's about to leave the country. Soon a car pulls up, and suddenly I notice it has parked beside a large suitcase. I thank him.

"You're not going to find anyone who will tell you anything," he says. "The people have nothing but fear to tell, and besides, many of them actually believe the story about infiltrators and traitors." He is silent for a few minutes, and then introduces himself to me. He is an Arabic teacher, travelling from Baniyas to Greece.

"Everybody knows these stories from the net," I say.

"And what makes you think that people here ever see the net?" he asks with great despair.

He gets in the car and disappears. I turn to the fidgety driver and tell him we have to try a different way. Maybe we can still reach the women at the sit-in. He shouts he is going to leave me there if I don't get in because there are snipers stationed up by the Marqab Castle, and all over the place really, that they had already shot and killed a lot of civilians as well as security forces and army officers.

The sad angry officer is panicked and annoyed to see me so he heads towards us and barks, "Come on, get out of here!"

"Why are you shouting?" I ask.

"Because people are dying here," he says, "and the next bullet might be aimed at you."

"Who are those snipers?" I ask.

"How should I know? They're killing ordinary people, security forces and army personnel."

"Aren't the snipers actually a bunch of *shabbiha*?"

"What *shabbiha*?"

"Who doesn't know about the *shabbiha*?!" I say, and then, too frightened to continue, leave him to stand there watching me, as anger spreads through him.

We head back towards the international road, preparing to head for Jableh. Baniyas is behind us.

Twenty-four hours before, we were near Baniyas, and things were very different. During that first crossing over the mountains we had to loop around the city because the road was closed, and the army had it surrounded from within and from without. We got in by way of the mountain villages, and I wasn't convinced by what they told us at the police checkpoint, that it was too dangerous to cross on the international road.

"Why's that?" I asked.

He said there were snipers inside the Marqab Castle and that the army was there to protect the people.

"All right, then, if they army's there to protect us..."

"The road's closed," he said. "Go back to Damascus, or cross over the mountains."

On the other side of the mountains, there was a timorous joy awaiting us: an explosion of green in the mountains and the valleys, and when we got past the green an exposed earth with overlapping layers of red. Beneath the villages inhabited by Christians and Alawites were the Sunni villages, closer to the sea. Once we passed through the villages of Daher Safra and Qarqafti, the village of al-Baida was directly below us: the thermal power station, the refinery, the deep valleys. Popular committees formed by leaders of the Ba'th party factions were being deployed along with security forces and soldiers. A five-year-old boy carrying a wooden stick on his back like a rifle stood there; his skin was scorched, his eyes shone, and a long honey-coloured beauty mark covered his forehead. He looked like a painting. I smiled and handed him my ID. After scrutinizing it, he handed it back to me and motioned for me to continue. Fighting back a smile, I asked him, "Who are you with?"

"I'm with you!" he replied.

It was the first time I had laughed in the many days since the bloodshed had started in the cities and the villages. I laughed out loud and winked at him as the car rolled past.

The checkpoints reflecting the people's fear aren't too much of a burden for me, because I understand their fear and actually believed what they told me about armed gangs that frighten them by opening fire in their valleys and from their mountaintops, but the question remains: "Who are those gangs?" I ask one of the villagers, most of whom are simple and poor and panicky.

"I think the story is not the way they say it is," I tell him. He looks at me with bewildered eyes and offers me a cup of maté after I step out of the car to sit down on a bench with him outside his house.

"No, my dear, you don't understand. They want to kill us. The army's here for protection."

"But you can protect yourselves," I say.

"It's all right, the army's on the front lines and we cover the rear."

"Where are all the women, and why is there no life in the village?"

Leaning on his bruised hand, he says, "We protect the village here and we take care of our women."

"I heard it's the *shabbiha* who are killing people and intimidating them," I say, and then fall silent.

He pauses before saying, "Whoever they are, by God they'll only get near our houses over our dead bodies."

The people of the village are anxious and on high alert, and with so many search checkpoints, the mountains seem to be in a state of war. Nowhere did this seem clearer than the area surrounding Baniyas, where the popular committees from the coastal villages come out at night in order to protect the villages from the feared gangs. The checkpoints – comprised of several varieties of security, military, the people and the popular committees –respectfully and carefully search people. There is a car behind us in which I saw a young man fingering a pistol. As we had already passed through several checkpoints, I ask the officer why there needed to be so many additional searches; he asks me to wait at the side of the road so the car that has been behind us since the start of the mountain road can pass. Four young men are inside, a type I recognize because they have begun appearing lately in Damascus, the faces of killers I know all too well. They are all playing with guns. The officer stops them and asks them to step out. The driver does not respond at first, nearly running over a soldier, but the officer stops him and they all get out, affronted – doesn't he know who they are? I have a sixth sense about this; I never fail to recognize these men who deploy in the streets of Damascus and Latakia: puffed-up muscles, tattoos, broad chests, an arrogant gaze, death. The officer speaks as the soldiers search them; one of them angrily scowls at me. I am scared. They seem to know I already informed two checkpoints about them. When the officer permits them to go on, I am shocked, shouting, "You even search my computer files and my bags, but you just let those armed men go!"

"Please, be on your way, Madame," the officer says calmly. "They have a security assignment."

I hear their screeching tires, like a scream, and a cloud of dust is kicked up as their car speeds away like a shot, with people jumping out of the way to avoid getting hit.

"But they're criminals!" I insist. "And they have three guns."

He turns his back, leaving me with his soldiers. The soldier who was nearly run over seems upset, but he approaches me and says, "Calm down, sister. We can't do anything about things like that."

Things in al-Baida are becoming clearer. After enough time passes, history will record how human beings here were carted off to prison like cattle, how women came out to defend their husbands and their children, how children shouted even as they were being arrested, how blood was spilled in the streets, and how bodies were left out in the open air.

I gaze longingly at the place. Al-Baida is directly below us. Plastic houses extend all along the coast, obscuring Baniyas and polluting the air and the sea. I can imagine what happened: The people got scared. They panicked. They no longer thought about what was happening. The security that the army could provide them with became their only concern. Events blended together. Stories and rumours swirled around. Fear of the ancient humiliation long endured by the Alawites, fear of homelessness and oppression brought them closer to the regime narrative, forcing them behind it with all they possessed. They were poor, believing whatever they were told, and even after many decades they had not got used to this horror. A small number of them were against the violence and killing that were taking place. They started telling the people in Baniyas that the whole thing did not just concern the Sunni community alone. When the Islamists came out to demonstrate, they were peaceful; they did not open fire on anyone. Even some Alawites joined them. Some of those Alawites were subjected to additional oppression by the security forces, as a means of intimidation; their reputations would be smeared. Some of them were arrested; others would be warned against creating moral scandals. The greatest tragedy was excommunication from the sect, being called a traitor. Some of them were compelled to leave Baniyas under pressure.

People from Baniyas tried to find out who the armed fighters shooting at them were, those who spread out along the rooftops as snipers, intervening and arresting people from al-Baida. They were the ones who made the people believe that the ones being arrested were traitors and infiltrators who wanted to slaughter the Alawites. But that was not the case. Maybe it is true that what happened inflamed sectarian sentiment in Baniyas, turning the place into hell, but it all started with those *shabbiha*; they were the ones who shot at the minaret. A number of Alawites in Baniyas related these events to me, about how they left their houses behind, fleeing collective punishment.

Today is the Friday of Perseverance. Fifteen people are killed in Latakia. In Damascus the security forces cut the arteries connecting streets and squares with security and military checkpoints, especially around Abbasiyeen Square. The security opens fire on demonstrators coming from Jawbar after being joined by people from Douma and Harasta; they are prevented from reaching Abbasiyeen Square. Despite the demonstration of hundreds of thousands of people, security does not open fire on demonstrators in Dar'a. The people of al-Rastan fell a statue of Hafiz al-Assad, who remains the greatest figure in Syria. In Latakia security forces try to infiltrate the demonstrators; when the demonstrators oppose the presence of weapons, the infiltrators tell them they only carried them for self-defence, but the young men seize them when it becomes clear that they are from the security forces. They wanted to make it look like an armed demonstration. The security and the army would loot businesses. The city of al-Dumayr is surrounded; security is heavily deployed throughout. The suburb of Douma is still surrounded, and the daily toll of arrests is nonstop.

Now Baniyas is empty. The streets are deserted; the shops are closed and many have been looted; city hall and the post office have been torched. Tomorrow the people will call for the army to be sent in and for the security to leave; tanks will remain stationed throughout the city; soldiers will deploy in the streets. There is fear that sectarian clashes may break out at any moment. They have succeeded in framing what happened, as if it marks the beginning of a sectarian civil war that it is incumbent upon the regime to prevent. But many city residents know that this is not the case, that there were invisible hands behind what took place that would like to turn the peaceful demonstrations that came out of the mosques into treasonous activity by armed men who are conspiring with foreign elements. Perhaps that was the only reason the regime could come up with to justify killing the people of Baniyas. But who was killing the army and the security forces? And the snipers, who were those snipers? Maybe figuring out who was behind these actions will be simple enough, but how they managed to pull it off is still unclear. All these thoughts come and go as I enter Jableh, intensifying my anger, my pain and bitterness, but the small happiness I acquire from arriving safely after such a nightmarish journey over the mountains makes me think the time has come to take a break. I do not know this will be my last visit to Jableh.

Now that I have crossed paths with death, I am prepared to see more of it.

29 April 2011

In besieged Dar'a falling hailstones get mixed up with the sound of bullets whizzing past. Not far from this calamity, land is being surrounded, buried, all alone and drifting beneath the darkened sky, as if in a painting by Dalí; its wounded people slowly die while their mothers watch, mothers whose bloody trembling fingers are wrapped with perforated bed sheets. Before the martyrs' eyelids are closed, the mothers moisten their throats with a few drops of water. People watch the young bodies strewn all around the square disintegrate from behind their windows. After the electricity has been cut off, stenches rise from the dead in the darkness. All people can do is stare at those bodies, which were once beloved and beating with warmth, as they turn to dust.

Not far from my window, hailstones fall, and my heart turns into a hunk of scrap metal in the face of my impotence, as Dar'a is slowly dying for all of us to see, while the whole world watches. Among those of us who comfortably tuck in our children before going to sleep, there is a thin imaginary line separating real pain from hypothetical pain, and no matter what we say about feeling the sorrow of those mothers, it is a lie. Pain appears in the wake of actual loss. Pain is not purely coincidental now.

Not far from Damascus, just an hour by car, there is a calamity taking place that seems more like the stories we read about in the papers, one we cannot believe is actually happening here. Entire families are surrounded by tanks and soldiers and snipers. Women hide out in their homes, shaking and shuddering from the popping sounds of gunfire, the gunfire that never stops. Anyone who dares set foot outside is a potential martyr. Nobody is around to bury the bodies lying outside the al-Umari Mosque in Dar'a. Even as voices start to rise up in the city calling upon the authorities to let the martyrs' families bury their dead, the wounded remain holed up inside the houses for fear of being picked off outside or bleeding out in the open without any first aid. I manage to confirm that several pharmacies have been bombed and burned. Why are they setting the pharmacies on fire? So that people won't be able to treat the wounded, of course. Some residents escape the city and flee the country by crossing the Lebanese or the Jordanian borders, leaving death and destruction behind. What does today have in store for the city? Will demonstrators go out this Friday, this Friday of Rage that has been called for by demonstrators in every Syrian city? Will a single one of them dare cross the threshold of his house, with tank turrets and snipers' machine guns all around them?

Last Friday Damascus was a ghost town. It wasn't Damascus.

Despite the calls spreading throughout the Syrian cities for people to come out and despite the death of so many young people, security forces were deployed in all the squares, the number of their personnel and platoons rose into the thousands. With the road to Jawbar closed, my female friend and I drove through Abbasiyeen Square, and there was a strange deadly calm. As we circled the square, the security was just starting to gather; it wasn't yet time for the demonstration. My friend drove us through the streets of Damascus as we looked for signs of life. My eyes played tricks on me, and I cried to see the city empty except for the screams of death and those murderous eyes that were gathering, the eyes of young people who stepped off government-owned tour buses. They carried sticks and chains. I thought about how I had lived in Syria for 40 years but had never seen anything like those faces, their dusky complexions, petrified wooden bodies, hate-filled eyes.

Was 40 years enough time to create such a frightening genera-tion of murderers?

During the afternoon, on our second time around, the situa-tion in Abbasiyeen Square was different: the number of security forces had increased, even along the side streets, and as our car looped around the square, we saw military checkpoints blocking the Jawbar road. There were many different groups assembling and somebody said shots had been fired. We didn't hear any gunshots on our entire trip, but the next day when I met up with a friend,

I tried to find out from her what had actually happened in al-Zablatani, not far from Abbasiyeen Square. She told me she had been there and saw a group of young Christian men standing and demonstrating right in front of the security forces, only a handful of them, no more than a few dozen. One of them had taken off his shirt and bared his chest to the security forces' machine guns. He stood there for nearly a minute until the sound of gunfire rang out and brought down the young man. I asked her what happened to him. Although they were only monitoring the security forces from afar, and from behind a balcony even, she said that they opened fire and ordered everyone to go back inside, as those who remained on the street fled. Then the square was empty except for security forces, the sounds of gunfire and the bodies of five young men who had fallen on the ground. State television would later report that the security forces had captured five saboteurs who were killed during armed clashes.

What happens in this moment between when the shot is fired and when the bullet hits the bare chest? How are the two related?

What was that young man who exposed his chest to death thinking about at that very moment?

How long will it take us to understand the language of life? How much sadness do we need in order to endure this fresh blood in a country succumbing to the forces of death? Did the bare chest of that young man, standing there alone in front of them, without uttering a word, frighten them? What did the machine gun that killed him and his friends do after this assignment?

Questions upon more questions, and that afternoon, driving towards Barzeh, a checkpoint appeared in front of us. It was a different kind of checkpoint: there were not a lot of men, five of disparate ages, and it was obvious they weren't security, but they and their machine guns moved closer to us despite the fact that the car wasn't the least bit suspicious. One of them was a young man who could not have been more than 25, his machine gun barrel was pointed straight at us; his eyes were lethal. My heart quaked as we turned around. Beyond that checkpoint there was killing and gunfire. We weren't allowed to enter Barzeh.

That was last Friday, and just as I was about to start recording these diaries, pain prevented me from doing so. I was too nervous to focus on writing. I wandered from friend's house to friend's house. I avoided going home in order to evade detention, because the security apparatus had fabricated more reports about me and posted them on their websites. It was getting difficult for me to go to Jableh or to move around freely in Latakia. I was a traitor to my sect for being on the side of the demonstrators. I wrote two pieces about the protest movement, in which I talked about the practices of violence and killing and arrest carried out by the security forces. They responded by posting articles on a *mukhabarati* website discussing my relationship with American agents, a ready-made excuse the security apparatus would always resort to in order to clamp down on people who have their own opinions. I was bounded by my own anxiety and fear, by my daughter and my family, who came under direct pressure from the scandal that ensued in my village when the regime told them that their daughter had betrayed her sect and her homeland. I could not write. The daily news of killing was more present inside of me than any emotion. Then there was the news of my friends getting arrested. Finally, there was the atrocity that ended with the siege of Dar'a, which continues until today, the Friday of Rage.

I awoke to the sound of hailstones rattling against the window. It was early. I had come home; I simply had to, despite the threats from the security forces, despite all the rumours that were being spread about me among the Alawites, provoking everyone on the coast against me. I must remain calm in order to make sure my daughter is going to be all right even after being threatened she would come to harm. Despite this, I decide to become even more active on the ground with the young people of the uprising, whether at demonstrations or in terms of providing assistance to those young people who had gone underground in order to work for the revolution ever since the security apparatus started following them. These days require a lot more effort, especially in light of the policy of media militarization to which the regime has resorted. We need voices to convey to the media what is actually happening, but most of the young people have been locked up, or will be arrested immediately after appearing on any satellite network.

As of today the Syrian border with Jordan has been closed for five days. The Syrian authorities closed it, and all economic life between Dar'a and al-Ramtha has stopped. 50 martyrs in one week, and the news is still ambiguous. Under the weight of the security forces, the soldiers and the *shabbiha,* the people of Dar'a live in obscurity and darkness. News about them is vague, but the stench of death is obvious. Two days ago the son of a representative in the People's Assembly appeared on television with tears in his eyes, saying, "No matter what's happening in Dar'a, why have they cut off the electricity and water, why are they starving the people, why won't they let people bury their dead, why won't they help the wounded?" Of course, it is obvious that the regime wants to teach all of Syria a lesson through Dar'a, even if they have to exterminate every last person in the process.

Still no news in the afternoon. The army surrounds Damascus, its trucks and its soldiers patrol the city. Daraya is cut off from its surroundings and we hear that the power has been cut, as the people there fear the snipers who deploy up on the rooftops at night. The full strength of the army mobilizes along the Lebanese and Jordanian borders. There are major incursions in several cities. Now, at two in the afternoon, there are demonstrations in Amuda and Latakia, and there is perpetual news about gunfire. I am still waiting.

I sit at home next to my daughter after she returns from two weeks back in the village. She tells me impatiently, "They're going to kill you. In the village they said they're going to kill you. Everybody's saying that, everybody's cursing you and insulting you, and in Jableh they were handing out flyers accusing you of treason!"

I assure her that I am not going to leave the house, that I will stay there with her. She is happily following the marriage of Prince William and Kate. I try to find out online what is going on in the Syrian cities but she asks me to get off the computer and sit with her. I remain silent as she cries and accuses me of abandoning her. I try explaining to her what happened to me, how the security apparatus has smeared my name and incited people to kill me in order to silence the voice of truth. She argues that the situation isn't worth sacrificing my life for, and that she doesn't have anyone else in the whole wide world except for me. I fall silent and go to my room to cry. I don't want her to see my tears, even as she continues yelling. I let her yell as long as she wants, because I know how much pressure she has been under in the village and in Jableh.

Now security prevents people from making it to the demonstration squares in all the cities of Syria. In Homs security surrounds the district of al-Bayyada and imposes a curfew.

In al-Qamishli the people come out to demonstrate. People emerge from the mosque in the al-Maydan district of Damascus. There are tear gas canisters and ten buses filled with security agents who beat up the demonstrators scattered throughout the neighbourhoods chanting for freedom and for the siege on Dar'a to be lifted. They are unarmed. There are about a thousand demonstrators, but they quickly disperse because of the violent beating and the tear gas.

I hope there will be very little bloodshed. Every Friday I have an appointment with pain, not simply pain as an aggravation, but the kind of pain that keeps me awake. Ever since the uprising began I can only sleep with the aid of sleeping pills: Xanax.

Now there is news from Dar'a: heavy gunfire, snipers are still up on the rooftops, nobody can move, there is a flour embargo. Why are they doing this? After the electricity and the water and the medicine, they'll even cut off the bread?! Are they just going to let the people die from hunger? All the eyewitnesses who come forward confirm that the snipers will kill anyone who moves in the city. In the Damascus suburb of Saqba there are also huge demonstrations demanding the fall of the regime.

It's pouring with rain in Damascus now, and there's news about the Jordanian army shoring up its forces near the border. My heart is in my mouth.

I still pace around the house like a madwoman. I feel powerless. I can't go out into the street, the net is shut off, there's no news about what's going on in the outside world. Hailstones pound the windows. My heart clenches. I feel dizzy. The rain keeps falling. Large hailstones. I think about the demonstrators caught out in this downpour when suddenly I receive a text message from a childhood friend: *Dear traitor even god's with the president and you're still lost.*

I am not going to respond.

The internet connection is finally restored.

There are demonstrations in all the cities. They're calling for freedom and the downfall of the regime.

The southern entrance to Damascus is closed as the army redeploys to al-Ma'damiya. The people of Homs hold up olive branches. The news reports that people went out to demonstrate in spite of the stormy weather. But I am nervous. News of the dead still hasn't arrived and there are reports of heavy gunfire in the al-Saliba neighbourhood of Latakia. How much Syrian blood will be spilled today? This mighty people that came out to die will not go back to the way things were. That is the message that arrived today. The Syrian people will not go back to the way things were before. For the first time all of Damascus went out, its centre and its periphery. The news still isn't clear, but what is clear is that the people went out into the streets in force and the security apparatus carried out a sweeping arrest campaign.

Today will not end without bloodshed, that's what I assume anyway, but I hope for the best. News from my city of Jableh reports women and men coming out, forces from the Fourth Division and fire trucks are present. What is happening right now in those streets where I grew up? I know all too well what the *shabbiha* and the regime goons are willing to do in order to stir up the Alawites against the Sunnis; they will shoot at the Alawites to make them believe the demonstrators want to kill them. I wait for civil war to break out in Jableh at any moment; it still hasn't happened, but the regime won't hesitate to make it happen. Maybe they are waiting a while just to play on Alawite fear and stir up even worse sectarian strife.

Now there is confirmed news that demonstrators are coming out in Aleppo. Here is something that will frighten the regime, in light of the city's commercial and strategic significance. I see a report about demonstrators coming out in Hama, the city that still bears so many memories of death and destruction from the early eighties.

My fingers start to tremble. I am under siege in my own home. I want to go out into the streets, but my daughter's tears hold me back. Now I must make her feel safe, even if only a little. But nobody can feel that way amidst our daily fear.

I have been thinking I shouldn't stay here much longer. In two days I'll move to a house in the middle of the capital.

The Arab and non-Arab channels broadcast the wedding of William and Kate. I'll go down and get some supplies. I tell my daughter I have to leave her for an hour, just a car ride through the streets of Damascus. On the verge of tears, she shouts, "Don't go! I know where you're going." Then the tears spill from her eyes. I respond by sitting down next to her.

I wait there until the end of the day, when I learn that the number of demonstrators killed is 62.

30 April 2011

....

The cities of Syria are under siege. Water and electricity have been intentionally cut off for two days, and now there is a growing threat of humanitarian disaster. People began sending calls for help on behalf of children who might die of starvation. That all started yesterday, even as reports about the use of live ammunition against the people were still ringing in my ears.

I am not all right this morning, either. I go to see a friend from Baniyas, I want to hear something true from him. He had left his house and his family behind because he was an Alawite who stood with the peaceful demonstration in Baniyas. My friend is staying with his wife in a small room in al-Mezzeh. He is a lawyer and his wife a public employee; he is an old friend of mine and I can relate to the pressure he is under because I suffered from the same thing, even if my story has been better publicized in the media, more distorted and more like an incitement to kill. The Alawites of Baniyas consider him a traitor, but as far as I know most of the Alawites in Syria think I am one. Entering Mezzeh 86, I am terrified. I happen to know that most residents of that neighbourhood are Alawites who had been brought together in the eighties by then President Hafiz al-Assad's brother Rifaat in order to form the Defence Brigades, which were the forces that carried out the massacres in Hama and at the Tadmur prison. I tell my girlfriend accompanying me, "If they find out who I am, they'll tear me to shreds!"

"Kurds live side by side with Alawites in this neighbourhood," she says. "Nobody's going to know who you are."

I am so worn out I start to feel woozy and weak inside my own skin. Today 50 women hold a demonstration outside the Syrian parliament calling for the siege of Dar'a to be lifted, and security confronts them and arrests some. Reports of killing are still coming out of Dar'a: the shelling of the city, six new martyrs, pictures of dead children and women who were put into a vegetable refrigerator. Images arrive from Dar'a, and finally there is news of arrests. But the most disconcerting thing as far as I am concerned is the feeling of despair that starts working its way through my heart, all the signs of life informing me that the situation in Syria is going to last for a long time, there will still be a lot more death and killing and bloodshed before the regime falls, or before another crazy situation can take its place. I am unnerved by the latest threat – they hacked my Facebook page and deleted all the comments, insinuating that my daughter would be harmed. I had reached the point where I resolved to stay home and write these diaries in order to understand how the uprising began. Going out for the demonstrations has become impossible, but that means nothing to me compared to my tragic feeling of powerlessness. It is all I can muster to write down what happened in Baniyas. I also have an appointment tomorrow with a journalist who managed to break through the siege of Dar'a, and who promises to tell me everything he knows about the accursed day when the massacres took place.

Today it is cloudy; this is enough to change my mood. Imagining that at any moment while I am out somebody could break into the house and take my daughter just like they threatened to do, I decide not to tarry too long at my friend's while recording his testimony.

Even in the middle of the afternoon Damascus looks miserable. Security forces are still deployed out in the streets, at military checkpoints on the bridges and intersections, all around government buildings. Hesitation and caution is inscribed on people's faces, and something indicates that everyone is in a hurry: they just want to get home or wherever they are going. After hearing sporadic gunfire elsewhere in the city we get scared that cars carrying armed men who would open fire on us might pass by at any moment, randomly shoot people and then disappear as if nothing had happened.

We sit there in the one-room apartment. It is a painful meeting, and my exhausted friend is not able to tell me much, but I write down enough of what he says to make some sense of how the events in Baniyas got started.

I.H. says: "The demonstrators set out from the al-Rahman mosque in Baniyas. It was 8 March after Friday prayer when A.S. called on the people to go out of the mosque against tyranny and in order to demand freedom. As about 200 to 300 men came out of the mosque, three were detained by criminal security and taken to the police station over by the bus terminal. The demonstrators followed them in order to demand their release, and on their way down there people poured out into the streets, heading for the garage and smashing up the buses. The demonstrators tried to prevent any vandalism but those thugs got in their faces, and so they immediately started collecting donations to repay the bus owners. They managed to raise some money that they gave to those who had sustained damage. Those thugs were Sunnis who smashed up Alawite buses, but the damage in that initial demonstration stopped there.

"At that point Alawite security forces started stirring up sectarian sentiment. Regime goons and *shabbiha* known for their sectarianism started coming out and chanting that the Sunnis had attacked the Alawite businesses in Baniyas and that they were going to burn everything in sight, especially in the al-Qusoor neighbourhood. Then phone calls were made to the thugs up in the Alawite mountains. A whole bunch of them arrived at the political security branch that was located along the border between the Alawite and Sunni neighbourhoods, and they started making some provocations and threats, until a decision was taken by the political security forbidding clashes between Alawites and Sunnis so they withdrew to the Alawite neighbourhoods, but the provocation by the security forces and the regime *shabbiha* continued.

"The next day those who called themselves the Voice of the Alawites started mobilizing and communicating with one another. With a directive from political security they came together and tried to get in touch with Shaykh A.I., a Sunni *shaykh* they called 'the voice of truth' in Baniyas. It's important to note that throughout the demonstration and the assemblies the security would roll out some prominent Sunni personalities in order to contain the crisis and convince the demonstrators to go home, so this one time they brought the mayor, but the demonstrators chanted, *Get out, get out you thief, get out!* They say the mayor paid millions of liras to get that position, that he paid off a group of Ba'thists and security agents. Then they brought Shaykh I.H. and another imam, who received the same shouts from the demonstrators: *Get out of here, you liars!* They were also corrupt men.

"At this point the demonstrators asked the security forces to bring Shaykh A.I., because he could be trusted and because he was a Sufi. The people of Baniyas gave them a handwritten letter with their demands for Shaykh A., which he read. Their demands included: the release of prisoners, including Tal al-Malluhi, the abrogation of the emergency laws, the return to work of women who wear the *niqab*, the re-opening of the *shari'a* high school, forbidding the mixing of the sexes as in every other Syrian governorate, complete freedoms, the replacement of the head of the port of Baniyas because he behaved like a security officer and imposed taxes on poor fishermen who could barely make ends meet..."

At this point I.H. stops talking and I receive a news bulletin from Damascus about more killings:

Internal source in the army: Under a total media blackout an army hearse delivered the bodies of at least 42 civilians from the village of Tafas outside Dar'a who were killed near the housing bloc of the Fifth Division as well as the body of a soldier from the Fifth Division Housing Bloc who is believed to hail from the coastal region. The bodies were delivered to the Tishreen military hospital at approximately 3 p.m. The 43 bodies had been shot in the head or in the chest by a single sniper firing from a great distance (the sniper's bullet was small both upon entry and exit).

Another bit of news to add to the chain of news stories about killing. My friend stops talking and his wife remains silent, frightened. I am stunned. It takes a few minutes for the conversation to start up once again. We flip through channels as night starts to fall. My daughter starts to call. She is scared. I tell her I will be home soon, that she should lock the door well and not open it for anyone. Then I ask I.H. quickly to finish his story.

"After these events," he says, "and with both direct and indirect orders from the security, rumours started whipping around the Alawite street to the effect that those who came out to demonstrate were sectarians and Islamic fundamentalists who had no other goal than to strike at the Alawites. The proof was what they had said about the women in *niqab*s and the *shari'a* colleges, or even the issue of gender mixing, all of that helped to exacerbate the sectarian mood between Sunnis and Alawites, and caused the Alawite sect in Baniyas to further cling to and wrap themselves around the regime and the security.

"The next Friday," I.H. continues, "there was a demonstration of approximately one thousand people, and a group of Alawite individuals were there. A young Alawite woman named A.I. got up and made a politically pointed speech in front of the demonstrators that confronted the regime head-on, and she received a warm welcome from the demonstrators as all the slogans were patriotic and decried sectarianism. Until that moment there hadn't been any slogans calling for the fall of the regime. It was 15 March."

Exhaustion written all over his face, I.H. says, "Maybe we can pick this up again some other time."

"First I want some news about al-Baida," I respond. "State television is reporting a massacre never took place there."

"But it did," he says, "and what you saw on that video is real. They completely occupied al-Baida, they killed and arrested and insulted people, and what appeared on that video is just one small fraction of what actually happened."

"What about you?" I ask.

"Every person who isn't sectarian at this point is accused of treason. I know that the Sunni neighbourhoods in Baniyas were shelled for more than four hours, while relief supplies were smuggled into the mosques without anyone knowing who was shooting. There were snipers."

"Do you know who the snipers were?" I ask.

"Everybody knows that the snipers are drawn from the regime's *shabbiha*. It did turn out that some Sunnis brought weapons to defend themselves, but they were never aimed at the chest of a single Alawite. They were only for self-defence. We should bear in mind that the worst sectarian rancour in Syria is centred in Baniyas, the situation there is dangerous, but not a single sectarian incident has taken place yet. The Sunnis in Baniyas later insisted upon announcing that Baniyas has no Salafis, that the people of Baniyas never fought against the army, and that it was the security forces and the *shabbiha* who went to the Alawite villages and told them that if they wanted weapons, they would bring them some."

"But who shot at the bus transporting officers and soldiers? Who blew it up?" I ask.

"They say terrorists blew up the bus that was transporting army personnel, but it had been mobilized under such strange and incomprehensible circumstances. The real question is, why was that bus there in the first place? Who had given them orders to pass through? And why had it changed course? High-ranking officers were involved in bringing that bus there and, besides, someone had to order the personnel to get off. Who's capable of ordering military men to go and die like that?

"Do you know that five agents carried out an investigation in Baniyas about this matter? With officers and soldiers from a unit in the 23rd Brigade, which is part of the air force that is primarily stationed in Baniyas in order to protect the oil refinery and the thermal power plant. Everything they said points to an officer working on behalf of Maher al-Assad, who used to work in the very same military division as the soldiers who took part in the fighting. They think he was the one who gave the orders to deploy, and that it was the *shabbiha* who carried out the assassination."

It is getting late, and I must hurry home in order to sort out all the details of the past two days.

Today a broad arrest campaign has swept up even a moderate group in the opposition as well as hundreds of young men. Al-Zabadani is besieged. Dar'a is still buried. Over the past two days there have been demonstrations in all the cities of Syria, including Damascus, Aleppo, Dayr al-Zur, Homs, Hama, Latakia, Qamishli, Amuda and Daraya. Government websites have been hacked, including that of the People's Assembly and the government-run

Tishreen newspaper, in order to leave a message – *Ba'thist Crimes Exposed!* – or else to upload pictures calling on the people to demonstrate. The arteries of Damascus are cut off and checkpoints are set up all around them and between the surrounding suburbs. Four soldiers are killed in Dar'a and the security forces storm a private clinic in order to arrest the wounded, many of whom are in critical condition. The situation in the al-Qala'a and al-'Aweyna neighbourhoods of Latakia is very bad: arrests, shots are fired directly at people, a little girl is killed by her window in the al-Saliba neighbourhood. In the town of al-Tall the women call for a sit-in in the public square until their incarcerated sons are released. In al-Zabadani thousands go out to demonstrate despite the ongoing siege of the town by security forces and the cuts in electricity, water and communications. There is an intense siege all over Jableh even as demonstrations continue; a heavy siege upon the neighbourhoods of al-Dariba and al-Saliba, and massive gunfire and fire trucks at the entrances alongside the demonstration. In Salamiyah security forces break up the power of the demonstration using electric prods. And news keeps pouring in: a massacre in al-Rastan, in which three people are martyred and scores wounded.

The residents of Baniyas are demonstrating with flowers as Syrian television broadcasts images of saboteurs in Jableh. The al-Rastan martyrs are simple young men. The first, Y.H., supported his mother and his sisters by working in a roastery on Jirkis Street because his father was dead; he worked from morning until night and everybody knows him and knows he isn't a terrorist or a Salafi or anything like that. The second, Y.M., sold vegetables from a street cart; and the third I.K. was also a vegetable seller; they were poor and made just enough money to feed their children. There is no end to the news of gunfire everywhere, as I sit here biting my nails. Ten youths are martyred on the Sidon bridge in the Break the Siege massacre, which the security forces carry out against peaceful protesters who pour out to support the people of Dar'a. In Hama, there are two security agents disguised as ordinary citizens at a demonstration, who suddenly try to open fire. The men of Hama pounce on them and beat them up until a political security patrol comes around to save them.

In the end there are 83 martyrs, including women and children in Dar'a, where dozens of houses are bombarded.

Is there any other news left? Is there anywhere else left in my heart for death?

Now I am home at last, my daughter is upset, and I can't feel anything but upset either.

A moving corpse, I smell rusty odours, and my eyes never stop watering. The taste of rust is in my mouth. I remember I have an important appointment tomorrow with the journalist who managed to break the siege of Dar'a.

And so, in utter despair, I fold in on myself and sit down, to sleep for an hour right where I am. I open my eyes some time after midnight, sitting there until dawn smoking cigarettes, stoking my anxiety in anticipation of imminent death.

4 May 2011

....

I begin my day with this headline: *"From a reliable medical source: Security forces transported 182 civilian bodies from Dar'a to Tishreen hospital in Damascus on Saturday, and 62 bodies on Sunday; 242 bodies in all. In addition, 81 bodies from the army arrived at the same hospital, most of them were shot in the back."*

That's how things are in this country...

Sheets of agony are the dividing lines between the sea and the desert, between the mountains and the valley, hung on thin thread-like ropes supported by poles in the sky that vanish into thin air.

That's how things are in this country...

Every bit of territory is separated from every other and tethered to the abode of the Lord's blessings. The mountains are suspended over the open veins of the earth. Beyond the veil of death is the screen of prayers and pleas for relief. Eyes accumulate like soap bubbles floating behind the windows; unafraid, they have lost all their fear. Eyes open onto the void, hunger and anger; they cannot make out anything but a dreary wall blocking their sight. The veil – we live according to the roots and branches of that magical word. The veil grows and grows until it becomes an entire country.

A few days ago, before becoming a creature besieged by the death of my loved ones, I had been in the city and at the seaside. I had thought about getting closer to the body of a tank. I say 'the body' because when I was a little girl and would see them in pictures or on television I liked imagining they were giant amphibians, which would disappear as soon as we filled the bathtub with water and plunged in. Children have such a vivid imagination. I try as hard as I can never to give it up. I am always struck with wonder, which is why my childhood remains a witness to all this pain. It was an odd military checkpoint. We might have expected it near a border, for example, or in a movie when two enemy countries are at war. But what a sight to see their artillery aimed right at domestic windows.

It never occurred to the miserable soldiers hovering around the body of the tank that I might approach them. Soldiers are also waiting for unfathomable death, just like all the unarmed people, who want to know the answer to one question: Where are all these murderers coming from?

One of the soldiers told me he was sure he was going to be killed by a sniper's bullet.

"You'll find out someday," I told him, a painful lump in my throat. Should I have said instead, *You're a sitting duck, you and everyone else in this country, everyone who fails to obey the orders of the security forces and the ruling family*?

I wanted to touch the metal. I placed my hand against the tank, closed my eyes and listened to an exquisite wet hissing. I touched it a second time; my fingers trembled as the coldness of the metal transferred to me. I jumped with a start and opened my eyes: the soldier was standing right there in front of me, watching in bewilderment. I didn't budge; just let my hand rest there on the metal. The soldier laughed. Backing away a little bit, I glanced over at the artillery turret aiming at the houses. The mountain looked down silently in the distance. Greenery enfolded the place. A green mountain with reddish earth against the blue sea – had it not been for the cold chill of the metal I could have been looking down on a gorgeous painting. Tell me, what kind of dialogue is supposed to take place between an artillery turret and an unarmed house? Hmmm, let's see…No dialogue!

As I reached out my hand once more, the soldier seemed to be getting annoyed with me. I tried to strike up a conversation with him, but he was exhausted. What if I spun a spider's web just then and picked up the tank like a toy? What if the whole thing was just a game? What if…and what if?

We have never got used to the sight of those metal bodies among us, here where time allows us to hide in thinking up questions or in the idiocy of a response. Here where I must shut my eyes against all the measures likely to be taken by monsters that multiply and divide like cancerous cells that thrive upon the death of others, like life and its cruel natural law of evolution. This is another morning, and still we fly through a country with clogged arteries, paved over with the capacity to invent bullets and love, the capacity for anything from this moment forward…anything except silence.

The details of this country have imprisoned me, with deceptive rays of sunlight or the rustling of cinchona leaves as I pass underneath those gargantuan trees and head out into the streets of Damascus. Suddenly a white Suzuki rolls by with three masked men in its open trunk, two of them carrying machine guns and erratically firing into the air. Yesterday there was heavy gunfire near the house, and two men were wounded on the opposite side of the airport road. Today the white car zooms past, and it isn't inappropriate for it to be white, the colour of a death shroud. It isn't strange for me to try to hear the rustling sound of cinchona leaves after the deafening silence, when people on the street suddenly disappear, turning the scene into a silent painting – the armed men disappear and the silence and the void remains.

That's how things are in this country…

Like debris we float through the rays that split away from one another, soaring like fire sprites, disappearing and then reappearing all of a sudden, burning up and plummeting without asking any questions.

Today legal activists release a report saying that the daily average number of arrests is at least five hundred people. Students are arrested for demonstrating outside the business school in Damascus. Telephone lines are cut off in the city of al-Tall after the security forces move in and arrest eight hundred people. 30 tanks and six troop convoys are on the move from the Ya'foor region, heading toward Damascus. House raids and detentions continue in Daraya, while in Baniyas thousands of demonstrators have come out demanding an end to the military siege of Dar'a.

That's how things are in this country…

My childhood is being stolen from me these days, as if I am being told, "Wake up, little girl, this isn't the Neverland of Peter Pan." I do not understand how a child's stomach can rumble as it contracts in hunger, or how an entire city can be wiped out, only a few kilometres away.

5 May 2011

. . . .

These critical days are going to continue. My daughter will refer back to them like a scrap of tattered lace in the closet. Beautiful girlfriends will tell me how I stumbled like a cartoon character whenever I walked. I'll continue roaming the streets, nervous, out of breath, frightened, biting my fingers. I'll wilt like a wild mountain plant as I watch your priceless death. Years from now I'll walk even more hunched over, but every day I bow to you, Oh courageous Syrians, and I'll continue to bow down until my lips touch the dust left behind by your pure remains. I'll always be ashamed of my temper when I think about the coolness on your faces in the moment when the bullet passed from the barrel into your chests.

These memories... images of the dead...are going to kill me.

I know that now, as I worry about going to sleep in my new bed after moving downtown. There are no people of conscience opposed to the regime who haven't had to leave their homes. I know that most of my male and female friends who are former prisoners and spent long years in Syrian jails fled in order to avoid getting arrested, because they never want to go back to that savage injustice. Things were more complicated for me amidst the campaign of detentions and raids and house invasions, since I was also trying to protect my daughter even as she heard them call me a traitor and accuse me of being a spy. I wanted to wipe away the burdensome black days she had spent in the village, when I had to leave her there for fear she might be detained along with me when I left the house for the first time. We lived in fear, not fear in its familiar sense, but the kind of fear that makes me think about my daughter's destiny and how I have endangered her, and about my family who have patiently and painfully suffered the consequences of my life in a conservative society, especially when I learned that my brother had started thinking about shooting himself after being subjected to attacks from people in the village because his sister was a traitor to the sect. My heart stopped for a few seconds. I realized this was a situation where I had to do whatever I could to protect them, despite the fact that they were with the regime. Like most Alawites, they had been intimidated by the security forces and the Ba'thists into believing that the Sunnis would kill them all if Bashar al-Assad and his regime were to fall.

I was confused, as dry as a scarecrow. I couldn't find the time to write in my diary and I started feeling there was no use in writing down what was happening to me anyway. But I soon discovered that these diaries were helping me to stay alive; they were my walking stick these days. I had to go on writing if only to keep my spirits up and to bear the pain of leaving home as I moved into an anonymous house downtown. I was sure they didn't want to arrest me, just tarnish my reputation and make people believe that what I had written and what I had done recently had nothing to do with my rejection of the regime or with the fact that I wanted to record the truth of what was happening at the demonstrations, but rather was because I was part of a foreign conspiracy, that I was being paid to write, the same ridiculous talk they repeat on state television about the opposition. But how can I believe what they say when I have seen with my own eyes how they kill people, when I have seen the 'armed gangs' they are talking about? Every time I went out to the demonstrations to monitor what was happening I didn't see anyone but peaceful protestors.

Now it is becoming more difficult for me to move around, not only because my daughter would shut the door on Fridays and burst out crying if I tried to go out, but because the security services know what I look like as well. Maybe the last women's demonstration I went to convinced me that going into the street from here on was like walking myself to jail. Truthfully, I want to stay out of prison as long as possible, at least until my daughter finishes her exams and as long as I can be useful for the young people's movement. I have been cut off from my family, I have been torn by them and from them. I know how much pressure is on them but I won't pay the price for the tyranny and brutality of this regime. I will not surrender to their sectarian blackmail. And so, just like every other moment in my life when I have found myself at a crossroads, I bend towards this fate, towards my freedom. This is a moment like the one in which I ran away at the age of sixteen, like the one in which I divorced my husband and took my two-year-old daughter to live in Damascus. It is like many moments I have experienced; it has nothing to do with any political position or bias toward one party or another. It is, in all simplicity, a tilting toward my own freedom – who I want to be, how I am going to think and write. But none of that means anything. In the end I am just a woman in this little world living alone with her daughter. How narrow this place is for my soul. I can almost reach my hand outside of it and touch the sky.

A woman like me makes life difficult.

Nevertheless I decided to go out into the street again a few days ago. I intended to stay far away from the women's demonstration that had been called. About five hundred women were supposed to meet at Arnous Square, in the middle of the al-Salihiyyeh district, a sensitive location with great commercial significance. A demonstration like that, calling for an end to the killing and an end to the siege of Dar'a, would present a challenge to the regime and its toadies. To me, it was a very important demonstration, because it had been organized by Syrian women. It was absolutely imperative for me to be there. One of my girlfriends refused to let me go alone, and even though she had decided to remain neutral she went down with me anyway. We arrived in the al-Salihiyych shopping area at around 2:30 p.m. There wasn't much activity in the market, most of the shoppers were women, and it had to be admitted that the economic situation was starting to deteriorate. The shop owners were apprehensive about the current state of chaos. One of them told me, "If the situation continues like this for another month or two, we'll be ruined, bankrupt!"

We strolled through the shops, casing the area; the most important thing we needed to find out was, where were the security forces centred? Did they know about the demonstration or had it remained secret? The demonstrators have stopped announcing exactly where they are going to gather, exchanging the time and place in passing on the street instead, as I used to do with the young men. Whenever we want to get the word out about something, we meet in the street for a few minutes, and then everyone takes off in a different direction.

There was no security presence. We searched the place thoroughly and went inside several stores, scrutinizing people's faces and monitoring the movement of men in Arnous Square. I spotted some other women doing the same thing, even some male friends who were loitering around the square, as protection for the demonstrating women. I won't deny the fact that I felt a little bad to see them hovering around the young women demonstrators like that, a light sadness, like homesickness, or the yearning for contact with another living creature. Human beings worried about others, people protecting other people, maybe it was the solitude and the extreme independence that made me feel this way, but I felt better when the women started assembling. I observed some male friends watching from a little bit further away. I left my girlfriend with another friend of ours, and the two of them moved aside as I lined up with the other demonstrators.

There weren't a lot of people there, maybe 60, even though five hundred women had been expected. I knew a lot of the women there, all different ages and types, mostly unveiled. Veiled women also went out to demonstrate two days ago, but this demonstration was different. That's the way the Syrian street is, no matter what happens it will continue to harbour diversity and difference; that's part of its essence. The signs being held up brimmed with life, reading, *Stop the killing, End the siege on Dar'a* and *No to Death, Yes to Life*. Signs count off the basic truths of life, the ABCs of living. The women were all fired up, holding their signs up high and clear. We had only been marching for about ten minutes when a strange vibration rippled through the atmosphere. I could sense it; I was very aware of it as it was happening; I had developed the instincts of a threatened animal. I saw a man walking towards us, and another gesturing at me. Turning to leave the gathering, I started running, certain that they had recognized me. How could the security forces sprout out of the ground so suddenly? As I started running away, men pounced on the demonstrating women, beating and cursing and kicking them.

They broke one woman's finger and slapped her in the face before arresting her. The rest of the women took off, scattering.

How could those men attack us like that? How did they come so quickly? Has half of the Syrian population been turned into security forces? It always happens like that: men in civilian clothes, frightening in their appearance, surging up out of the ground. Syrians know who they are now, the Syrians who come out to demonstrations anyway. As I was running away, I saw my girlfriend and our young male friend. They pushed me out in front of them and we ducked down a side street. We ran as fast as we could until we found ourselves outside the al-Hamra Mosque. The young man left us there and went back to see what was happening with the other young women, after begging us to get out of there as quickly as possible because the security forces were fanning out on the side streets, arresting people and beating them up. We hurriedly jumped in a cab and asked the driver to stop at the edge of Arnous Square. I wanted to find out what was happening to the other women.

Even though only five minutes had passed between when I started running and when the taxi pulled up, I couldn't figure out what had happened. Security forces had broken up the demonstration; they were the only ones left in the square; we are more likely to see them than ordinary people in the streets of Damascus these days. I told the driver to wait there as I phoned one of the women, telling her, "I'm parked off to the side. If anyone gets in trouble, bring them here." She said she was fine, and that they had left the scene right away. Watching the square, I noticed one of the young women standing off to the side, where security was present, and suddenly three agents appeared, dragging a young man in his early twenties behind them, beating him violently. They smacked him in the face. Every blow is directed at the face, as though they mean to insult anyone they beat up. How else can a person be known except from his face? They kicked him, yanked his hair and cursed him, people just stood there watching; they were scared, panicked. The taxi driver asked, "Does that guy work for the government?"

I told him to get closer. I wanted to find out where they were taking him. The driver grumbled, but I said, "I'll pay you double, get closer."

The security forces stood by a small white van, but they couldn't seem to get the young man inside; he was remarkably strong. But there were just too many of them. They beat him again and again, severely, his head got smashed against the side of the van, and finally they tossed him inside. Just then I cried out, I couldn't stop myself. The man who had just been banging the young man's head turned to face our car as soon as he heard my shout. I stared into his eyes, which were like every other murderer's eyes that have appeared these days, eyes I had never seen before in Damascus. How could all those murderers be living among us? I know that I am repeating this expression a lot in my diaries, but I never get tired of it. The man's complexion was dark and his features hinted at a kind of foreignness we were all starting to wonder about.

"Get out of here, quick," I ordered the driver.

His eyes locked on the car window as we sped away. He would have needed only a few seconds to grab me by the throat, which is what his hand craved to do, because I had stuck my head out the window to watch what they did to the young man. The driver quickly drove us away, and after a little while he stopped and kicked us out of the car. My girlfriend was scared and so was I – my entire body was heaving. We looked out at the street and started running toward a friend's office not far from where the demonstration took place. I thought we could stay there until things calmed down.

The women were trapped there for about ten minutes, getting beaten and kicked – one would get hurt, another would get arrested. A lot of other women managed to evade the security forces. They had said what they wanted to say. These were the best circumstances we had for demonstrating in Damascus: military checkpoints, tank barricades, machine guns, security forces, thugs and murderers – all of that just to confront people who wanted to step outside, unarmed, empty-handed except for their demands for liberty. In that moment I returned home with a whole lot of bitterness and not so much joy. Standing up and remaining steadfast to tell the regime what we wanted to say had only cheered us up for a few minutes.

Today I'll prepare myself a little bit more for the next few days, for my new home and my undefined new life, for the financial burdens, more frustration, more of all these painful things. I have to be ready. Tomorrow is the Friday of Defiance, and it will be a turning point for the protest movement.

7 May 2011

....

Today I sit down to write about yet another massacre. Tanks besiege Baniyas once again; they shell al-Baida and al-Qumsiyya. Baniyas is a ghost town. The army and the security shell the city on a sectarian basis, bombing only Sunni neighbourhoods. I try to make a phone call, but the lines are disconnected, so is the internet. People are surrounded on all four sides in a square that is no larger than four kilometres.

What's going on? Is the regime occupying the cities? Do they intend to kill their own people in broad daylight?

Latakia is sliced in four. All communications between the cities are cut. We're in a state of war, that's right, we're living in a state of war. My blood boils. I've lost my nerve. Let me try to clear my head, one siege has barely ended when another one begins. They start targeting women. Three women are killed in al-Marqab, outside Baniyas. My internet at home is shut down, and it's going to be hard for me to get out to an internet café because the security forces monitor them, arresting boys and girls at random. I find it's better just to stay home. What I am able to document on the Friday of Defiance is that a total of 30 people have been killed in all the Syrian cities, killed at demonstrations by the security forces' bullets. I try better to understand the course the army is taking in its joint operations with the security forces, especially since Friday afternoon when they started shooting people at precisely the same moment in every Syrian city.

This policy is an obvious declaration of war. There is no longer any uncertainty – the regime has made up its mind to kill its own people without making any attempt to listen to what they have to say. The military and repression options are abundantly clear, and perhaps the worst possible scenario is becoming even clearer, the scenario I worried the country might fall into: a sectarian war, in which people are killed indiscriminately. That would mean Syria drowning in a pool of its own blood.

The endless telephone threats make me increasingly nervous. What more do they want from me? I keep silent, I have fled my house and am living in hiding, my relationship with my family has been severed, I even write in silence. Maybe they know I am actually moving around on the ground and among the people.

Now I want to calm down, to try and focus on the details of what has happened, on compiling more testimonies from the people who assembled in various places on the Syrian streets, but even that seems too difficult. The obstacles people face in getting in touch with each other, the security's surveillance of the phone lines, the shock and the sadness that weigh upon the people – all these details are very difficult to deal with right now. I even cancel my appointment with a journalist I was supposed to meet after he had to flee his house for fear of being arrested. And so I have decided to spend these two days calmly studying the Syrian situation, from the beginning of the protest movement right up to this very moment: What had actually happened on the streets? And why had the regime started right away with such repressive tactics? How did the incident involving those young boys in Dar'a first get started? What had Atef Najib done to them? And what about the echoes that still reverberated about Maher al-Assad opening fire on Vice-President Faruq al-Shar'a? Before closing this file I am going to try and call people in Baniyas. The lines are still disconnected but I manage somehow to get through to someone who lives near the sea. They tell me they don't know anything. I would guess they are afraid of the *mukhabarat* listening to Syrian mobile phones as well as their ordinary eavesdropping. We have all started keeping our cell phones more than ten metres away from us because we believe the security forces are carrying out surveillance even when our devices aren't in use.

What kind of a siege is this?!

We breathe the security forces in the air.

It isn't true that we don't feel terror. After seeing how readily they shoot to kill, I tremble whenever there is an unfamiliar sound.

I have somehow become both more fragile and stronger at the same time; that's right, both those states have become deeply anchored in my heart, to the point that last night, as the wind blew fiercely outside, I heard rattling noises up on the roof and couldn't fall asleep. The whole time I imagined someone coming. The senior officer warned me they would let me flop around like a fish, in pain and fear, before arresting me. I knew the regime would do the same thing in Baniyas that they had done in Dar'a: besiege the city, detain people and kill them. But such a move worried me because Baniyas remained an epicentre of sectarian tension, which the regime had been working to feed recently. I know the people of Baniyas won't remain silent forever, that they are arming themselves, and that a sectarian war is looming on the horizon. As usual, in addition to bombing and terrorizing the city, the regime will resort to turning the Alawites into human shields, taking advantage of the tension that was starting to intensify. Now I get a phone call from a friend, and suddenly information regarding what happened today in the village of al-Marqab is confirmed by people at the heart of the city and its people, including the names of the women who were killed in al-Marqab-Baniyas: Ahlam Huwisikiyyeh, 25; Layla Taha Sahyuni and Amina Taha Sahyuni, both in their forties; fifteen women wounded. The army had moved in and detained people in al-Marqab. When they finally pulled out, women came to demand the return of their detained children. The security forces and the *shabbiha* started indiscriminately shooting at the women. My source at the heart of Baniyas also adds: The bombardment isn't only by tanks, there is also gunfire, and two men were killed in the heart of the city, one from the Rustum family and a second from the Qarqour family.

In Jableh, too, the women have started coming out to demonstrate now that the houses are emptied of their men; sons and husbands are in prison and women have taken over the task of demonstrating.

I expect more violence. The number of people killed has now actually risen to six, and it is not yet nine o'clock in the morning on the seventh of May.

I write down the most important things that have happened

since the beginning of the uprising. Two months in and the protest movement is growing. It started in February in a small way. In March it spread, and then there were the events in Dar'a. 25 March was the Friday of Dignity, when the first person was killed in Damascus, and many were killed in Dar'a. Then there was the president's first speech and his talk about a conspiracy against Syria. On the Friday of Steadfastness 37 people were killed. The students in Damascus started to mobilize, then the students of Aleppo.

The Friday of Perseverance took place in the middle of April, and Good Friday saw the largest harvest of victims; then there was the Friday of Defiance and the organizers were punished. Thoughts I try to put in order: eight hundred civilians killed by the security forces, a large number of army officers among the dead. The rhetorical posture of the protest movement in Syria is growing and growing. There are so many details about pain and subjugation and death, about fear and the consecutive breaths of life... the life that is slowly expiring here before the eyes of the entire world.

8 May 2011

··

I didn't wake up as early as usual today. Now that I am addicted to Xanax, I sleep more deeply these days, missing the sunrise I was once accustomed to watching. It's 9 a.m. as I sit high up on the fifth floor balcony across from Arnous Square, looking out on al-Hamra Street and the districts of al-Shaalan and al-Rawda. From my new home I can see in all directions; besides the safety, this is its main virtue. I try to reconstruct my memory, which has been fraying ever since the protests broke out, and ever since killing became an everyday occurrence in this country.

Today I need to be more focused, but there is news from Homs, where the electricity has been turned off in some neighbourhoods, a siege tactic the regime depends upon, and news about heavy gunfire there causes me to lose my focus again. What drives me even crazier is the internet disruption. I have to do something, the problem requires a quick fix or I won't be able to find out any news from the protests. The siege of Baniyas is surely ongoing, the electricity and water and communications lines are still interrupted, but there is no news yet about any more dead. The arrests continue. I am extremely irritated. I am headed, quite possibly, for a major depression. My fingers tremble. I have no desire to see anyone or anything, to follow the news or even to write. I am shaking.

This morning my bad luck seems to be getting worse because the first scene I see on television is a sniper action against a young man running down an empty street – the image is shot from far away, there are trees on both sides of the street, the sound of gunfire, and suddenly the young man drops after being shot from behind, in his back, falling down like a scrap of paper. I shake even more. That young man has a family, friends, a name. I don't know who he is, but I know he had a life, and that he is a Syrian citizen, killed by another Syrian citizen.

How has the blood of this united country's people become so worthless?

How did the security services make people so savage?

Memories of the first protests come rushing back, when I was able to move around more easily. I wasn't prepared for all this violence, and I don't just mean the metaphorical violence that came crashing down when I was accused of being a traitor and other kinds of defamation, but violence in its material and tangible senses, real violence. I never thought that murderers could just sprout up out of the streets like trees. Even Baniyas, that magical city, is now besieged by tanks and bullets, the city I know street by street, tree by tree, and house by house, the city whose beautiful imperfections I know by heart, Baniyas, where I can roll all the way down from the peak of the al-Marqab Castle to the edge of the sea without my body getting shaken up because of the soft slope that nature has made between the mountains and the sea, where I can hear the cicadas humming at the end of alleys that connect all the houses, and where I could sit for a hundred years and write novels without getting tired of the sight of that city's beauty. Now Baniyas has been turned into a series of military checkpoints, which separate the neighbourhoods, Sunni from Alawite, where the army and the security forces arrest people and kill. Now the connecting arteries of Baniyas have been cut, just like the rest of the country, occupied by soldiers and security forces and murderers. I can no longer conjure up the shape of the Baniyas coast or its inhabitants or the sounds of the vegetable sellers. Now the only imagination I have left is bullets and killing and images of people being killed and beaten and arrested, the women who were killed. I can't laugh or do anything at all. Syrian cities are besieged one after another – Dar'a, Baniyas, Homs.

Just before going out to meet a female journalist, I call her number, but her line is out of service. At the same moment a friend calls to tell me that she has been arrested by the security forces and that I need to be more careful. I stop for a moment in front of al-Hamra Street, thinking about how I had just seen her yesterday and how we had talked for a long time. She is getting ready to write an article about me. I feel all shrivelled up. A shouting Chinese woman snaps me out of it, as she spreads her wares out on the sidewalk. Al-Hamra Street is funny: the elegant shops open and their owners sit down outside them, while Chinese merchants display their cheap products along the edge of the sidewalk. Everyone is heading towards the Chinese goods. I laugh at the sight: a market inside a market, goods of all different kinds – clothes and shoes and wallets and accessories – and the funny Chinese women who chat with their customers in broken Arabic and move around vigorously. I walk back a little bit and look at my house right in front of me. That young journalist is now in jail. I tell myself it is a good thing she doesn't know where I live. Her arrest must have had something to do with me. Every day somebody who I have been with or who I am going to meet gets arrested. Thinking about the journalist who had scheduled two different appointments with me, and how I didn't show up for either one, I call him impulsively; the phone rings and he picks up, we talk for a little, and I feel a small happiness. The arrest campaign is ongoing, and there are more deaths and a slew of arrests in Homs today.

The meaning of death and the meaning of fear change by the day. The fundamental meanings of our lives were changing with every passing moment. I need to focus and think about what I am going to do with no internet, unable to move around. It's like they're amputating our limbs while we're still alive.

On my way home, imaginary funerals swirl in my head, and I long to hear just one bit of good news amidst everything that is happening, just one bit, however small, that might make me less anxious, maybe even a bit of news that would give me the strength to go on living, to sleep like a normal human being, without Xanax. The only news I heard was of army tanks invading the town of Tafas near Dar'a and the death of twelve civilians; the army's assault on Homs on the Friday of Defiance in which nineteen people were martyred; and, finally, an eleven-year-old boy among those arrested today in Baniyas.

The dead and the funerals become new funerals: every time the Syrians mourn a martyr another martyr falls, and that's the way funerals drag along behind them...more funerals.

I get a call from a broadcaster friend, and I ask her if we can meet.

The brutality of the regime knows no bounds. It does not remain neutral towards the people here; it creates beasts in its own image out of ordinary people who might have been neighbours instead. Even more dangerous was the fact that the fundamentals of humanity and the ABCs of life have been eviscerated from the hearts of many people here. State television destroys human compassion, the sort of fundamental empathy that is not contingent upon a political or even a cultural orientation, and through which one human being can relate to another. The al-Dunya channel stirs up hatred, broadcasts false news and maligns any opposing viewpoint. I wasn't the only one subjected to internet attacks by the security services and the Ba'thists, even if the campaign against me may be fiercer because I come from the Alawite community and have a lot of family connections to them – because I am a woman and it's supposedly easier to break me with rumours and character assassination and insults. Some of my actress friends who expressed sympathy for the children of Dar'a and called for an end to the siege of the city were subjected to a campaign of character assassination and called traitors, then forced to appear on state television in order to clarify their position. Friends who expressed sympathy for the families of the martyrs would get insulted, they would be called traitors and accused of being foreign spies. People became afraid to show even a little bit of sympathy for one another, going against the basic facts of life, the slightest element of what could be called the laws of human nature – that is, if we indeed agree that sympathy is part of human nature in the first place.

Moral and metaphorical murder is being carried out as part of a foolproof plan, idiotic but targeted, stupid yet leaving a mark on people's souls. I recorded an interview with one of my friends who used to work for Syrian state television. The poor girl had been conducting a kind of schizophrenic life, torn between what she saw with her own eyes and what she was involved in disseminating on television. She agreed to grant me an interview as long as I do not mention her name, no matter what, not now, not ever, and I agreed. Here is her testimony:

"Official media discourse has divided the Syrian people into two camps: with or against. This means that even if you're a demonstrator who hasn't been accused of being involved with the armed gangs then you're a traitor. For example, when news is reported of people being martyred 'by the monstrous hands of treachery,' we in the media know that such expressions are only used when we're talking about Israel/Palestine. The last time was in Gaza. When a son is forced to publicly disown his father on the al-Dunya network for being in the opposition, this hits the core of human feelings. Meeting with the families of the martyrs, all the weeping and wailing, the horrifying and soul-destroying pictures of the military dead, without showing comparable images of dead civilians, all of this creates awful hatred among the people, and people everywhere have started saying, 'May God never forgive them.'

"State media gives voice to these emotions, then militarizes them. There is the focus on militaristic, jingoistic anthems and love for the homeland, which only ever means love for the president. Unfortunately, most calls in from the people are love poems to the president. One time, a little girl recited a love poem for the president live on air. I asked her, 'Sweetie, why do you love the president?' The little girl was silent for a few moments. She didn't respond so the guests we had on, who were regulars, filled the dead air. With the outbreak of the protest movement they had been transformed into superstars on the Arab satellite channels and the Syrian satellite channel as well, and they served as mouthpieces for the regime.

"Following recent events the media discourse has become more ideological and more didactic. Practically speaking, on the media side of things, I can't say there has been any reform. On the contrary, the first news we always had to report in our broadcasts was about the president's ongoing meetings with the people; the second most important story was always the continuing pursuit of the armed gangs; this would be followed by statements from the Interior Ministry and international news. There has been only one significant change in the official media discourse, in that the focus on Palestine has taken a backseat to the Syrian situation. We as journalists asked to go out into the streets alongside the security forces and the demonstrators in order to find out the truth, but our request was denied for safety reasons. We asked because we couldn't tell true from false, and we were flatly denied. Besides, what we were reporting and broadcasting was nothing other than whatever SANA was telling us. Reuters was absolutely banned, as was every international and Arab news agency, but only concerning the Syrian situation. SANA is an outlet for the Republican Palace, and from the beginning of the events until now we wanted an official to meet with us, as journalists, in order to discuss a media strategy given the exceptional circumstances. Orders came over the phone because everyone was afraid. During this crisis some Lebanese spokesmen for the Syrian regime contributed by making visits to the radio and television station in order to talk about what was going on inside Syria, to take part in political discussions. One time one of the Lebanese guests even asked, 'Why is there no voice opposed to the regime here with us?'

"The fact of the matter is that, as a government media organization, our discussions were always muted by a unified perspective, and careerists couldn't reconcile two different voices, because the news was dictated from on high. We were merely employees earning a wage, not journalists. For example, a broadcaster can't be hired for television without security connections or a recommendation from the Regional Command of the Ba'th Party. The interesting thing now is that they are relying upon radio broadcasters who have been transferred to television, and they have a religious outlook, coming from old Damascus families and the old neighbourhoods. I think that was done in order to attract the residents of Damascus over to the side of the regime, and in order to deny the overwhelming presence of Alawites on Syrian television. Lately they want to create balance in the media image, just as they have done in allocating seats in the administrations of the television, radio and media.

"News would come to us printed and ready to go. Even when we had a question concerning the shape the news was going to take, the answer was always ready for us: Here is what SANA or the news bureau is reporting.

"Our media isn't real journalism, it's an instrument that adheres to classical and harsh strictures. From the shape of the news to the selection of guests, everything is subject to security censorship. The hosts of political talk shows must be cooperative with the administration and the security first and foremost, even at networks such as al-Dunya that call themselves private, but which are owned by pro-regime businessmen and do even more of a disservice than state media by distorting the reputation of the opposition and inciting people to hate others based on their position vis-à-vis the regime, making up rumours and poisoning the atmosphere. Or, for example, over the last two months or so, we have a new device in the radio and television building that takes fingerprints from anyone who enters the building, under the pretence of keeping track of who keeps regular office hours and who is playing hooky, knowing full well that there are radio and television employees on the security forces' payroll earning their salaries by staying at home. The television reports are produced by regime supporters, by those who are very close to the regime and the decision-makers. For example, the person who now conducts local reportage about the protest movement is the nephew of the minister, and we all know there is a directive regarding what people have to say in order to make it on camera."

The broadcaster's testimony ends here.

I check in to see what has happened today: there is extensive security deployment in the town of Saqba; troops have moved in. Tanks in Dar'a remain where they are as the security and the army are deployed and snipers are posted on top of the buildings. The minarets ascend above them even as the arrest campaign continues.

9 May 2011

....

I have finally been able to catch hold of the threads leading back to where the protest movement began; its simultaneous origins in more than one city, how the protests surged out with simple demands for a dignified life using various protest tactics, how all those threads came together around one essential thing: the dignity of Syrian women and men confronting the injustice and humiliation practiced by the security services.

Every city began with the same demands, and when the security forces and the *shabbiha* started arresting and killing people, the protest movement started changing and simple quality-of-life issues were transformed into a single demand: the fall of the regime. As I met with people day after day, the view became clearer. Today I am going to finish up with Baniyas. One of the young men who had been at the heart of the events when they all came out of the mosque is coming over to my house with a lawyer friend of mine from Baniyas. Maybe it's dangerous for me to tell them where I live but it would have been impossible to find somewhere outside where we could meet, so I opted to get together in private. My friend promises me this young man is trustworthy but there is no room for trust here, because imprisonment and torture can tear a person away from himself.

The young man shows up. He is in his twenties, skinny and of medium-height. He won't shake my hand but he is polite, well-spoken, calm and measured. After five minutes I can tell his belief in fate was unwavering, but his mind seems inclined towards reason, which makes me feel better. In addition, he ends up talking to me freely, without getting flustered and without my feeling like he is talking at a woman inside a frame, as would many fundamentalist Muslims. Maybe this is what they call moderate Islam. He tells me his name is Abed and without any further introduction I ask him to talk about what happened in Baniyas, or about what happened afterwards, about the first and the third Fridays I had already written about. He says:

"I was at my grandfather's house, and there were about 50 soldiers stationed in the Ibn Khaldoun building, 200 metres past the municipality in the centre of Baniyas. The army was sleeping up on the rooftops and we showed them hospitality, at first the people of Baniyas and the military cooperated. In al-Marqab the army carried out searches and sweeps, then they withdrew. It was the security forces that did all the killing. I saw the battle with my own eyes, the battle on Sunday. When the army launched their attacks from the international road, I was standing up on the roof with a telescope, the army units started to attack, out in the open on the international road. It was a weird formation. I don't think armies usually behave like that. They were like death squads. The army hit the houses and the water tanks and the Ra's al-Naba'a bridge. Bullets were pouring down like rain. They moved into the city in the afternoon and then continued pounding the houses at random. We didn't know what was happening, some guys who were closer to the action told me that security forces and *shabbiha* opened fire on people and beat them up. Something like twenty bullets whizzed right past me. That was in the afternoon.

"The next morning at dawn, I went up to the top of the minaret at the mosque and saw security forces on the rooftops. When they saw me watching them I left the minaret. The army moved under the al-Qawz bridge, we ran out of the mosque and the security forces disappeared. An agreement was reached that security forces wouldn't move in, but that the army could enter the city. On the same day as the battle, some soldiers started turning themselves in to us and to the people. One of them said, 'They told us we were going to be fighting a gang, but when we saw the *muezzin*, we realized there was no gang. I knew it had all been one big lie.' One of the inhabitants of Baniyas told the soldier, 'We're the people of Baniyas, we're not a gang.' Some army soldiers got killed turning themselves in, and others were killed before they could even leave the army. All their injuries were either from behind or directly to the head."

I ask him about the images we had seen of people dancing on top of bodies in Ayn al-Baida, "Ayn al-Baida and the pictures that came out, what the state media is saying, what do you have to say about it?"

He laughs mournfully and says, "Of course it's all real, and what actually happened is even more disgusting than those pictures. That video was leaked by the security forces themselves. One of them sold it for a ton of money and the video went viral. They were filming themselves just to show off, those are security agents. Anyone in Baniyas who had weapons didn't want them, and I doubt there really were any except for those that were used in self-defence.

"The army reinforced its presence in Baniyas and didn't come out at first. Baniyas was beyond government control, there was no police presence. We the people were protecting the city. The canteens were only open when necessary. We set up essential roadblocks to protect property but not a single act of vandalism took place in the entire city and the people remained calm. At first there was a limited number of soldiers and it was the people who decided where the army would be stationed. Seriously, when the army first moved in we felt protected and secure and there was amazing cooperation between us and them, but apparently there were others who weren't so happy with that situation."

"Who were those others?"

I want to add my own sentence here —the others are Hell, the others are the dead who plunder life from us – but I am still playing the role of journalist, so the novelist in me backs away as I await his response.

"People inside the regime weren't happy about it. I have an interpretation of the situation, which suggests the existence of two factions within the government; the first is violent and the second is peaceful. I believe the violent current won out over the peaceful and reformist trend. Anyway, the army fully pulled out and a new force arrived in al-Marqab. It was the security forces that killed the four women and wounded scores of others. Then they moved into Baniyas two days later. This army had more equipment and greater numbers. They detained entire families. I think this operation was intended to force the entire city onto its knees because it had been completely outside government control and the protest movement there was strong; the regime asked for the demonstrations to stop but the people refused. We knew the names of some of the *shabbiha* and the security forces shooting at the women, and they included the following: I.S., H.Z., and I.M."

"What about the social situation, what was Baniyas like during those days?"

"We were constantly on alert, rotating shifts late into the night in order to protect the people. When the phone lines were cut, the women would prepare for war. There were incursions every couple of days. We weren't afraid of the army, we were afraid when the security forces carried out their raids. When the army moved in, the people would cheer for them. The security forces were the people's real problem.

"It's been said ever since the start of the protest movement in Baniyas that it has a sectarian quality."

"Every society has people who are simple-minded and stupid, who don't understand. I'm not going to tell you that among all the people of Baniyas there isn't a sectarian colouring – sectarianism is present among some individuals, but it had no place in the demonstrations. We were against sectarian slogans. I attended all of the sermons in the mosques and none of A.I.'s sermons had any sectarian incitement and there wasn't any sectarian character to what we were proposing. An Alawite professor came with us during the demonstrations and we were chanting alongside him and behind him. M.Y. and the people from the village of H. were all there."

"What's the story of Nidal Junoud? And why was he killed?"

"He was there in the graveyard with a sniper's rifle and the people found him after coming under heavy gunfire. The guys told me he had been killing people. I think it was a case of revenge but I also think it was an isolated case of violence."

"Who were the young men who captured him?"

"They were ordinary young men, illiterate; they hadn't been with the demonstrators. The city was in a state of anarchy, anything could have happened with all that violence. We demonstrators captured somebody from criminal security, but then we left him alone. One of the soldiers as well; we held him and then let him go. We aren't sectarian, we aren't violent, we weren't inciting people to violence, but there are incidents of violence and ambiguity that take place during such situations. When the guys took control of an army convoy they handed it over straight away to the army; there were papers and maps of Baniyas inside. There was something odd about that bus where soldiers and officers were killed, because the soldiers stepped out in a completely natural way and then suddenly, the shooting started. The bus had come from Latakia and it was shot up for an entire hour. I saw it all with my own eyes and I found it very odd. I couldn't tell exactly where the shooting was coming from. I was down a way, towards the sea. I watched the soldiers calmly step off the bus. They weren't prepared for combat. They looked like they had just received orders. They were completely calm. And then they died. After getting off they just stood there until the shooting started, it was machine guns, mostly, and I saw them with my own eyes, they were shooting – it was the *shabbiha*, I just told you some of their names a little while ago. They were the ones who killed the soldiers along with some others who were with them."

I think about the fact that the people of Baniyas know who the murderers were, how they live alongside them and how their silence, despite knowing who they are, is not cowardice. I know the city well, I know how proud and self-respecting its people are. They remain silent so as not to respond to murder with more murder, to protect the peacefulness of their protests.

"Were you there when the demonstrations started?"

"Yes. Even before 15 March, Shaykh A.I. would talk about taxes and the rising injustice against the people through this theft they were subjected to by the state. He talked about the pollution from the Baniyas refinery. Then the demonstrations started to spread throughout the Syrian cities. During prayer on 18 March we noticed a lot of cars outside the mosque and people were streaming inside. Shaykh I. said, 'By God I didn't invite anyone to come, I simply spoke the truth.' Some people, including A. S., left because they didn't like what the *shaykh* had to say. They wanted to start demonstrating. The demonstrations were spontaneous and unplanned at first, at the municipal roundabout. But after the events in Dar'a and the incursion into the al-Umari Mosque on Wednesday, the people rose up once again, and they were energized by what was happening in most of the cities in Syria. We started trying to calm people down and tried to get them to delay making their demands and the *shaykh* decided that nobody should go out into the streets, telling them, 'You'll be turning your backs on God, telling God to shut up.' But they wouldn't listen, the energy was intense and Dar'a was under siege. The people didn't respond to what the *shaykh* was saying. In the al-Qubayat Mosque, when Shaykh Mustafa Ibrahim described the demonstrators as riffraff and anarchists, the people brought him down from his pedestal and then they got together and the demonstration happened. We tried to calm everybody down but the people started going out to demonstrate and to demand their rights."

"When did the army first cooperate and make contact with security and the *shabbiha*?"

"I don't know the exact date but it could have been the first Saturday in April. Before they moved into al-Baida, before the communications were cut and the people started getting themselves ready and getting scared. We started setting up roadblocks before dawn. There were threats but no police, no security, no protection for anybody; it was just political security. The women were scared and carried sticks to defend themselves. After dawn prayers people were coming out of the mosque and I was in the garden when I heard the sound of heavy gunfire. I saw someone shooting from a car, bullets were raining down everywhere and I heard from the guys that somebody named A.S. had been wounded in the al-Qubayat neighbourhood. Four others and I tried to treat him, but he died. The guys followed after the car that had been shooting, when suddenly the driver jumped out and left behind the car, which the guys set on fire. We took the car registration. It was owned by *shabbiha* of the Assads, from the family of S. and the family of H. One of them was named I.S., and we were informed that those guys weren't just *shabbiha*, they were very close to the security services. We took pictures of the security agents under the al-Qawz bridge and pictures of some *shabbiha* pointing out certain locations to the security forces. The *shabbiha* were armed the whole time, even after this assault."

"Where was the shooting at the army coming from?"

"From behind. All the soldiers who were killed were shot in the back. The shooting came from the house of a well-known man named F. H. He was close to the *shabbiha* and the security forces. Baniyas had been shut down for a month. There was a lot of recrimination among the people, who were now ready to die after all this killing and injustice. I mean, in the al-Baida incident, people were subjected to a lot of injustices and humiliation. You wouldn't believe how many bullets were fired. The army assaulted them and said they were out searching for weapons. Where were the weapons, though? During their search of al-Baida, the only person who got killed was a Christian man named Hatem. Where were the Salafis they were talking about? One of the guys told me that before he was killed the man had said, 'I swear to God I'm a Christian.' He had nothing to do with what has going on yet they shot him on the spot! I personally recorded some footage of a 60-year-old woman. I filmed her house and the pictures spread everywhere; it later appeared on the internet. There were hundreds of bullet holes. They demolished her son's house and hers. I filmed a man sitting in a wheelchair, they broke his chair, broke his cane and stole what little money he had; it also got circulated on the internet. The people who did all of this weren't from the army, this was the security forces and agents who they say were loyal to Hafiz Makhlouf.

"I also videotaped three meetings with three girls who were twelve, thirteen, and fourteen, who all told me how the security forces had brutally tortured them. What had those little girls ever done? They tortured a nineteen-year-old. He said their heads were cracked by the security forces' shoes, 'They stamped on us,' he said, and they smashed them down on the pavement. There's another story from Baniyas about the practices of the security forces there: three visitors from Aleppo and Baniyas were quickly passing through the city. The security forces captured them, broke their ribs, stamped on them and stood on their necks and their faces. They mutilated the face of the guy from Aleppo who had just stayed with his friend from Baniyas and then he died under torture. When he arrived in Damascus his face was pummelled beyond recognition, his nose was gone, his eyes were missing. He had kids, too. The face of the guy from Baniyas who had been his host, A. S., was also pulverized, but he didn't die. Another guy from the S. family was hit by a strange bullet, which pierced him and came out leaving a gaping hole. The back of his body was torn wide open. This was an explosive bullet that the security forces were using to slaughter people; they used the same bullets in Jableh and Dar'a and Latakia."

His face goes slack, and I feel like there isn't any air left in my lungs. I pour him a glass of water, light a cigarette and motion to see if he is ready to continue, and he nods.

"Did all the media coverage of what happened in al-Baida play a part in preventing the region from being completely surrounded?"

"First of all there was recrimination and anger about all the practices that took place in al-Baida. The state media ignited the people's anger because it claimed the pictures were fake. We were trying to calm the situation down but the al-Dunya channel and Syrian state television played an incendiary role in stirring up hatred among the people and making them afraid of each other. We alerted the authorities to what the state media and its security appendages like al-Dunya were doing. Abd al-Halim Khaddam was banned – as far as we were concerned he was a traitor – which comes through in our slogans at the demonstrations, *No Salafiyya and no Khaddam*. There were rumours propagated by the regime and if the people were left to their own devices there wouldn't be a civil war, but what the security forces and the *shabbiha* were doing was going to lead them there. They didn't use any guns. Even Nidal Junoud, who did get killed, was killed with knives. There's an unlikely story going around that the people defended themselves with sticks of dynamite."

"How did the army search the houses?"

"They moved into al-Baida on 12 April, searching house by house but they didn't find any weapons."

"What's with the story that some demonstrators came out wearing shrouds?"

"People got a little too excited, they began to prefer death over humiliation. I would have liked for the city of Baniyas not to carry out this kind of initiative."

"There's a geographical divide in Baniyas between Sunni neighbourhoods and Alawite neighbourhoods. Don't the Alawites sympathize with their neighbours, didn't they stand side-by-side with them?"

"Yes, at first, but they were frightened and intimidated. Recently there was a young man who wanted to come out to the demonstrations with us but they threatened to demolish his house and kill his family."

"How much intermarriage is there between Alawites and Sunnis in Baniyas?

"Not that much. Baniyas is divided geographically and there are a lot of ex-prisoners from the Iraqi Ba'th, the Muslim Brotherhood, a lot of exiles and fugitives. Historically, Baniyas has been oppressed and marginalized by the state, but not in sectarian terms. What happened in Baniyas wasn't against the Alawite sect; it was against the Syrian regime. It's the practices of the state that feed sectarianism. The state is responsible for whatever sectarian strife is taking place. The Alawites in the villages around Baniyas are very poor, they suffer the same injustice. We must recognise that sectarian tension has become a reality ever since the state started nourishing it. On 18 April, I saw a gathering of young men. I asked them what was going on and they told me that the young men from the al-Qusoor neighbourhood were going to come out to kill Sunnis. I told them that someone from the J. family who was part of the *shabbiha* had told the Alawites that the Salafis were coming from Latakia to defend the Salafis in Baniyas, that they were already at the Seville restaurant and that they were going to slaughter Alawites. I ran over there to see what was happening but didn't see anything at all. When I got back and asked if anything had happened, they said the Alawite guys were coming down. So as we got ready, I pulled one of the guys aside and found out what was going to happen; the people weren't going to remain silent. Afraid there was going to be a sectarian massacre, I took a scooter and went up to al-Qusoor, an Alawite neighbourhood. Seeing the roadblocks, I asked someone, 'What's going on?' He said, 'Nothing.' Then I went back and Shaykh A. I. said, 'There is no sectarian strife,' and asked the Sunni guys to go home, but they didn't. There were thousands of people hanging around but nothing happened. The ones who wanted to stir up sectarian strife were the *shabbiha* and the security. The people were smarter than that. Somebody told me that a man from the Alawite village of Barmaya rounded up the Alawite guys and asked them to go home. And that's how the rumours would grow, fed by the security and the *shabbiha*, in order to terrify the Sunnis and the Alawites at the same time."

"Al-Marqab is known as an area for smuggling weapons. Could the people retaliate against what was happening with violence?"

"Anything's possible, violence begets violence, but you saw how they didn't retaliate. Besides, it was the people of Ra's al-Naba'a in Baniyas who mobilized and not the people of al-Marqab, despite the fact that that half of the population of al-Marqab is from Baniyas. The army moved into al-Marqab. They had spent three days getting ready. Its forces were concentrated in several locations. We got news that there had been a mix-up in the orders given to the army. The army withdrew and then advanced and when they finally moved in, they came from the direction of the village of al-Zuba.

There were *shabbiha* sniping at the soldiers and one soldier got killed. The army moved in with gunfire and the people started demonstrating in the direction of the army. As usual, the army announced through bullhorns that they wouldn't harm anyone, that they just wanted to search. The army moved in, searched and arrested about 200 or 300 people. The mothers went out in order to demand the return of their sons and husbands who had been arrested even as the prisoners sat on the buses. Then the security forces sprayed gunfire chaotically. The people said that some of those who were killed were wounded from behind, which means there had to have been snipers. They arrested some of the mothers and children and four women were killed. There were four axes to the assault on Baniyas, from the thermal power station and al-Marqab. Two young men were killed and three were critically wounded. I think they're dead now, but how can you be sure when the phone lines are all cut, just like the water and the electricity? Even though there was a curfew and random arrests, the women started demonstrating and wouldn't give in to all the killing and arrests."

Silence.

The young man stops talking. I wait. I don't push. Today Baniyas is cut off from the outside world, a chunk of earth floating in the void. Today the Syrian authorities will not let delegates from the United Nations enter Dar'a. State media says they had gone in for hours. I remain silent out of respect for this young man. My hands are tingling from writing so much. I don't feel good about recording what he has to say so I transcribe everything. But a friend of mine videotapes and records him, and I memorize what the young man says.

I wanted to say, 'So, in brief, Baniyas is occupied,' but I hold back, and everything inside of me retreats into a deep black pit, bigger than the black hole of existence. He does not wait long, apologising and saying we would have to finish up some other time, but I doubt we ever will. All the young men I meet with say the same thing, and then they disappear.

10 May 2011

. . . .

What a strange morning.

I wake up and touch my skin. I am just an idea, a character in a novel. I drink my coffee and believe that I am only thinking about a woman I'll write about one day. I am a novel.

I am living through a more realistic novel than I could ever write. Yesterday evening a few young men and women who went out to demonstrate on al-Hamra Street near my house were arrested. My friends no longer tell me the time and place of the demonstrations because they have lost faith in me and don't believe my promises that I won't participate in them anymore, that I'll be satisfied to watch from afar in order to keep writing. The last women's demonstration made them worry about me. I received quite a few reprimands. The demonstration passed nearby my house and I could hear the ambulance sirens spinning around the place. From afar I could see people pushing and running. The demonstration started in Arnous Square. When I met up with my writer friend who had participated in the demonstration she reported the following details:

"We all assembled in Arnous Square. I thought I wasn't going out into the street because we were all being watched after all. I had been thinking about working in some way other than going out for demonstrations, but I thought it was important for us to go out to demonstrate in the squares and not just inside the mosques. My girlfriend and I went out, we were all over the place, monitoring the presence of security forces. We went and sat on the steps in the square and started singing patriotic anthems. Then young men gathered around us and we all sang for the homeland, for Syria. There were about 150 men and women demonstrators, we videotaped it, we started singing the national anthem, *Guardians of the Realm, Peace be upon You,* unfurling and holding up high the banners upon which we had written, *No to the Siege, No to Violence, We Want a Civil State.* Then we started marching with our banners, singing the national anthem and heading towards al-Salihiyyeh. When passed through the middle of al-Salihiyyeh, the people in the market stopped on both sides of the street to gawk at us in amazement and fear and some in sympathy. We stayed there for about seventeen minutes singing *Guardians of the Realm Peace be Upon You.* Then the violent attack by the security forces began. They surrounded us. When they attacked we all started running, and people fell down on the ground. My girlfriend fell down too. I helped her up, and a man outside the glass storefront of one of the shops hit her. One of the al-Salihiyyeh shopkeepers rushed over and hid her inside his shop. Then a security goon broke into the shop while we were hiding inside. The shopkeeper told him, "There are women changing inside." The shopkeeper came and showed us a safe route for us to escape. During the demonstration there was a young woman filming and the security forces attacked her and took away her phone. One of the young girls got arrested. They pulled out all the young demonstrators from inside the shops. Then they parked a bus outside the shop and put the young men inside. The people had all started asking what was happening and the security forces told them, 'Nothing to see here, folks, these people are thieves.'"

"They brought the young men out of the shops, beating and kicking and shoving them. They were beating them with spite and violence and brutality, and the people watched in silence. The ones who got arrested were: G.N., M.N., A.Q., I.K., I.D., M.T., I.I. I watched with my own eyes as a security agent picked up a thick baton and started hitting I.D. fiercely and violently right on his head. Inside the bus they kept on beating them violently and harshly. We confirmed what happened on video. Afterwards we watched the harmful beating the young men received.

"Everyone who got detained is still under arrest. The security forces are everywhere, the regime resorts to turning city employees and government workers into private vandals and security agents, deploying them in the streets and squares in order to inform on the people's movements and assemblies. They're being threatened with their daily bread, with being fired from their jobs if they refuse to cooperate with the security forces."

My girlfriend's testimony and her description of what happened stops here. I get nervous thinking about the strange and interlocking threads of my life, the strange fate that put me directly on the front line of an explosive situation, and about the madness my life had become from the moment I turned fourteen. The funny thing is that I have always thought I inhabit a unique space, and I have no desire to change it or to incline towards one side or the other. My perspective approximates the sarcasm of fate, or of death making fun of life. I am in a funny situation, one that drowns in its own blackness. If only the Syrian security services had known that I am related to Osama Bin Laden before they started calling me names and fabricating stories about me on different websites. Maybe they could have used that against me. I laugh as I sip my coffee, thinking about Najwa Ghanem, my mother's relative, Osama Bin Laden's first wife and mother of his beloved boys. I knew Najwa when I was a child. Thinking about the death of Bin Laden and about the *mukhabarat* file that had been fabricated about me, I laugh.

Decades ago Osama Bin Laden's father married a woman of intoxicating beauty named Alia Ghanem. This young lady had a brother, and it was he who married my mother's cousin, Nabiha, with whom he had two daughters and three sons, the oldest of which was Najwa, who would later marry her young cousin Osama Bin Laden, who in turn would become a famous figure in modern political history. I spent some distant days of my childhood at Najwa's family's home, where I saw her children. Once I went with my aunt to visit the chalet in Latakia where she was staying. I was just a little girl then but I still have vivid memories about that family who went to live in Latakia, where they still reside. Najwa enjoyed protection from the Syrian security apparatus and Fawwaz al-Assad himself, who lived near the villa where she and her children resided.

Now here I am in my house, suspended up on the rooftop opposite al-Hamra Street, living in anxiety and fear, clinging to my daughter out of concern for her because of the threats that I receive over email and on the phone. Despite the fact that I adhere to strict silence, I am scared. I am the daughter of a well-known Alawite family, a family that supports the regime absolutely and that now considers me a traitor and a shame upon them, to the point that some members of the family announced on Facebook that in Jableh I am no longer considered one of them, publicly disowning me. That wasn't their first public statement. According to their social mores, my leaving home when I was sixteen caused multiple scandals. I had consecrated myself to the promise of a mysterious freedom in life. I never cared what they thought about me. But my nuclear family had always mattered to me. Despite my perpetual disagreement with them, I had always been connected to my mother, father and siblings in an emotional sense, in such a way that made the situation all the more tragic and painful.

The mere mention of those days – my mother's crying eyes – causes me to break down in hysterical tears. Just thinking about how the regime has turned the Alawites into its own human shield sends me into a bottomless pit of sorrow. Sometimes it seems as though everything that is happening in Syria, everything within its four walls, is happening against me.

In everything that happened I am the big loser. Among my family and my childhood friends, amidst all that is right and true, I am a dead woman, yet still present somehow. My life has irrevocably split in two all at once. I am alone. My life has become the most realistic novel. I'll write all about it one day if I manage to survive. Then I will be the one preserving secrets about the Makhloufs, the Assads, and all the Alawite families who strayed from their religious path in order to decimate the Alawite sect.

About a week ago I wrote on my Facebook page: *Our grandfather, Aziz Bek Hawwash, was the leader who refused the establishment of the Etat des Alaouites by demanding that France safeguard the unity of Syria. My grandfather on my mother's side, Uthman, fought in the resistance against the Ottomans, and the people of the mountain and the coast know of his many acts of heroism. My grandfather Ibrahim Salih Yazbek gave all his possessions and land to the peasants. That was before the land reforms of the sixties. That's right, I'm the granddaughter of those men, the granddaughter of al-Makzun al-Sinjari, of al-Khasibi, of Ikhwan al-Safa and al-Mutanabbi. You all are the grandchildren of truth, you are not the grandchildren of a mistake.*

That comment shook things up even more with my family and with the security forces, who had been deleting most of the comments I wrote. For a second time they announced they disowned me, the heretical traitor. It wasn't only my family. A number of families in the village announced they disowned me. Once again I started receiving threatening letters and obscene phone calls. The senior security officer summoned me again. In that comment I wanted to mention one more time who the true luminary Alawites were, as I had done when I wrote before about how Imam Ali bin Abu Talib chose truth over power and paid for it with his life.

I was sending a message to the Alawite Ba'thists and security agents who were handing out leaflets about me in Jableh and the surrounding villages to stir people up to kill me and get rid of me. I was also sending messages through interviews and meetings with some Alawite clerics, but that was in vain. The situation was only getting worse.

I arrived at the first meeting with the senior officer on the verge of collapse, because the two men who had accompanied me from home in a white car had blindfolded me, which was something that confused me. I hadn't thought of telling anyone. My daughter was still in the village. At that point, I thought my detention was sure to come soon, and that it would last a long time.

I arrived in a strange place, perhaps it was in al-Mezzeh, I could not be sure, but I found myself in a big office with the senior officer. He scowled at me, looking me up and down in disgust, as if he were staring at a squashed bug or a disintegrating corpse. Then he drew closer, grabbed me by the wrist, crushing my hands and burning my skin and suddenly he slapped me in the face, knocking me to the ground. Then he spat on me. *Cunt,* he said. My eyes were shut and I could hear a loud ringing in my ears from the blow. I felt like I was losing my balance, like I was convulsing. I didn't get up. I didn't even try. He shouted at me to get up but I really couldn't, my body was frail. I lost my balance. What a joke, a single slap could make me fall down. He shouted, *Get up!* I didn't move. I threw my head back, closed my eyes and thought to myself, *I'm not getting up, let him do what he wants.* The knife that I carried around in my purse was under my bra, the same small switchblade, and I thought about how if he or anybody else tried to insult me, I wouldn't hesitate to plunge the knife into his heart. Up until that moment I had been thinking I was going to be detained for a long time. I knew their anger at me went beyond every kind of anger. I heard the sound of footsteps, and I felt his hand reach out and pick me up. I didn't exactly feel how he sat me down in the chair, but my head fell, and when I straightened myself out, the spinning in my head stopped. He laughed, "Well well well, what a hero, you went down with just one slap." I opened my eyes. I didn't cry. I wanted to cry, the slap was an insult, but I wouldn't let him see my tears. I stared back at him. After running his finger along my cheek, he said, "Isn't it awful when such an angelic face gets hit."

He slapped me a second time. Then he returned to his seat and launched into a long tirade about ties of blood and kinship, about family and about betrayal, the same claptrap I had been hearing for years, about my betrayal and the shame I had brought upon all those around me. When he stopped talking I was staring at his palm and his fingers that I felt had left marks on my cheek, red marks that would turn blue in a day or two.

"What's wrong, cat got your tongue?" he asked. "Your long tongue should be torn out." And he hit me again; the slap was lighter this time. I stood up and pulled out my knife, brandishing it in his face and I told him that if he continued beating me I would plunge this knife into my heart, and that I wouldn't let him or anybody else insult my dignity. He stood up, stupefied, staring at the black knife, and backed away from me a couple of steps. I flicked the switch, the blade swung out and I touched it against the centre of my heart, which I could hear beating.

A heavy silence. He was staring in shock. He drew near me again and I backed away a step, saying, "Don't come any closer."

He stopped. He was staring in astonishment and I stared back at him without blinking.

"What do you want?!" I shouted.

"We're worried about you," he said. "You're being duped by Salafi Islamists if you believe what they're saying."

"I don't believe anyone," I said. "I went out into the streets time after time and I didn't see any Salafis. I saw how you kill ordinary people and arrest them and beat them."

"No," he said, "those are Salafis."

"They weren't Salafis," I told him. "You and I both know that."

"If you keep on writing," he said, "I'll make you disappear from the face of the earth."

"Go ahead," I said.

"Not just you, but your daughter as well."

In that moment, my heart stopped beating.

Sitting down behind his desk, he said, "Put the knife down, you lunatic. We're honourable people. We don't harm our own blood. We're not like you traitors. You're a black mark upon all Alawites."

"I don't want anything to do with you and other Alawites like you on the outside."

"All right, what do you have to do then?" I didn't respond, and he said, "Go on Syrian TV and we'll agree on what you're going to say."

Before he could finish, I shouted, "I won't do it, not even if you kill with me with your bare hands." Staring him in the eyes, my sharp tone infuriating him, I said, "Save your breath. I won't do it. Just leave me alone."

"*YOU* LEAVE *US* ALONE!" he bellowed.

I was silent.

"And those articles in *al-Quds al-Arabi*, on Facebook, your activities with the people, the demonstrations?"

"What can I say, I'm inclined towards the truth," I said.

He let out a resounding laugh and looked at me with pity.

I put my knife away. I knew he wasn't going to harm me, not this time anyway. Later on, when I started compiling testimonies of male and female prisoners, I would learn that they had spoiled me. His phone rang. He stepped out and didn't talk in front of me. He came back after a few minutes. I was sad and afraid.

"This is your last warning," he said. "From now on, you're aligned with the enemy."

"I'm not aligned with anyone," I said. "I'm aligned with the truth."

He laughed disdainfully and said, "By God, I'd let the people spit on you in the street. I'd let your friends in the opposition spit on you, let you flop around like a fish out of water before even thinking of arresting you. Go on, get out of here."

Two humongous men came into the room. They were standing there at the ready, dressed in civilian clothes. One of them to the right and the other to the left. The senior officer pointed at me and the two men stood me up. They weren't violent. They held me like an object that was easy to move. As they lifted me up from the chair by my shoulders, I didn't resist. I stood up. I found what was happening strange. Were they finally going to arrest me and put an end to this nightmare? Even that would be better than this madness. The officer looked at me scornfully and I looked back at him, trying to judge what was about to happen. I was trying to divine the future from their eyes, from the movement of their bodies and their behaviour. He remained impassive, staring at a fixed point in that cavernous room. The two men placed a blindfold over my eyes, or that's what I assumed because darkness suddenly blanketed my world.

Blindfolded, I smelled a strange odour on the piece of cloth. Then a powerful hand took me, a hand balled in a fist around my elbow, and pulled me. I moved sluggishly, then stopped and shouted, "Where are you taking me?!"

He replied calmly, as if croaking, "Just a short trip, so you'll write better."

I was sure they had decided to imprison me, but I wasn't scared. This was their ultimate recognition of my place in the opposition and it removed me from all the acts of madness which they had been taking pleasure from torturing me with over these last few days. I was pretending to hold myself together. I just wanted to discover that what had been happening for months was only a nightmare and that I was about to wake up from it soon. All those thoughts shot through me in less than two minutes. I almost fell down on the ground despite the presence of the two men, one on each side, who were holding me up, calmly and elegantly. They must have had orders from him to behave like that, but when I almost fell again and they picked me up I realized we were going down some stairs. One of them had to let me go; apparently it was a narrow staircase. I tried to see out underneath the blindfold but it was on too tight and I started having trouble breathing. I felt like we had descended several flights. I couldn't be sure. I started to get dizzy as putrid stenches mixed with strange odours that I had never smelled before. We stopped finally. That searing pain shot up my back. I shuddered, knowing how frail my body was.

A hand undid the blindfold from my eyes. I hadn't expected what awaited me to be so dreadful, despite the fact that everything in front of me was dark. Prison, everything I had heard and imagined, everything I had tried to write about – none of that meant anything compared to that moment when my eyes opened: It was a long corridor, I could just barely make out the cells on either side and I almost felt like it wasn't even a real place, just some kind of void in my head that was sick from too much writing. But it was real. A hallway just wide enough for two bodies side by side. Blackness surrounded its edges. A corridor separated from being. I looked behind me but couldn't see anything. In front of me...pitch black. A corridor with no end and no beginning, suspended in the void; I was in the middle of it and the doors were shut.

The man standing in front of me opened one of the doors, a sharp creaking that began quickly and ended with slow, sad beats that reminded me of a melody I once heard in a Greek bar. The man took me by the elbow and I saw three people inside. He continued holding my arm as the door opened, and in there I saw them: two or three people. I couldn't tell, but I am pretty sure I saw three bodies hanging in the middle of nowhere, but I couldn't understand how. He moved me even closer. I was dumbfounded. My stomach started to seize up. The three bodies were almost naked. A faint light seeped in; I didn't know it was from a hole in the ceiling but it produced dim lines of visibility that allowed me to see young men who couldn't have been more than twenty years old, or maybe in their early twenties, their tender young bodies clear under all the blood, their hands hanging from metal clamps, and the tips of their toes just barely touching the ground. Blood coursed down their bodies: fresh blood, dried blood, deep wounds carved all over them, like the strokes of an abstract painter. Their faces hung downwards, in a state of unconsciousness, swinging there like sides of beef. I recoiled backwards, but one of the men held me there, as the second pushed me forward in absolute silence. Suddenly one of the young men sluggishly tried to lift his head and I saw his face in those dim rays of light. He didn't have a face: his eyes were completely shut. I couldn't discern any gleam in his eyes. There was a blank space where his nose should be, no lips. His face was like a red board without any defining lines – red interspersed with black that had once been red.

At that point I collapsed onto the floor and the two men picked me up again. For a moment I was swinging in a sticky place, floating, and I hung there for a few minutes until I regained my footing on the ground. I heard one of them say to the others, "Come on man, she couldn't even handle one slap. She'd just die if we gave her the tire!"

Then that smell rushed in: the smell of blood and piss and shit; the smell of rusty metal; a smell like disintegration; a smell like the mouth of a cell, that had to be it.

Suddenly they took me out of that cell and opened another one. The sounds of screaming and torture rang out somewhere, somewhere both far away and nearby. I was trembling. I had never heard such sounds of pain, coming from some place deep inside the earth, burrowing into my heart. The sounds didn't stop until we left the corridor. The second cell opened and there was a young man inside whose spine looked like an anatomist's sketch. He also appeared to be unconscious. His back was split open, as if a map had been carved into it with a knife.

They closed the cell. And that's what it was like, cell after cell, holding me up by my elbows, shoving me inside, then bringing back me out again. Bodies strewn behind stacked bodies – it was Hell. It was like human beings were just pieces of flesh on display, an exhibition of the art of murder and torture that was all for show. Just like that, young men who weren't even 30 reduced to bits of cold flesh in cramped, dank cells. Heads without a face, bodies with new features.

As they were tightening the blindfold over my eyes again, I asked one of the two men, "Are those guys from the demonstrations?"

One of them rudely replied, "They're traitors from the demonstrations."

Annoyed by my question, he grabbed my elbow and squeezed it so hard I felt like he was going to crush it. I didn't know what was going on in their minds but my stomach started growling again. Holding onto me the man pulled me along and though I tripped and fell he didn't wait for me to get up, but continued to pull me after him. My knees were all scraped up on the stairs and then he started becoming even rougher, finally just dragging me along like a sack of potatoes. The pain in my bones was searing as I thought about the young men who had gone out to demonstrate. I shuddered a second time and the quaking was centred deep inside my gut. The stenches were in my mouth, the images of the cells coating the darkness in front of my eyes. When we stopped and they took off the blindfold, I saw the officer sitting behind his neat desk and that's when I realized this wasn't a nightmare. He looked at me contemptuously and said, "What do you say? Did you see your traitor friends?"

At this point something rapidly started rising up out of my bowels, as though I was trying to jump out of my skin. In real life, I tell my girlfriends, "A man's touch doesn't make you shed your skin like a snake, not a loving touch." I can say that there are other things that make our skin crawl – unravelling towards death, hurtling toward the abyss. In that moment, instead of soaring, I threw up. I fell down on my knees and they were furious. The officer stood up and looked in astonishment at the fancy furniture that had been soiled but I continued vomiting. My eyes were wet with some kind of liquid, they weren't tears, of that much I am certain, tears fall in droplets and what was coming out of my eyes wasn't like that. I kept having the same thought: Anyone here who goes out to demonstrate in the streets is shot, has to live on the run and in hiding, or else gets imprisoned and tortured like they were.

What kind of courage sprouts so spontaneously, seemingly from nowhere?

My voice was weak but I heard it say: "You're the traitor." I knew he had heard it too, because he bent over and slapped me hard and I fell down onto the floor once and for all. Then things started to fall apart and, before I lost consciousness, I was able to feel that my mouth was open, and warm blood was oozing out onto the ground. In that moment I knew the meaning of the expression, "I swear to God I'll make you spit up blood."

After they hauled me out of there, I went home. I wasn't the person I had been before. I observed myself going into the house, a woman caught somewhere between life and death. I saw her toss a bunch of keys on the table and then light up her cigarette. The woman closed her eyes and put the blindfold back on, as though she were on stage, and those images of the mutilated bodies returned. The laughter of her little girl and her mother's beautiful eyes flicker in front of her, a furtive glance of fleeting hope as she squeezes the blindfold hard enough to blind herself. She feels that deep horrible hole starting to form inside her heart, and as the hole grows, this woman reaches her fingers deep inside, all the way to her neck. The woman becomes a chasm of blisters and pus.

Two days after the incident, one of their websites described me as a traitor and a foreign agent. Then a few days passed and leaflets were thrown in front of the houses in Jableh and the surrounding villages, about my being a foreign agent and a traitor, inciting people to kill me.

What do they want from me now? I have already fled my house to live in secret. I no longer publish articles. Do they know about my activities with the young men and women? I don't think so. I was really scared for my daughter. I didn't go to my summons, I thought maybe they would forget about it amid everything that was happening, but I got a phone call. It was him, and in a raspy voice he said, "You bastard, even if you go to the ends of the earth, we'll get you."

Trying to buy myself some time in order to catch up with what was happening in real life, I said, "I haven't done anything."

"This is your last warning," he said.

I was about to explode with rage. I had tried to hide. I refused to enter into any dialogue session with the authorities, even as some lines of communication were opened between them and some of the opposition. I even disappeared from Facebook. What did he mean? Was it just to frighten me, to scare me into madness?

89

It is as if I am living in a real-life novel. The characters and events need to be fleshed out and the plot needs work if I am going to be able to pull myself together, be strong and take up the strands of my life once more. That's how writing toughens me against the hardships of life. As a novelist I can be more accommodating with myself and with the interlocking strands of my life that are so hard to separate. I am untying a knot the way I would animate a puppet, but the difference is that I am the puppet and the strings and the big, mysterious invisible hand.

I tried to focus during those ten days when they came to my house, three or four men, and placed a blindfold over my eyes so we could all go back to the same officer's room. I didn't know whether that was really his office and whether we were actually in the al-Jisr al-Abyad neighbourhood in Damascus or in Kafr Sousseh. Distances had become meaningless to me ever since I moved. As the car went round turn after turn and then stopped, I would lose my concentration. The fourth time I went down to the cells, they didn't arrest me and they didn't leave me there. I just wandered around. One day I'll write all about those hellish journeys. I'll try to recall all the details of what happened, how I would come out of the house and they would place the blindfold over my eyes as soon as I sat down in the car and in that moment the world would turn into a black hell. My soul suffered in silence as I was stuffed between two strange bodies, smelling their odours and becoming increasingly panicked. With the blindfold on, I would imagine I was being forced into blindness, as I waited for hands to run all over me. In that pitch-blackness I would take courage in similar situations I had read about as images rolled by in front of my eyes. One time, and here I knew I had lost my wits, I believed blindness could be like a window shutting out the outside world, a secret door through which to enter the gloom, an opportunity to meditate upon the furthest reaches of the soul; blindness became philosophical justice. And that's how I would fight back against the black blindfold covering my eyes. I would pretend I was a character on paper, not made of flesh and blood, or that I was reading about a blindfolded woman forcibly taken to an unknown location, to be insulted and spat upon because she had the gall to write something true that displeased the tyrant. At this point in my fantasy I would feel strong and forget all about how weak my body was, about the vile smells and the impending unknown.

11 May 2011

....

Syrian tanks shell the Baba Amr neighbourhood in Homs. Security forces invade houses and rob them. The shelling lasts for hours; nineteen martyrs are killed. The regime is going to announce that it is in the process of putting together a committee in order to draw up an election law.

Damascus is calm now, but it is the result of a plot by the security forces. Today international pressure on the regime is building. Catherine Ashton says, "The Syrian regime has lost its credibility." Ban Ki Moon calls on the president to have a dialogue with the demonstrators and expresses his disappointment at what the regime is doing to its own people.

Baniyas regains its electricity, water and telecommunications and 300 prisoners are released there. There is a report that around 11,000 prisoners are still in jail.

My morning begins with news of killing and bombing in Homs. I have barely opened my eyes, made my coffee and turned on the television when I see the news: a researcher from Homs is talking about the Baba Amr neighbourhood, where poor peasants live. News is coming in from all directions. How can the tanks shell the houses of Syrians? Once again the murderers are being murderers. Last night I had fallen asleep transcribing the testimony of a journalist who sneaked into Dar'a during the siege and woke up with tears on my cheek, the lines burning my eyes. I had got used to crying fits but I cannot take it anymore. I feel like I want to die, that I will never finish meeting all these people and recording their testimonies and that I should just leave my daughter with her father and go into hiding. The insanity of all this blood is marching me towards madness. The bouts of agony in my head do not stop without the Xanax tranquilizers that knock me out.

Last night at midnight I got threatened, yet another threatening phone call. It was a young boy. I don't know exactly how old he was. It had been two days since my last threat.

I secretly planned a trip with one my girlfriends to Jableh, my city; I am not supposed to set foot there right now because security forces and Ba'thists have decided it is off-limits for me. We decide that we will take a friend's car and that I will conceal my identity. It is enough for me to put on a headscarf and thick glasses and to wear a long dress. I need to get into al-Dariba – supposedly the anti-Alawite neighbourhood as the security forces tried to describe it to the Alawites – in order to meet with people. But the truth of the matter is that it also is also the neighbourhood where the protest movement began.

O great sky, support me against this recurring death. It's not going to be easy for me, the daughter of a well-known Alawite family in Jableh, to get into that neighbourhood. Any group might try to kill me, perhaps a Sunni fundamentalist out of revenge for a death in his family or one of the Alawites who thinks I am a traitor, or a sniper, or maybe somebody else? So many questions. I recall the scene in Baniyas back at the beginning of the crisis, when some extremist Alawites showed up in trucks wanting to demolish Shaykh Abboud's house, despite the fact that he was one of the oldest residents of the city, just because his son was aligned with the demonstrators. His son had been arrested and kept in jail for three days, but that wasn't enough for them. Salafism isn't only a Sunni phenomenon; there are Alawite Salafis as well.

As we emerge from the heart of the neighbourhood, my friend gets nervous and says that she shouldn't be risking her life like this. We see security forces every which way we look. After all the trouble of making the journey from Damascus to Jableh, my visit is a failure. My quest ends in half an hour. The young man who is supposed to come to meet us where we wait for him never shows up. My friend turns the car around and we head right back the way we came in. We stop for a while in front of the entrance to the old covered market when several members of the security forces start moving in our direction. As we hurry out of there, she tells me, "They're asking to see IDs, if they find out who you are they won't show you any mercy."

I have already postponed returning to Jableh until my daughter is finished with her exams. Two more weeks. Now I wait for news, like the stump of some ancient tree.

There is no internet. My movements must be kept to a minimum. I have to remain calm and wait for the security forces to forget all about me, for me to drop off their radar, but will that ever happen, even while I lie low in silence? My friends want me to leave the country right away, they plead with me in anxious phone calls and express concern about my wellbeing. I can't do it, but I do have to think about how much money I have saved up. The rent on this downtown apartment is expensive. I also have to think about what I am going to do when the three-month lease is up, how I am going to take care of my daughter and myself. I want a morning without any bloodshed, just one morning when I don't feel saltiness churning in my throat, when my fingers stop trembling and I can stand still staring into the void. I try to transcribe the interview with the journalist, M.I., who broke the siege of Dar'a, writing it down first and then transferring it directly onto the computer.

The testimony of M.I.
"A veterinarian got me into Dar'a. I didn't go there as a journalist. Army personnel were stationed at intersections throughout the city. There were military checkpoints and security forces everywhere. We got stopped and searched a lot. It was a long journey, in spite of the short distance. The army had lists of names they were scanning. It was only after searching us thoroughly that they let us pass.

When I was finished talking with the doctor, we took a tour around the city and then went to the al-Umari Mosque. There was a demonstration, or people beginning to gather for one. I saw Ma'n al-Awdat and I said hello to him. There was a large security presence just waiting to attack the demonstrators, even though there was supposedly a cease-fire that day in order to carry out the demonstrators' demands before Friday. There were about a thousand people demonstrating. We didn't really feel like sticking around so we went to the house of one of the notable figures who told us what happened. It was the story everybody knows about the children of Dar'a who had their fingernails pulled out and were brutally tortured. The notable figure repeated what Atef Najib had said to them: *Come get your children and let your wives make new ones*. And so, after their honour and reputation had been slandered, the demonstrators, who were tribal *shaykhs*, decided to carry on their opposition and in addition to punishing whoever had tortured their children, their demands included the abrogation of the emergency laws and a crackdown on corruption."

M. stops talking here, and stares straight ahead. Then, all of a sudden, he says, "By the way, they weren't tear gas canisters. It was nerve gas."

He stops talking for a second time and I wait for him to continue but he remains silent.

"Then what happened?" I ask.

"The notable figure, who had been part of the nationalist current in the sixties, emphatically said they weren't armed, that they didn't have any armed gangs among them – contrary to what the regime claimed – and while I was talking with them, there was an 'alarm', and an 'alarm' is when there is a call to save demonstrators who are being attacked by the security forces. I took my camera and went out with them. Everything I'm telling you is backed up with pictures. When a thirteen-year-old boy threw a big rock from up on the roof onto the ground to break it into smaller stones that could be used against the security forces, the demonstrators shouted at him and scolded him, because what he was doing was violent and they only wanted peaceful demonstrations. I went out with them and started filming. By that stage, France 24 and the BBC had been expelled. They asked me who I was. The notable figure told them, "He's with me." That was the password and the people protected me themselves. I told them I wanted to be with them. I didn't want any protection. I conducted a lot of interviews during the demonstrations, which I still have. The main point the demonstrators talked about was their pain and frustration at the president of the republic. After all the killing and the bloodshed in Dar'a, he had paid a visit to nearby Suwayda but never mentioned the blood of the martyrs. One demonstrator told me, "We are the ones who protect Bashar al-Assad, not the security services, just let him try us in the

Golan." When another one said, "The snipers are from Hizballah," someone nearby shouted back, "Don't say things we don't know for certain, brother, that's inaccurate talk." A man with a long beard, who looked like a fundamentalist Islamist, came over to talk about the Sunni-Shi'a issue, but the demonstrators rose up and told him to be quiet, so he was. They only talked about the practices of the security forces and the repression. The women asked to come out into the streets to sit-in and the men agreed, so women and men sat in together in the mosque. That was before the massacre.

"I forgot to mention something, going back to the notable figure, I asked him to listen to a second opinion, and I.S., the previous *shaykh* of the al-Umari Mosque came over. I can't tell you exactly what he said, even though it's on tape, because I promised him that whatever he said would only be made public if he died, or if he gave me express permission to do so. That's why I hesitate to publish what he said, in spite of the fact that he's in prison right now, after they killed his son.

"A relative of one of the arrested children, I think it was his uncle if I remember correctly, came up to me and said, "They took the children to prison for writing on the walls. They gave them the 'special treatment.'" M. falls silent for a moment, then asks, "Do you know what that is?"

I shake my head.

"That means they raped them. I'm not sure how accurate that information is because he refused to let me quote him directly. By the way, inside the notable figure's house, he had pictures of Hafiz al-Assad and Bashar al-Assad and Gamal Abdel Nasser on the walls. Security forces were breaking into the houses and confiscating people's cameras and mobile phones. At one o'clock in the morning, maybe 12:30, one of the protestors called from inside the al-Umari Mosque and told me, "We assembled here and there was a massacre." M. stops talking and then says, "Even then there were medical supplies inside the mosque but after the massacre the demonstrators improvised a field hospital inside the mosque in preparation for other massacres. That was on a Thursday or Friday in March, when the famous clip appeared on satellite television saying: *Is there anyone who kills his own people? You are all our brothers.*"

M. continues: "The security forces were at the outskirts of every neighbourhood in Dar'a at the time. I saw that with my own eyes. They had cars and armed men, which made it impossible for an armed gang to get inside the mosque and kill people or carry out that massacre, because the security presence was large and solid. When I reached the entrance to the mosque I saw security forces. Central Security was in a state of total demobilization. They weren't doing anything. It seemed clear that they had no intention of attacking."

"So who carried out the attack then?" I ask him.

"Maybe it was the Fourth Division," he says.

"But they're saying the Fourth Division wasn't there..."

He interrupts me: "I think it was one of those divisions of private forces."

"In your opinion, who did the killing in Dar'a?"

"Security, the security forces were killing people."

"Did the army kill anyone?" I ask him.

"No, I don't think so even though they were at the front. There are confirmed sources saying that anyone in the army who disobeys orders would be killed by the security forces. I have some videotaped testimonies I'll send you."

"But that means the army was killing people, because even if some wouldn't carry out their orders, others would."

"Yes, sometimes, but what I mean is that there were orders for the army to kill the armed gangs. That's why they were fighting, and anyone who disobeyed orders when they found out what was really going on got killed."

M. falls silent. I feel tired as I write down his words that ooze with bitterness. He says, "I heard a story about a mother in Dar'a whose son was wanted by the security forces even though he was only twelve years old. He was her only child and she kept him hidden him in a strange way, by moving every day from house to house like a ghost. The security forces were not able to capture him. Then all news about her dried up. They told me security would invade the house where she and her son were staying a few minutes after she left. Despite the intensity of the siege and the heavy security presence she managed to protect her only son somehow. That was very unusual, but strange things were happening. I have some of them on tape. After demonstrators torched the military security detention centre during the siege of Douma, security forces attacked a funeral procession, making it all the way to the coffin and even opening fire on the pallbearers, wounding three of them critically. The people ran away, and the coffin was left on the ground by itself. Amidst the heavy gunfire I saw a little boy, who couldn't have been more than ten years old, standing behind his father. We could barely hear each other, but I asked him, 'Why did you come here, little guy? Go home.' His father looked at me, and after a long stare, said, 'He isn't any more valuable than his father.' Then he pounded on his chest. 'You're right,' I told him. 'I'm going to get my son, too.'

I stop writing in order to light a cigarette. I am a wreck, fumbling for some comment to make after hearing all these stories but once I had lit my cigarette he adds, "Listen to another story from Douma. Everybody knows that the town of Douma is religiously conservative, especially the women. One time I was passing through there, the demonstrators were on one side and the security forces were on the other. A young girl passed by, I had my camera with me so I filmed her. I imagined she was going to walk by the security forces, in order to avoid the hordes of male demonstrators, but she chose to cross through the demonstrators. I said to someone near me, 'Isn't it strange how that girl passed right through all these men?'

"Maybe this is how we are with our women," he says. "Did you see anyone leer at her or harass her? Even if things are messed up here without any law and order, we are still men of conscience."

"Real life is in the little stories," I tell the journalist. "How could it be any other way under these circumstances?"

"There are strange stories from al-Rastan," he says, distracted. "I was there, the demonstrators knocked down a statue of Hafiz al-Assad and stamped on it because of the anger and the recrimination and the injustice they had suffered for decades. One of the inhabitants of al-Rastan told me that when the people of Talbisseh came to pay their respects they showed up on motorcycles, which is how they get around, and while they were at the mourning ceremony their motorcycles were stolen. One of the fathers of the martyrs confirmed this to me. One was stolen right in front of me, so I went to the police and made a complaint about the theft and said I had seen it happen. At the police station they told me that that man was locked up. In other words, the theft must have taken place through collusion between the police and the prisoners, with the profits split between the thieves and the police the same day the motorcycles were stolen. There were no security agents, and there was no police in al-Rastan. So the people of al-Rastan went and told the people of Talbisseh, 'We're going to get you your motorcycles back.' The mourners said, "That's all right, we'll figure something out." But the people of al-Rastan insisted that the people of Talbisseh wait there, while they disappeared for about half an hour. When they came back they had the bikes with them. The people of al-Rastan had tracked down the thieves and gathered them all in one place, telling them, *Either your lives or our guests' bikes*. They handed the bikes over to them." M. is silent for a moment after finishing the story and then says, "This means there was no government and that the people were solving problems themselves the right way." I wait for him to say something more. "I'll give you the rest on tape," he says. "I'm worn out."

"That's much better anyway," I say.

I felt grateful to him because there were moments while he was telling me those stories when I had to fight back tears. Now I am released from that awkwardness.

15 May 2011

....

I didn't sit down to write on Friday as I had intended to do, nor the next day. What's happening now is bigger than what I can write about. I need some more time in order to be able to focus on what's happening. Since running out of Xanax, which had been very difficult to get here anyway, I have been awake for two days straight, from Thursday night until right now...I do not sleep.

I could fall asleep for two hours, which was enough for me to be able to focus, if only a little. What happened? It happened on Thursday, when my daughter and I were sitting there, a half-confirmed bit of news; nothing is certain these days other than the curses of death, the torrent of bullets and waiting. The backdrop is our nonstop bickering. I tried every means possible to calm her down but I had failed, until that moment when the man came and told me to leave the country at once, out of fear for my life because he had solid information about the impending liquidation of certain Alawite figures, about accusations of belonging to armed and Salafi gangs, and that my name was on the list.

The man spoke openly in front of my daughter and I believed him. I knew he was concerned about me but I was surprised by what he said and I sensed the enormity of the mistake I had made in letting my daughter hear this. She turned yellow, went to her room and slammed the door. The man left and I was there, alone with her silence and fear. My friend who also overheard the conversation tried to convince me it was essential for me to leave immediately, even though I insisted to her that this was crazy talk, especially now that the regime was starting its manoeuvres, pulling the army out of the cities and announcing a round of national dialogue. On the one hand, it wouldn't do them any good to carry out acts of violence now; on the other hand, I couldn't leave without my daughter, and she would staunchly refuse to leave the country anyway. It was impossible for me to leave without her. I wouldn't have the strength and I resolved not to go unless my daughter agreed, even if that cost me my life. She refused to speak to me at first. She wouldn't say a word but then she said bitterly that the only way I could make her feel better was to appear on state television and proclaim my loyalty to the president, so that our life could go back to normal. I stood there, stunned by what she said. I tried explaining to her, I tried to convince her that this meant suicide as far as I was concerned and that I wasn't worth more than the blood of the people who had already been killed, but she refused to listen. She knew the power she exercised over my heart.

"I won't do it," I snapped at her.

"And I won't leave with you," she retorted.

The new house we had rented was strange: two bedrooms opening onto a living room, separated by sliding doors. I could hear her footsteps when she was in her room, pacing anxiously, breaking things, screaming. I began thinking that the time had come to force her to leave, especially after having met with my friend who was close to Hizballah, whom I trust, whom I trust is not corrupt, who leans towards secularism in his life and who is with the regime although he is not on their payroll. Still, when they posted what they did about me on the *mukhabarat* website, he got very upset and called me to say he wanted to see me. He came to Damascus, and I met up with him and his girlfriend last Saturday afternoon. I was upset. Things were quiet but he seemed agitated and asked me to calm down, telling me he had just seen the very people who were making up stories about me, fabricating rumours; simply put, he had been in touch with the deciders, with those engaged in the media and psychological war against the uprising and its supporters. He seemed very concerned as he asked me to calm myself. When he learned what had been happening to me over the past few days, he became even more uncomfortable and asked me if I needed anything. I screamed in front of his girlfriend, apologizing to her from time to time for being so loud, wishing they would just let me be. That's all I wanted, for them to leave me alone, to quit monitoring me night and day.

"It's not so simple," he said.

"How's it not so simple?"

"Just write something that says you're against what's going on in the street."

At that point I stood up. I felt like my body was about to shoot through the cement ceiling. I know I can get as enraged as a psychopath, but in that moment, on the brink of death, for them to make up stories about me, for me to have had to flee my house and be terrorized night and day, for them to publish lies about me and to incite every Alawite in Syria to kill me, after all of that, how dare they ask me to write an article in support of the regime and its president? I screamed in his face.

"They're never going to leave you alone," he said. "There were two opinions in your case. Your story was discussed at the highest levels. There's a faction who say they won't ever leave you alone because you're one of them and another faction say you have to be punished more severely than anyone else, that prison is too good for you and they have resolved to make you regret what you've done. They're all displeased with you, the most powerful people in this country are very angry at you."

I sighed and repeated that the most powerful people in this country are very angry with me, they're calling me a traitor, intimidating me and forcing me into hiding like a hunted dog.

"You have to get out of here," he said.

"I wrote what I saw. I didn't make anything up and they know it."

He didn't respond to what I said, just pleaded with me to leave Syria as quickly as possible, saying that the group trying to come after me might back off. After a moment of silence, he added, "You're in real danger, in their minds you're a traitor and an agitator."

"Tell them I'll be quiet. Won't that be enough?"

"Just write something to get them off your back."

"I won't do it," I said. "After all this injustice they expect me to betray my conscience. I won't do it."

Our conversation ended there, he said goodbye to me with extreme sadness; he called me later several times to ask if I needed any help, repeating his well-mannered plea for me to leave Syria at once. After he had gone, I went straight up to my balcony and looked down at the two men who were following me. I had discovered them 24 hours before. An article about me by a female journalist had appeared in the Lebanese *al-Safir* newspaper on Friday, and after it was published I got a phone call from abroad, threatening me with my last warning. I had promised to remain silent but I had broken my promise. I thought the one threatening me might have been from outside the security apparatus. Perhaps it was ordinary Alawites who were calling all the time and threatening my daughter and I. But I became seriously afraid when I discovered the existence of the two men in front of my new home. How had they found my new place so quickly? Why were they so focused on my movements amidst such difficult circumstances? Apparently I was infuriating them, stoking their rage. What would prevent me from provoking their anger? Silence. But it was just a newspaper piece about me. And what if the editor hadn't deleted my last line? *The real question is, who is it that is killing both sides? What I mean to say is, who is killing both army officers and civilian demonstrators?* The editor at *al-Safir* cut it, I think, in order to protect me and the journalist who wrote reasonable things about me. Nevertheless, the article stirred up their anger and the man on the phone with the angry voice said, "If you don't disappear, Samar Yazbek, I'll make you disappear from the face of the earth."

That was Friday night. I was getting ready to write in my journal. Then the man came and talked in front of my daughter about the liquidation of some Alawite figures. I could not write. I sat out on the balcony, which was actually the roof. The streets of Damascus were empty. Friday had been turned into a day of horror for Syrians, in which life itself nearly disappears as the security forces spread out, everywhere, until finally, after some demonstrations, security forces are posted in even greater numbers. I was smoking a cigarette as coldness whipped me and my body felt like shifting sand. What was I going to do? I was unable to write and my daughter was in her room with the door closed. All contact with my family had been eerily cut off: after I was labelled a traitor they stopped calling me, and I no longer called them. Days would pass without my hearing from friends or their hearing from me. I had no internet, my movements were becoming more infrequent by the day and the witnesses who I was trying to meet with in order to archive their memories of the uprising had started to go missing as well.

I poured myself a glass of white wine and sat beneath the cold sky. I tried to think seriously about what I had to do. I wasn't prepared for all this violence coming for me, against me first, and against the people second. I wasn't prepared for all this intimidation, but I had to remain calm and think in a rational tone. The warmth of the wine began spreading through my limbs. The one feeling that made me cry bitterly that evening was loneliness, not fear. I had been experiencing fear in every moment, but that night, and before I went into my daughter's room, I truly understood how a person can be utterly alone, how the four corners of the earth can be too narrow, unarmed save for a heart and a weakly moving body. In that moment I also understood how important it is for a human being to be capable of regenerating herself and bringing her dead cells back to life; this may seem like a line out of a book but it's a real feeling and not a metaphor I write down in words here.

Truly, I was a dead woman, bones encased in dry skin, cells that need to be regenerated – something straight out of a science fiction movie. I stood up and stuck my head out over the balcony. I breathed in the cold air, feeling the blessing of being liberated from the sensation of living, of being transformed into an inanimate object. At first I felt like I was dead, but then I pushed the thought away and had the exact opposite thought. It was only a moment, maybe more, a moment in which I pushed my body towards the edge of the balcony. As half of my body hung there in the air, it was a moment of freedom, awesome and clear, like boundless flying. Just then I craved a moment of even greater freedom, to fly through the air towards the abyss. The only true freedom is in death. I closed my eyes but I didn't find the strength to flap my arms in the air. I closed my eyes and imagined those flying drawings that would come to me in my dreams from time to time, the flying drawings that I dreamed about for the first time after I watched *The English Patient*, when Katherine comes into the cave with her lover and they find the drawings on the wall, those drawings that fly and swim in the eternal darkness. That deadly pastime of swimming in the void. I incarnated them for a moment, and then they disappeared. I opened my eyes and the passing moment of magic that would transport me to the unknown, to a quick flight up in the air and then into eternal slumber, was gone. Out of complete cowardice I was unable to jump and fly towards the repose of death. My daughter was on my mind. As long as she was, she would save me from dying.

I went back inside and closed the balcony door. As if tranquilized, I didn't go to my own bed but to my daughter's. She was still awake, her eyes all red from crying. I snuggled up next to her, wrapped her in my arms and cradled her in my lap, just like I used to do when she was eight years old. We cried a lot that night. Everything that had been missing in my life until then, I cried it out and she cried with me. We slept on our tears and when I awoke after about half an hour, she was fast asleep in the same position. I started getting anxious. I thought about writing…and I started to write.

That was *al-Nakba* Day, but because of the revolutions and the uprisings across the Arab world it was no ordinary anniversary. Young bare-chested men confronted the Israelis. In this place young people are fated to welcome death in a very particular way, either from the bullets of their despotic regimes or the bullets of the Israelis.

I haven't written anything yet about the Friday of Free Women or the six people who were killed by security forces in various Syrian cities. I could no longer keep up with the news as I had become accustomed to doing, so I did not bear witness to the women who were martyred in the Palestinian Intifada on that special day of solidarity, nor did I see the slogans highlighting the presence of women in the Syrian protests either. The Syrian regime claims to be preparing for national dialogue even as it continues its killing and its arrests. The tanks withdraw from Baniyas and Dar'a, but are then redeployed in the suburb of Daraya, near Damascus.

I think about what I will have to do tomorrow, going to ask if I have been banned from travelling, going to Emigration and Passports in order to get a passport for my daughter, and then, and then…

Now I can understand that cry: My God, why hast thou forsaken me?

16 May 2011

....

On this black morning I have sharp pains in my chest as waves of loud ringing swirl in my ears. I start to feel that I am truly in danger. A number of signs have pushed me to respond finally to my friends' pleas for my total silence, self-interest and dropping out of the public eye once and for all. Doctor A. told me that what I was doing was suicide, that I must keep a low profile. Everyone was telling me to stop meeting with people and demonstrators, to stop mobilizing on the ground at all.

I used to believe there was a simple sideline from which I could watch what was happening before my very eyes, or follow the people as they mobilized for the demonstrations but what had happened to me recently has made me stop. Then there was my feeling that I was living under house arrest – tapped phones, surveillance; everything, even my whispers, were being monitored. Yet it had remained possible for me to move around calmly, until that moment when signs started to appear that convinced me I needed to take a break.

The first sign came in the middle of the night about a week ago. My friend was sleeping over and I was with my daughter in her room. In all honesty I was fast asleep, having taking half a Xanax, when suddenly heard a scream, woke up in a panic and stood right up. My head almost hit the ceiling when I jumped up on the bed and for a moment I thought that my daughter had been kidnapped. I screamed, loud, and I was still screaming as I started to run around the room like a madwoman. It wasn't even midnight. When I lifted the blanket from my daughter's bed, it was empty. I screamed even more.

I wasn't myself, something savage was emerging from my chest. I was convinced that my daughter had been kidnapped, that their threat to hurt her had finally come true, when suddenly the balcony door opened and my daughter appeared in a panic. She had been out on the balcony. I was out of breath. My girlfriend was standing next to her, alarmed by my screaming. They both stared at me hesitantly. "Where were you?!" I demanded. "On the veranda," she said. I left the two of them and went back to bed. My heart was racing, I was shaking, my entire being shook. Both of them remained silent. I didn't cry. My eyes stayed wide open until morning. I couldn't remember the last time I had been able to fall asleep in less than an hour.

The second sign came at dawn two days after the previous incident. At 4:30 in the morning I was out on the balcony watching dawn break across from my house over Mount Qassioun and the slums stretching up above the al-Muhajireen neighbourhood. I was cold but took pleasure from the captivating silence and peace. Nobody could take that moment away from me. I went inside and made a pot of coffee. A moment later I walked across the living room to enter the bathroom and wash my face. I would look out of the back window at the dilapidated buildings with their details that amazed me: old Damascene houses, shacks scattered between the tumble-down earth buildings, roofs paved with old decorative stones, half-collapsed – these were the backs of commercial establishments. The view from inside them would cause some unhappiness, especially the Damascene plaster of Paris house being eaten away, decaying, left to rot. Looking down at those houses I would strain to hear the raspy sounds they made. I turned my head away from the bathroom window to pick up the towel and saw myself in the mirror. I saw myself clearly. I was standing there in front of myself, looking at her, feeling frightened. I didn't scream and I didn't move, it was just a moment. I stared into the depths of myself, and I stared into my eyes for a long time but she wasn't angry, I mean I wasn't angry as I looked at myself. It was just a harsh, blind stare. Then I ran into the living room...and she/I disappeared.

The third sign came yesterday. I had been upset by all the messages that were pouring in for me: some people in the opposition sent me letters in which they accused me of disappointing them by remaining silent but in reality I hadn't been silent. I found those letters so strange. Letters from Alawites, accusing me of treason. There were death threats from regime supporters. I even received a bizarre letter that read, "Dear unveiled infidel, the Syrian revolution doesn't want an Alawite apostate like you in its ranks."

Letters pour in from all directions. I am caught in the crossfire.

The third sign was harsh. I was home alone, screaming, kicking stuff around and cursing the clock that forced me to live here inside such narrow horizons, pacing back and forth between the balcony and the sitting room. I could see myself sitting there in anger. As I watched myself, that woman who was me opened her mouth and whispered. It was less a whisper than a hiss, and she watched me with a devilish expression. I was me, but for a few seconds I didn't realize I was not myself. At that moment, the woman tried to get up. She was holding something in her hand, trying to turn towards my chest, and my hand was holding my heart. It didn't last for more than a few seconds. I closed my eyes and it disappeared at once. I thought that when I opened my eyes again I would be dead. She didn't kill me, I didn't kill me, but piercing sirens rang out in my head.

Today the dead reach as far as Lebanon. A picture of a boy screaming and a woman being killed, another woman wounded. Bullets are fired from the Syrian side: a Lebanese soldier is killed. Human beings running, streaming, escaping across the border, women carrying simple things on their heads, crossing over to Lebanon. The Red Cross asks for assistance and the refugees who arrive await the unknown. Tanks assault the wide town, pulling out of one city only to encircle another. The president says that the dialogue with the opposition is about to begin, the opposition stipulates from the outset that the killing and the siege of cities must stop and all prisoners of conscience must be released before any dialogue can begin, but the killing continues and the siege moves from one city to another. Confirmed reports arrive that the president has given orders to halt the military solution on the fifteenth of this month and that the reformist option has commenced. Yesterday, state television announced they had defeated the armed men; this news had to have come from general security itself.

Wasn't the president supposed to form a dialogue committee with the opposition? They were painting a Surrealist picture these days, but I knew that in reality it was all coiling like a snake around the uprising in the Syrian cities and towns. I know all too well that the real reforms being demanded by the demonstrators mean one thing and one thing only: the fall of the regime. The difference is that this fall would be peaceful, if they actually carried out their promises to hold democratic elections. But I don't believe they will simply relinquish the spoils they have come to expect from this country, they're going to fight to their last breath, even if they have to turn Syria into one big grave, for them and for the people.

Right now, at exactly nine a.m., sirens squeal in Arnous Square and the intersections connecting the al-Rawda, al-Shaalan, al-Hamra and al-Salihiyyeh neighbourhoods. Stepping out onto the balcony, I look for the source of those sounds, thinking they must have been ambulances but discover instead that they came from yellow cabs. People are scared, in retreat and the cars typically have a few men inside. Looking out from the balcony, I spot another yellow taxi with a group of men making ambulance siren sounds, zooming past stoplights, as people in front of them jump out of the way. We all come out onto our balconies; people in the street cower in fear. In reality, those are security forces doing that. Everyone in Damascus knows that most taxi drivers are hired to serve in the security apparatus. On the one hand, these actions are meant to be intimidation; on the other hand, they actually do arrest and kidnap young people in the street. I witnessed many such incidents with my own eyes, particularly during demonstrations. They would hunt down young men one by one, throw them into taxis and speed away, as the shrieking sounds of their cars resume.

With every sound I hear in Damascus, I imagine Syria being stripped of its freedom once again. Now, too, I can imagine what it means when cars shriek like that.

19 May 2011

....

Today the bombardment of Talkalakh continues. The images of refugees in Lebanon kept me up all night. The testimonies I hear from people who were at the heart of the action make me even more nervous. I can barely keep my cool or focus on a single thing. It's going to be hard for me to carry on like this. I have been trying to relax for the last two days, but I can't. The only solution is sleeping pills, but they turn me into a zombie who sleeps and wakes up, then wanders around the house like a vagrant only to go back to bed.

It is now 5:30 p.m. Stepping out onto the balcony, I look into the street to see whether the two agents are still outside my house. Maybe I am just imagining things. I don't see anyone. I haven't been out for two days. Today is day number three. I amuse the agents who are watching me, who oversee my surveillance. I am special. Thinking it's tragicomic for me to be besieged like this, I try to focus on what has happened over the past two days. Video clips on YouTube stress me out, so much news coming from all directions. My appointments with witnesses from various cities have been cancelled out of fear and I have started becoming afraid even to meet up with my friends because my presence could cause problems for them. The hate mail still rains down on me from all sides. Today I received a letter asking me to return to what I was doing before and not to disappoint them, not to leave the Syrian people to their inquisition because of my fear; the author says he had thought I was a free Syrian woman but now it seems the regime has been able to intimidate me, or perhaps that was because I am an Alawite.

Silent in the face of the letter, I am not going to reply. What could I say to him and his kind about courage anyway? Should I tell him how I have struggled just to stay alive? That they asked me to write an article of support or appear on state television in order to proclaim my loyalty? What should I say about the mail I get from Alawites asking me to stand side by side with my people and my family? Should I tell him that high-level officials in the regime want me to work for them? What do I say to the mail that keeps pouring in from the people of my city, threatening me with death and announcing that I am disowned by the people of Jableh? Indeed, what do I say to the mail asking me to return to the true path of Islam? I ignore all the mail. I don't reply to any of it. I try to get back to the testimony I took down from an anaesthesiologist who managed to get into Dar'a.

The man was so broken up that he was barely able to give me any information. Getting to see him wasn't easy. I had to change taxis three times, weaving through neighbouring districts in a town just south of Damascus as a precaution against being followed by security. It would have been hard for me to deal with someone getting arrested on my account; I would never forgive myself if something like that ever happened. I got into one last taxi before arriving for my meeting with the young friend who was going to take me over to the doctor's house.

The idea was for me to get in and out of that town quickly. I wasn't going to be able to live like that for very long. Every day I woke up there feeling as though my heart was about to stop, that I had reached the brink of madness, with bouts of headaches that could only be stopped with tranquilizers. The place was normal. Damascus and its suburbs and a lot of places seem normal, as if nothing is happening, but everything is poised to explode at a moment's notice. This morning I met up with a writer from Suwayda who told me about the collective punishment wreaked on the people of his village and his relatives because he had gone out to demonstrate and how one of his neighbours said she was going to hand him over to the security forces for being a traitor. He told me how in Suwayda they felt an unbelievable kind of *schadenfreude* and rancour towards the people of Dar'a, which only intensified my sadness and anxiety. He left his house and came to the capital, fleeing the collective punishment. He said he was going to write down everything that had happened to him in order to be a witness for posterity. Thinking about what he said, the first thing I am going to do is send these memoirs to a group of friends abroad in the event that they arrest me or kill me as I heard they were preparing to do, or in the event that something else happens or a war breaks out. Anything is liable to happen here, but all the possibilities are black and don't bode well. We were living in anxiety, protecting it and nourishing it, dying in it. I return to my notebook and begin to transfer my conversation with the doctor from Dar'a.

"We founded a secret medical centre to treat the wounded," he says. "We did the same thing here in Damascus, when it was necessary, and in Bosra there's an entire hospital controlled by the youth of the uprising. We founded the medical centre during the first week, on 21 March. Previously I went three times per week to a medical centre to work as an anaesthesiologist, but when the events started, we founded this centre."

"What did you do at the centre?"

He is silent for a bit when I ask him that, he steps back and sighs. More agitated than at first, he says, "In Dar'a there were atrocities that never happened in Musrata or even Gaza, the only difference is…(raising his voice) there was phosphorus in Musrata. In Dar'a the killing was direct, we saw various cases of murder but most of them were killed with bullets in the head or in the chest. Do you know what I heard from security as I passed through the checkpoints? They said they were going to teach all of Syria a lesson in Dar'a. That's why they focused the killing and collective punishment there. One thing I found out about recently was the mass grave of the Abu Zayd family. Do you know their story?"

He continues, "This family had a beautiful house, security wanted to take it over but the owner resisted and wouldn't leave, so they killed him along with his children and took the house, not only the Abu Zayd house but many houses in Dar'a. Every neighbourhood was cut off from every other by tanks and military checkpoints. There was a Palestinian woman bringing in medicine and food to those neighbourhoods from the Palestinian camp. The people were helping each other."

"How many patients was the centre seeing daily?"

"There were several other centres besides ours. The young men were always working, the women who were still alive and the men over 50. Everyone else I swear to you was either locked up or had fled or was dead. Imagine that; for fifteen days, anyone who stuck their head out of the window of their house would be killed. They turned Dar'a into a giant prison, the electricity and water and communications were cut off twenty hours a day. I saw a vegetable refrigerator that the young men had put corpses in just to preserve them in preparation for burial because of the curfew. I asked the young men where all the corpses were. They said that they were in the vegetable fridge so that the security forces wouldn't steal them. As for our centre, there were about 80 dead bodies and approximately 250 patients. We had about four different centres there."

"How did you get through that military and security siege?"

"We would sneak in through Bosra."

I can sense that he doesn't want to give me any more information, so I stop there, asking him, "Were there women and children among the dead and wounded?"

"90% of the dead were young men and the killing was done with regular bullets, I was impressed by all the young boys between 15 and 16 years old. I felt sorry for them. Their moustaches were just starting to grow, it was like fuzz. They were just children and they were shot in the head or in the chest."

He stops talking. Swallowing hard, I light a cigarette as I always do whenever I am on the verge of tears. A hissing sound sneaks out of my throat as I hold back my tears, Oh God this is so hard for me. For the thousandth time I tell myself, I am not ready for all of this, I am going to die soon, as in one of these stories. He stares at me and I tremble. I imagine the young boys laid out on the ground, the soft fuzz on tender lips, shaking even more as I think about how I was a mother of one myself. I am going to cry as soon as I get out of here, as I return to the taxi all alone I will cry for all the Syrian boys being killed by Syrian men. My eyes will be all red when I get home and my daughter will look at me and say, "You were listening to a story." She'll bring me a glass of water and grumble, "Oh God, Mama, everything upsets you!" I'll pull her close to my chest and cry. She'll stroke my hair without understanding what I am feeling, but she'll hold me for a long time before making me a cup of tea.

The doctor continues, "After Salkhad we continued walking to reach Dar'a. It was a straight path to Bosra. In the village of M. there was a man with a pick-up truck in which we could carry food and medicine. I was responsible for the medical side. We'd sew up the wounds and the surgeries under lanterns because the electricity was always cut. The people were so incredibly helpful. When we had to perform surgery once at two in the morning the young men went to ask one of the pharmacists for assistance, and he opened the pharmacy so they could take whatever they needed without asking them a single question. We were able to pass through Salkhad because there were no soldiers there, but security forces and *shabbiha* were crawling all over the place, and they were even more brutal than the soldiers. They extorted two thousand liras from the businessmen of Suwayda. I would enter the southern area, where the checkpoints and the tanks began. There were BMB tanks, which were Russian and could reach 90 kilometres an hour and T-82 tanks that appeared on television. So many tanks, tanks everywhere. So many foot soldiers, as if it were an entire army, an army in a war. Hundreds of tanks, every intersection in every neighbourhood of Dar'a had a tank. The BMB tanks were the most common even though Dar'a was empty, as if it had no human beings. Only tanks and dogs and security.

"There were also funny things that happened I would like to tell you about. You know, the situation in Nawa and Jasim was different from the situation in Dar'a, where it was bleak and where the killing never stopped. In Nawa miracles took place. Shirtless young men would come out and stand in front of the snipers and the tanks, in huge demonstrations despite the siege and the death. But in Dar'a they killed anyone who came out to demonstrate and arrested everyone else. There are stories of heroism that will be told for generations among the people of Dar'a: reluctant, non-sectarian and honourable people, old women stronger than tanks. There was a woman named Hajjeh A. who bumped into the tanks by coincidence outside the clinic and she thought they had discovered the clinic so she came out to attack them and push them away. The young men inside shouted at her to come back but she didn't listen to them and advanced in the direction of the tanks and the soldiers and the *shabbiha*. They were making fun of her, and the young men in the neighbourhood who were staying out of sight. She picked up a rock and threw it at the tank, then moved forward, raising her hand up to the sky. Of course it turned out the tanks and the *shabbiha* were cruising by in a show of force and they never discovered the young men or the clinic, but the Hajjeh stayed where she was until they were gone. Do you want to know what made me happiest while I was doing my work? It was when I was doing the intubation, which is an operation where we insert a tube into the lungs so the person can breathe again when the heart has stopped. The happiness when a person starts to breathe again, when people come back to life, those were the happiest moments of my life. You know what, I'm getting tired. This is painful to talk about, but I'll tell you one more thing. Here in Damascus, there's a security agent outside every door of every hospital, just go to the Ibn al-Nafis hospital and you'll see, they refuse to let any patient in the operating room without security clearance."

My conversation with this man ends and I go home to catch up on the events of the day. I am stressed out, so I take a sleeping pill and go to bed. Writing down what the doctor told me today reminds me of those painful feelings over what happened in Dar'a, and what is happening now in Talkalakh and Homs and Nawa and all the other besieged cities. I wait for tomorrow, *Azadeh* Friday.

20 May 2011

....

More than any other day, I feel free and unmonitored on Friday, when everyone is busy with the demonstrations. The demonstrators decided to name today *Azadeh* Friday, which means freedom in Kurdish. Kurds have been coming out in droves in spite of the fact that many were recently granted citizenship; the regime thought they would be able to buy them off like this but it didn't work. Since this morning, the news has reported gatherings in Qamishli and Amuda preparing to go out for huge demonstrations, and there is also word of a substantial security presence. Consecutive messages come in over email and Facebook asking about me and about the situation among Alawite intellectuals. Even though every word poses a danger to me, I simply must say something to those young men and women, and I write the following comment on my Facebook page:

> *If the price we have to pay on the path of speaking the truth is our lives, it has been preordained and falls within the natural order of a more just human existence. At this historical moment of rupture that is opening up days of bloodshed in Syria, what the regime is attempting to accomplish must be exposed: the notion that the popular protest movement sweeping across Syria has a sectarian character is an utter fabrication. Despite the well-known regime tactics, such as dividing cities militarily along sectarian lines or targeting certain sectarian neighbourhoods for bombardment instead of others, and despite the collective punishment and the intimidation and the label "traitor" that is applied to any free Syrian citizen who happens to belong to the Alawite sect, I say to all the young women and men of the other sects who have sent me long letters regarding this question: I am here and I know there*

are others. Let us offer our spirits up alongside them, and add our
voices to theirs. The fear of sectarian war has its justifications, and
it may be the price we have to pay if the rhetoric of violence and
murder continues unabated. But we have nothing to lose except
our lives!

Returning to my diaries I write down the following incident, which T. related to me, as his face turned red and he gazed up at the sky, repeating, "Oh God...Oh God, where are You?"

"Corpses were arriving at the Tishreen military hospital," he said, "along with people who were critically wounded and the occasional light injury. One young man who had been mildly wounded was asleep in his bed, and I was standing next to another bed when an officer in civilian clothes came in and sat down next to the wounded man. The two of them started talking. I couldn't understand what was happening at first, but I edged closer to the wounded man and heard what they were saying to each other. The officer asks him, 'Who shot you?' The wounded man remains silent, and the officer suggests, 'The armed gangs?' The wounded man remains silent, and the officer instructs him, 'You'll go on television and say that the armed gangs shot you.' The wounded man looks the officer straight in the face and says, 'It was security who shot me.' The officer repeats his order, only this time more serious and threatening, 'The armed gangs shot you.' 'It was security who shot me,' the wounded man insists, unflinching as he looks into the eyes of the officer. Suddenly the officer stands up, pulls out a gun, and places it against the wounded man's forehead. The wounded man doesn't blink, and the officer stares right at him, 'Who shot you?' The wounded man says, 'It was security who shot me.' The officer shoots the wounded man in the head and walks out."

....

I come out of my stupor, from my hollowed-out heart. Over the past few days I have been suspended between life and death as I try to get rid of all these sleeping pills. I met with a lot of groups who want to contribute to the mobilization, young and old, women and young girls under the age of twenty. Nobody wants to remain on the sidelines, everyone feels a sense of responsibility but the methodology of political action is lacking and most of those who are mobilizing and active must perpetually live in difficult circumstances. I feel anxiety growing in the pit of my stomach. We are mobilizing to set up some kind of movement even as people die like flies; the fact that murder truly has become an everyday occurrence was keeping me awake on a daily basis. Today I sit down to transcribe the interview I conducted with a young man from the A.Z. family in Dar'a. I met with him once, and I was supposed to continue the interview in order to follow up on what had happened in Dar'a but that turned out to be impossible, just as it had been with the young man who told me how the protest movement in Baniyas got started, who then disappeared as well. Two days ago I learned he had been arrested. I have no idea whether the young man from the A.Z. family was arrested as well but he disappeared all the same. I am particularly interested in Dar'a, compiling as many testimonies from there as I can, because it was the spark from which the Syrian uprising first erupted.

This young man in his early twenties says, "I was charged with belonging to a family in the opposition, at the military *mukhabarat* branch they would insult me and beat me."

I ask him to tell me how the events first unfolded. He was sad but despite his moving speech, his voice remained calm and clear as he said, "On 18 March 2011, when the people went to see Atef Najib in order to demand the release of their children, he said, *Forget your children. Go sleep with your wives and make new ones or send them to me and I'll do it.* Soon after they left, the inhabitants of Dar'a found out what had happened. They all agreed that on 18 March they would come marching out of the al-Umari Mosque and one other mosque. They came out chanting *Freedom, Freedom! The Syrian people won't be insulted!* and we all went out with them. Just then, sixteen helicopters landed at the new municipal stadium in New al-Assad City and we heard that Atef Najib had told the leadership there had been a coup in Dar'a. Those who got out of the helicopters were from the counter-terrorism unit, central security. There were security agents all over Dar'a. There were *baltajiyyeh* with them. I saw them with my own eyes. There must have been thousands of them. As the demonstration marched through the valley, they were sprayed with water from fire truck cannons and gunfire broke out, killing four people, including Mahmoud Jawabra and Hossam Ayyash. That Friday ended without any arrests and four deaths, and the security presence remained heavy.

"The next day, 19 March, at six a.m., the people shouted out the names of the dead inside the mosques and assembled for the funeral. We all went out in the way we would for the funeral of any martyr, hoisted the coffin on our shoulders. A huge number of people headed for the cemetery. As we buried them, Shaykh Ahmad al-Sayasina held the microphone and called for calm, saying that they were going to release the children within 48 hours. A young man shouted, 'The blood of the martyrs is on all of your heads!' The people rose up and started shouting for Atef Najib and the governor to step down. *O Atef O Najib, we all want to see you leave!* The young men set off for the al-Umari Mosque but there was a phalanx of counter-terrorism and riot police and *baltajiyyeh* and security forces waiting for us in the valley. They were only one hundred metres from us. Shaykh Muhammad Abu Zayd tried to calm us down. We didn't listen to him. We stood there for a long time, until one of the Dar'a elite and a supporter of the regime, Ayman al-Zu'bi, showed up and the young men started beating him. Then canisters started falling down on us like rain, tear gas canisters, and then they opened fire. Atef Najib and the governor were there, but they took off on a motorcycle. We all pulled back in the direction of the town of Hayy al-Karak. They lobbed canisters at us and we set tires on fire. We were set on staying there, which we did until eight o'clock at night, when we came under heavy gunfire and finally all scattered. On 20 March, the people of Dar'a al-Balad came out to criticize the people of the city of Dar'a for not having come out with them. On that day when the people of Dar'a al-Balad came out with us, there were canisters and gunfire again and the security surrounded us on all sides. We pelted the security forces with stones and they pulled back. The people looted a Syriatel centre. They didn't set the entire building on fire, but torched the assets of Rami Makhlouf. They brought out the equipment and burned it. Two people were wounded. We were only throwing stones at the *Palais de Justice*, it was the security forces who set it on fire. A fire truck never showed up. They were burning down buildings on purpose. Security forces gathered together at the governor's mansion. Dar'a was in a state of war. A lot of people were injured, but they occupied the hospital and any wounded person who went there would either be detained or shot. Donating blood was forbidden. Wisam al-Ghul, a Palestinian, went to donate blood and the security forces killed him on the spot."

My fingers started trembling, a condition I know all too well. Rarely can I finish recording a testimony without winding up crying or shaking. Rarely can I write down the words coming out of the mouths of the tortured without them washing over me as though it were happening for real. What sort of torture is this? In moments such as these I wish I were an ordinary woman. I long for my diaries to be transformed into the diaries of a vegetable seller on a crowded sidewalk and for my vision to become empty, blind, for me to follow neutrally in other people's footsteps, but that isn't the way I am. I am the one sitting here now beside this young man from the city where the revolution broke out, the one who had been imprisoned. Blood drips from his every word.

He continues, "We woke up on Monday, 21 March and the *Serail* had been torched. We were surprised by the military checkpoints and the sandbag barricades. There were security forces everywhere we went. People came out from all over for a sit-in outside the al-Umari Mosque. They set up tents, called for the release of the prisoners and children and for the abrogation of Article 8 of the constitution, for the release of female prisoners and for the murderers to be brought to justice. On 23 March (it was a Wednesday) there was a massacre. But before that, on 22 March, the people were sitting in and everything was fine; on that day the demonstrations took place without any incidents. But between 12:30 and 1 a.m. on 23 March, violent gunfire erupted. They broke into the al-Umari Mosque, opening fire on the people inside and killing seven martyrs. They smashed the tents and tore up the pictures of the martyrs even as the *shaykh* called for help. Anyone who moved was killed. The young men gathered together and the security showed up and started shooting at us, stamping on our necks, so that nobody would dare to open their doors, lest they get shot at too. The people of the surrounding villages heard what was happening and decided to help the people of Dar'a. They streamed in from the eastern villages and from west of Dar'a, and when they assembled at the train station by the post office roundabout, near the Ba'th Party branch, they were allowed to pass through without being stopped. Then the shooting started, they say 70 people were killed, but I am sure there were at least two hundred. There were bodies that couldn't be identified, we kept going back there for weeks and saw the empty shoes of the dead and so much blood. In short, it was a massacre.

"On Thursday, 24 March," the young man couldn't stop talking, as if pus was oozing out of his heart, "people were tallying up all the martyrs and dressing others' wounds. The mosque was occupied and everyone was in a state of shock and disbelief. About 100,000 shirtless barefoot men came out and the security forces and the army opened fire on them. They fled inside the houses. People opened up their homes and hid them. We discovered a large number of people had gone missing, and to this day we still don't know whether they're dead or incarcerated. Despite all the death and imprisonment people were brave. My father said, 'I'm willing to sacrifice the three of you as martyrs.' Then Bouthaina Shaaban made a speech wishing the people well. There was a wedding where people held up pictures of the president, these were security and

Ba'thists and party members who were bussed in to show their support for the president. The people mourning their children were incensed by these weddings. Inside the mosque, after security had pulled out, everything was ruined, and there were writings in Persian. I saw security forces with scruffy beards, which was unlike the security forces we knew. Some people later said that one of the two snipers they captured didn't even speak Arabic. On that day, 24 March, the crowds chanted, *The People Want to Topple the Regime!*

"On 25 March, the people congregated in big numbers at the al-Umari Mosque for the martyrs to be buried. There were huge crowds, more than 200,000 people. The people intended to go and assemble in Governor's Square. We had been promised we wouldn't be harassed by anyone from the security or the army, Bouthaina Shaaban herself said they wouldn't shoot at demonstrators. The people crowded together and shouted in unison: *The People Want to Topple the Regime!* They also yelled: *Hey Hey Maher you Cowardly Man, Send Your Dogs Down to the Golan!* During the demonstration we got news of a massacre in al-Sanamayn where more than twenty people were killed, and when it was confirmed, the people went mad. They jumped up and down on pictures of the president and tore them up, they attacked a statue of the president, pounding it and shaking it violently. There was heavy gunfire coming from the governor's mansion. There were snipers. In that moment women stood side by side with men, and when the heavy gunfire broke out the people froze. They stayed there until they brought down the statue and set it on fire. The shooting continued for two hours. People attacked the governor's house to bring down the snipers who were up there killing demonstrators, then they set the governor's house on fire and the blaze lasted for hours. When it was all over the people knew the punishment was going to be severe but they stayed there anyway, burning tires outside the governor's mansion.

"Thursday, 31 March: Local representatives talked with the people of Dar'a about attending a meeting with the president. 25 notable figures went. Hisham Bakhtiar had chosen fifteen, and the people selected ten, but before going out to meet with the president the women told those ten, "When you go out to represent us, their blood is on your hands." Among the demands made by the fifteen men who were collaborating with the security forces was the return of the women wearing *niqabs*. The people of Dar'a hadn't asked for that, and later on this demand was shelved. They met the president and were back in the afternoon. We heard the ten men selected by the people courteously greeted the president. When Dr. Hisham al-Muhaymid, whose brother Ali al-Muhaymid was martyred in the events, saw the president, he rapped on his own chest and told him, 'We were the ones who tore up pictures of you and knocked over the statue, because you killed my brother.' According to our sources, the president was diplomatic and a polite and sympathetic speaker, telling Dr. Hisham he was prepared to do whatever they wanted. They had brought pictures and CDs and videos with them, and after making the president watch everything, he told them he had no idea this was happening and promised to withdraw the security and the army, saying he would do whatever they wished. The army really did withdraw, and the prisoners and the children were released. But that was just another trap set by the president, who we learned later on had actually ordered them to open fire in the first place."

He falls silent, and my head is still buried in my notebook. I want to tell him, *That's right, it was the president and his family and his gang who gave the orders to open fire, and everything else was just a charade they acted out in front of the Dar'a delegation*, but I keep silent and just listen to what he has to say:

"Friday, 1 April. We felt like this was a victory, everyone from the villages came to Dar'a. Even people from Damascus came. We headed out from the suburbs for the city centre. There wasn't a single security agent to be seen, there must have been 700,000 of us, huge numbers. Even though it was very hot that day, people stayed out in the squares, in three squares and everyone was chanting: *The People Want to Topple the Regime!* People started protecting government buildings so there wouldn't be any vandalism. There weren't even any traffic police. People were picking up trash and cleaning the streets, protecting the town. Civil revolt was declared and we demonstrated there for two weeks without any security present. Then, on the Friday of Steadfastness, as people came out of the al-Umari Mosque and headed for the station, shots were fired and a lot of people got killed.

There's the story of Musa Jamal Abu Zayd, who was wounded in the leg so people took him to the al-Umari Mosque where they had set up a clinic. Everyone was helping each other. Even though Jamal had been shot in the leg he refused to leave the demonstration. He seemed to have inhaled a lot of tear gas. I think he may have been poisoned, so he was taken to the clinic inside the mosque again. The doctors chided him because he couldn't handle that situation in his condition, but he refused to stay away from the people and the demonstration. When he went back out, a sniper shot him in the neck and he died. Twenty people were killed and the whole time the security forces were killing people as they walked through the streets and the alleyways. One of my friends was killed when they indiscriminately opened fire. They were barbarians. Then there's the story of Muhammad Ahmad al-Radi, a college student studying library sciences who was born in 1986. He was leaving his fiancée's house, which was near the blood bank and also happened to be on the street where the massacre took place. He saw the wounded in the street and went out to help care for people and take pictures. With nothing but a rock in his hand to defend himself, he was shot in the stomach. He fell down on his front but the people weren't able to save him right away. The security forces got to him first, and made an example of his corpse. By the time the security forces were done with him, his head had been separated from his body. People came over to take him away for treatment but it was too late. His brain slid out of his head right there in front of them.

"On 25 April they moved into Dar'a. The invasion started at night. People could sense the danger and there were rumours saying that the security forces were going to attack. People started setting up checkpoints and organizing committees to protect the city. We didn't know they were going to enter Dar'a with tanks. They moved in at dawn with eight tanks. Electricity and landlines and mobile phones were cut off. They pounded the city with gunfire for seventeen hours, destroying the pumping stations that brought water from Mzairib and shooting up the water storage tanks before the army tanks moved into the neighbourhoods. There were 75,000 soldiers in Dar'a, out of the 200,000 in the entire Syrian army. They invaded Dar'a along with saboteurs from Dar'a whose names we found out later on. That was in downtown Dar'a. Meanwhile they hadn't moved into the suburbs of Dar'a yet. They broke in and searched the houses, detaining all the young men between the ages of fifteen and forty and all the homeowners who refused to let snipers up on their rooftops; they detained a lot of people, maybe as many as ten thousand. There were a whole lot more names of wanted people and the list just continued to grow. The charge was demonstrating and chanting slogans. The houses in Dar'a were pockmarked with bullet holes and most of the houses had been sprayed with gunfire inside and out. Then they demolished them in an appallingly savage way, eight days after entering the city. People fled from entire neighbourhoods where snipers were up on the rooftops shooting at anything that moved. During the siege it became difficult to bury the bodies and corpses decomposed. There was one morgue in al-Manshiyya and another in al-Nababta Square, two morgues full of bodies. People carried weapons to protect the morgues so that the security forces wouldn't be able to steal the bodies of their loved ones. After the security forces withdrew, the tanks came back four hours later and started shelling the houses. They opened fire on the houses that were next to the morgues."

The young man's testimony stops here. I had hoped to meet him once more, so that he could tell me how the people survived the siege and what happened afterward, but the guy never came back. I asked around about him and found out that he's sick and that ever since he got out of prison he suffered from infections resulting from the torture he had been subjected to.

8 June 2011

....

I sit down to write about the suicide of a soldier in Jisr al-Shughur.

The soldiers running sluggishly through the neighbourhoods could hear the sound of their own hearts beating and the heavy rumbling of their stomachs. A town resident that dashed over to try to help despite all the shooting and death noticed the seared scar line running along one soldier's cheek. The soldiers hurried on as the city was emptied of its inhabitants; many inhabitants of Jisr al-Shughur fled after the demonstrations were so violently repressed by the army, the security forces and the *shabbiha*. This came on the heels of many other incidents where soldiers and officers defected from the army and refused to follow orders. This forced the security forces and the *shabbiha* themselves to open fire on the unarmed people, those who had come out at the beginning of the demonstrations with olive branches and called for the fall of the regime. The response was as violent as it had been in other cities, killing, sniping and machine gunfire. But Jisr al-Shughur was different because people got their hands on weapons and tanks; we still don't know how many they were. Plus the army defected there. The city had to be taught a lesson, obliterated. The residents fled and became refugees in Turkey. Helicopters hovered overhead. There were orders to kill people and break into their homes, to set fire to the farms and agricultural land and to drain the water tanks – put simply, there was a scorched earth policy that was to be applied to the rebellious city. I was tracking the news, as I had done ever since the beginning of the uprising, and listening to the stories, writing them down and then finishing it all off with a cigarette and overflowing tears. This story in particular held my attention for a long time. I heard it from a frightened officer who didn't know whether he should have been talking to me but he told me anyway, crying:

"Nobody had any way out, everyone simply went there to die."

I return to the story of the soldiers:

Four soldiers who got orders to open fire and to break into a house in one particular neighbourhood were creeping along. None of them asked each other: Why are we moving so slowly? Over the past few days they had seen more than enough bloodshed and not a single one of them was ready to invade those narrow alleyways in the heart of Jamid and Ayn Maghmada, because those they were being asked to kill were their own people. Still, orders are orders. One of them said they had to carry out the orders without hesitation, that it was their job to protect the homeland and the people and they had to rid the people of the armed gangs.

One, who had been silent, looked over, his helmet glinting in the sun and told him, as the crying man later told me:

"But which armed gangs? I haven't seen a single gang, they're all people just like us..."

He stood there silently, his beard was quivering. The other responded, and he would come to regret saying this, later telling his commanding officer he would never forgive himself for what he said, "You coward...march!"

The soldiers marched forward. Those soldiers also had sweethearts, mothers and siblings, those soldiers also had moments of fear, when their hearts got weak and heaved in pain, those soldiers also cried at night and laughed like children. Those soldiers were children themselves once, and dreamed of having children of their own. But now they had to follow orders. The army leadership told them they had to break into the house in question and kill whoever was inside because it was a headquarters for the armed gangs. One of them veered off course and entered a nearby building that wasn't their target. Two others followed him surreptitiously. His eyes were closed. He took off his helmet and looked at his comrades with alarm. The fourth one watched in confusion. They were all staring at each other nervously. The one who had taken off his helmet started smashing his head and hands against the wall, and he kept doing that until his fists were all bloody, then he rammed his head against the wall one last time, tears shining in his eyes, before he fell down in a heap. His comrade tried to pick him up but his heavy equipment prevented him from doing so and he crashed down on the ground, which, along with the heavy gunfire in town, made an odd boom. The third soldier standing between the two of them backed away. The other one stood up in disbelief, his gun at his side, hanging down at his knees. He was swinging it back and forth and staring up at the patch of sky that was visible through the door, as the sound of gunfire grew louder. He heard screaming, picked up his gun and stuck the barrel right under his chin, staring into the eyes of the third soldier, a gaze without any meaning whatsoever, and a gunshot rang out. The bullet entered his neck and came out of his brain. When he fell down dead, the fourth soldier could smell it, a smell familiar to those who had lived with death. He looked down at the soldier crumpled at his feet and before he could move, he heard the sound of a helicopter hovering in the sky followed by long bursts of gunfire. He moved closer to the other two soldiers on the ground. He felt saltiness washing over his lips, then he collapsed onto the ground, surrounded by heavy gunfire.

When he came to, dust covered the entrance to the building, but he could still make out the wall of the house that had been their target, which had totally collapsed, demolished by other soldiers. He didn't know where the shots had come from. Was it a missile? Something else? Everything around him was unclear. He examined his two friends. One had died instantly from the self-inflicted gunshot. He could hear the other one moaning and he touched the blood that was trickling out of his head, the head that had been pounding itself against the wall less than fifteen minutes ago. The third one had vanished.

This was just one of many incidents experienced by the soldiers who invaded Jisr al-Shughur. Those that did not kill themselves and who refused to open fire on demonstrators, every last one of them was killed. Afterwards, news such as the following would be reported on internet sites and satellite television networks: "An eyewitness who is a field doctor in the military emergency force reported that he was with the medical division that discovered the corpses of more than 80 soldiers who had been killed by terrorists in the vicinity of Jisr al-Shughur." But in the medical examinations that followed, several factors would come to light that absolutely contradicted that official narrative. One of the most salient things said by the field doctor, who preferred that his name not be mentioned for fear of reprisal by the Syrian regime, was that most of the injuries were to the head. They had been shot from a distance of no more than two metres, which means this was a liquidation, an execution of these soldiers. Secondly, there were clear signs on some of the bodies of torture before they died. Thirdly, there was rotting and cracked skin and cleaved heads, which means the victims must have died more than a month and a half ago. Fourthly, the bodies were found somewhere where no fighting had taken place, there were no traces of gunfire in the area and there were no empty shells.

....

Not far from the territory where the monsters live, underneath the cracked urban sidewalks that are pounded by stumbling, angry feet that have never skipped for joy, there was a faint thin thread, a red winding string swallowed up by the asphalt.

The woman watching the novelist promised she would never again dare to bring her man a suitcase containing a red rose, not even in secret.

The woman who has become another, sitting somewhere inaccessible inside my fingers, also vowed not to sleep more than three hours per day. That was no figure of speech. I decided to sleep three hours without sleeping pills, a monumental achievement which would require a major effort. What helped me were my constant movement and the enormous quantity of food I resorted to eating before going to sleep. But it all seemed like a waste – I gained weight but couldn't gain any more sleep.

Recently I have been meeting with women in order to set up a 'Syrian Women in Support of the Uprising' initiative, which requires meetings and action. The aim of this group was to provide the demonstrators with all the support they need, particularly emergency care for the wounded and cover for the young men of the coordination committees who have been forced into hiding as a result of being pursued by the security forces. Additionally, some of the young people have formed a secular group. There are many different actions, especially among the young people who are not satisfied with some of the well-known names in the opposition. They believe the time had come to revitalize the spirit of the opposition. Everyone is active and resisting in his or her own way. Some young people work with the coordination committees in the suburbs of Damascus, others organize the demonstrations; women also organize demonstrations. The issue is no longer which actions we carry out, because the popular uprising is following the same course all over the country. This is an uprising of the countryside, an uprising of poverty and a protest against all forms of injustice. The murder the authorities always relied upon has been transformed into a daily massacre. The time for dialogue has passed, yet the regime comically calls for more dialogue. Some big names in the opposition responded at first, so that the country might avoid further bloodshed, but now more than ever, the domestic opposition refuses to convene any dialogue. Every day the regime commits another massacre, and the number of those killed at the hands of the security forces, the *shabbiha* and the army increases. The cities are being taken over, besieged, bombarded by aircraft – Jisr al-Shughur and before it Dar'a and Homs. How can we possibly have a dialogue with them? This is the most important question running through the meetings I have been diligently attending with figures from the opposition. There is no solution other than the fall of the regime. The regime does not want reform or any other solution. The regime is an assortment of gangs intertwined with the ruling family, who benefit from corruption and kickbacks. The regime wants to ignite a sectarian war and will soon turn the Alawite community into its very own human shield.

None of these trips and actions over the past few days has amounted to anything at all. As we expected, the outcome is weak. Just forming the women's initiative in support of the uprising makes me feel hollow, powerless, as I watch Syrians being transformed into refugees, as the people of Jisr al-Shughur fearfully flee the military siege and the massacres carried out in their city. Turkey takes them in, setting up tents along the border. Syrians are refugees in Turkey. During the invasion and bombardment of Talkalakh, Syrians are also transformed into refugees in Lebanon, but the Syrian regime is more present in Lebanon than anywhere else. The Lebanese government hands over two refugees and the Syrians become increasingly alarmed, because fleeing to Lebanon means fleeing right back to Syria. It makes no difference what we do now.

Turkey announces its disapproval of the regime and its barbaric tactics: repressing demonstrators, killing and mutilating people, making them homeless and refugees. How can the regime kill its own people? How can planes fly through the Syrian skies to bomb their own people? It's something incomprehensible to Syrians, that these massacres can be repeated day in, day out. The cities are annihilated one after another and the whole world is watching, criticizing and calling for reform while the Syrians die, quite simply. What matters now is that defections in the army ranks have begun. A lieutenant colonel in the Syrian Arab Army appears on the satellite networks and announces his defection from the army, claiming responsibility for killing security agents who killed civilians, refusing to follow army orders, calling out through bullhorns for them not to kill the innocent. This is something very serious in and of itself. I have not seen very much that is worth taking seriously.

I am frustrated, I won't deny it, a subtle sorrow has started to seep into my diaries, not regular everyday sorrow, but overlapping strands of everyday inability, total intellectual paralysis. Daily news of killing in the cities gives me barely any time to reflect. I am still lost. Last night I decided to go out shopping for a few things, not far from my new temporary home. I only intended to go out for a few hours. I just wanted to clear my head and think about what needed to be done regarding several things I was working on. As I strolled through al-Shaalan neighbourhood, in the spice market, I saw young women running away. People were running in all directions. At once I knew there was a demonstration. The panic in people's eyes told me what was happening. I ran forward and saw scores of young men and women gathered together and chanting for freedom. The security forces ran at them and pounced. They were singing the national anthem and shouting: *No to Killing! No to Violence!* My vision blurred and I could no longer distinguish the *shabbiha* all over the place, even though the *shabbiha* are generally the ones behaving the most savagely.

They jumped on the demonstrators and called on pedestrians in the street to join in beating them as well. I saw them crowd around a young man. More than ten of them were pummelling and kicking him. Just then I saw a young lady on the ground as one of the security agents beat her and called her the most vulgar names;

when a man who wasn't taking part in the demonstration tried to help her, the security beat him mercilessly. Many more agents crowded around him and started beating him as well. Then they arrested him. I was standing right there, listening and watching, my heart pounding. I stood there with those people, trying to be inconspicuous, thinking that if they captured me, not even God Himself would be able to convince them I hadn't been part of the demonstration. But I couldn't bring myself to leave. My feet were frozen as people surged forward, running away from the security forces. Some shopkeepers came out, yelling at the demonstrators, cooperating with the security forces and the *shabbiha*, and when one of them tried to give shelter to a young woman, the security forces and some other shopkeepers beat him up and smashed his store.

There was beating everywhere you looked, and everyone they beat would later be taken away and would disappear. I saw them throw a young man into a bus, then rush back out looking for more. The people watched all of this in terror since this was the first time such a demonstration had taken place in the al-Shaalan neighbourhood. Some young women who had been watching how the *shabbiha* mercilessly stamped on the young men's bodies started sobbing and ran away. All of a sudden I saw scores of young men and women approaching from the direction of Abu Rummaneh, holding up pictures of the president, clapping and chanting, *Abu Hafiz, Abu Hafiz*. They were all wearing white cotton T-shirts with a picture of the president and the slogan *We Love You* emblazoned on them. Once the security forces had broken up the demonstration, they calmed down and stood on either side of the street in order to protect the pro-regime demonstrators. The march continued all the way to the end of al-Hamra Street. They were calm, nobody tried to stop them and they kept chanting in unison, *Abu Hafiz, Abu Hafiz*. I watched for half an hour, pretending to shop. The security forces were still trying to read people's faces even though the demonstration had been broken up. The *shabbiha* of al-Shaalan strolled through the shops, watching. I noticed how different the *shabbiha* of al-Shaalan were from the *shabbiha* of Harasta and Douma and al-Merjeh Square; they were more elegant, cleaner, they wore gold chains on their wrists, they seemed to have been sculpted, with slender waists and puffed-up chests, like cartoon characters. But they kept their beards closely cropped. What they had in common with all the *shabbiha* I had ever seen in any other city was their eyes; the same dry, cold stare. No eyelids, no eyelashes. They were the same people who beat up one guy until he was covered in blood, even though it turned out later he was part of the security forces. They were the same people who attacked young men who refused to join them in beating up demonstrators. And so I had to go back home again yesterday without even thinking about buying my daily vegetables, without thinking about anything at all. I was running away from the internet and television news, from the killing, but all I found in the street was beatings and arrests and fear. What city is this that I now live in? With every step we take there is humiliation in store for everyone.

The paper woman in my fingertips told me, "Bloodshed or humiliation, it's either one or the other." I told her to shut up and just leave me alone for a little while, like a corpse calmly fighting against its own decomposition.

How can Syrian intellectuals remain silent in the face of all this? When the protest movement first started I felt sympathetic to the silent ones. I understood human weakness and because in a democracy mercy is one of those religious virtues that must be made up as we go along, I was silent towards them. But today, after the invasion and siege of the cities, now that the Syrian people are homeless and refugees, now that they have been killed and tortured and terrorized, I can no longer be merciful towards them. Today, those who remain silent are accomplices to the crime.

Demonstrations continue in Latakia and Damascus today, in Homs and Aleppo. What is new in Aleppo is that the security forces surrounded the University City after a demonstration there, and the *shabbiha* stormed on campus, shooting teargas canisters and live rounds into the air. Over the past 24 hours the number of Syrian refugees in Turkey has climbed to 2,400 people, and Jisr al-Shughur remains shrouded in obscurity.

Today a powerful video clip appeared: Demonstrators in the al-Qaboun neighbourhood of Damascus are burning a picture of

Bashar al-Assad, the video isn't clear, darkness and gloom. The fire starts in the middle of the president's face; the demonstrators hold it right in front of the camera as they shout until their voices get hoarse *The People Want to Topple the Regime!* then throw what remains of the scorched picture down on the ground. That's a portrait of anger and revolution against humiliation and poverty. I feel added anxiety. Burning that picture means there will be house invasions by the *shabbiha* and the security forces in al-Qaboun, which will also mean more killing and arrests.

10 June 2011

....

Friday of the Tribes

Today is different.

The defecting lieutenant colonel explains how the army uses people as human shields. The lieutenant colonel says there are criminal groups chosen by the security forces to carry out the killing. He appears on television and shouts it at the top of his voice. Clearly the ones doing the killing are with the regime. The lieutenant colonel who defected from the army and joined the ranks of the uprising says the Syrian army had assaulted his village in Jabal al-Zawiya and was going to detain his family and siblings in order to put pressure on him. The other shocking thing he says is that they relied on manpower from Hizballah and Iran. Lieutenant Colonel Hussein Harmoush goes on to say, "The security forces control the media." He calls upon the Syrian people and the free officers to stand up in the face of the regime in order to hold aloft the banner of freedom.

Signs of fundamental change appear today. On the Friday of the Tribes, unconcealed names openly speaking in the name of the coordination committees of the Syrian revolution begin to appear, and the name of the protest movement changes from the uprising to the revolution. And with the wave of army defections, the uprising enters a new phase. I follow what is happening on television. The situation in Damascus is calm. A demonstration goes out in al-Maydan, and outside my house Damascus looks like it is living under curfew. In the middle of the day there is nobody on the street. Last Friday was the Friday of the Children of Freedom, in which more than 60 people were killed in Hama, reminding people of the massacre that took place in the eighties under President Hafiz al-Assad, when the entire city was decimated and approximately 30,000 people were killed. How ironic that today happens to be the anniversary of the death of Hafiz al-Assad, passing by unnoticed for the first time ever in this country.

Death has enshrouded the cities for 90 days, and every day seems worse than the last. Every Friday there are more demonstrations. The number of dead varies from one city to another. The options available to the regime appear to have narrowed, because if the situation goes on like this, the demonstrations are going to grow into a state of total civil revolt. The Turks are hinting at a military option. Things are getting more and more tense, and the military response to the uprising continues apace. As far as the outside world is concerned, the situation seems different from Egypt and Libya and Tunisia. In Syria the promulgation of resolutions is postponed so the blood can continue to flow. The whole world is in agreement: Syrians must die alone. The regime knows how powerful it is, holding Lebanon in one hand and Iraq in the other. And so the regime justifies this violent repression to itself, arrogantly and stubbornly shooting people, and to the West, which is worried about Israel and its security.

Today on the Friday of the Tribes, 39 people are killed and one hundred are wounded. There are demonstrations in 185 different places – in Damascus, in its countryside and its suburbs, in Aleppo and its countryside, Homs and Hama and the governorate of Idlib, al-Hassakeh and the Euphrates region, the coast and the Hawran. Today for the first time since the beginning of the protest movement, I hear the sound of heavy gunfire at 1:30 in the morning, coming from the al-Rawdeh neighbourhood in the middle of Damascus. This is something new, because this neighbourhood is located at the intersection of Abu Rummaneh and al-Shaalan and al-Hamra and al-Salihiyyeh, that is, right in the heart of Damascus. This means danger could be anywhere, even in one of the wealthy neighbourhoods.

I cannot just change myself into a character on paper. Whenever I have to shut my eyes I open them as wide as I can inside my heart. Shutting my eyes is the same thing as the world all around me being hidden away so I can be transported somewhere else. The noises outside are making me nervous – punctuated gunfire. I step out onto the balcony. It might be three o'clock in the morning; the streets are empty. Arnous Square and al-Hamra Street. The shooting stops, and as I become a human being once again, fear does its work. I am more arbitrary than the dictators. I can erase the entire world just by closing my eyes. I stare out onto the empty square, which had been a stage for a number of 'flying demonstrations': How is it transformed overnight?

These places are beautiful, until the presence of human beings is contaminated by murderers who sprout up in the streets of Damascus. Then they become savage and terrifying spaces.

12 June 2011

....

My day begins with news about another defection within the army.

The army bombed Ma'arat al-Nu'man and the military security branch that defected from the regime. The bombardment of Ma'arat al-Nu'man is ongoing, paratroopers are dropped and the *shabbiha* have moved in to pound the city, where 150,000 people demonstrated against the regime. The security forces killed six demonstrators. After the electricity was cut, people fled in the middle of the night for Aleppo and nearby villages.

I scan for news of killing and death in other cities.

Jisr al-Shughur can still remember the massacre of 1980, during the term of al-Assad *père*; they have a new massacre in 2011. In the first massacre more than 97 martyrs were killed. During the popular demonstrations they chanted slogans against the regime and they were met with bullets. Meanwhile the events in Jisr al-Shughur were overshadowed by the size of the massacre that took place in Hama, the city of *norias*, two years later. No fewer than 70 people have been killed by the security forces' bullets in the massacre that is happening right now. Defection from the army has left in its wake a lot of dead soldiers and security agents. Jisr al-Shughur is surrounded, as helicopter gunships hover over it and security forces occupy the city. Conflicting reports are coming out of the besieged city. In other news, the number of refugees to cross the border into Turkey climbs to 4,300 today. The army forces stand at the entrance to Jisr al-Shughur, without moving in, waiting for the number of refugees to reach ten thousand. There is a video clip on television and YouTube of Syrians fleeing for their lives from Jisr al-Shughur. I feel as if I am shrinking, my fingers become sharp knives that scratch my skin. In images I have never seen before, I recognize the Syrians afresh, like pictures of Palestinian refugees we were shown when we were children: families searching for somewhere to live under the trees, families living out in the open, a family packing its kitchenware in a plastic box and staring at the camera in grief. Children huddle around their mothers, who curse the president, saying, "Bashar chased us out of our homes." The refugees look markedly exhausted and the tents people made for those who could find no space in the refugee camp look tattered. The scene is like a fantasy movie about people who are displaced and lost, stranded and hungry, eating out in the open, sleeping out in the open, in the forest, like prehistoric man who lived millions of years ago. Soldiers appear with the refugees, talking about how the security forces would kill them if they failed to carry out orders to kill civilians. Women appear, screaming how the tanks rolled in during the middle of the night, how the soldiers and the security and the *shabbiha* killed all the livestock and set their land on fire, how they even threw away powdered milk for children. I can't believe these atrocities. Even though I know they are true I just want to go back to my game of hiding. I know this is happening even as I sit here, panicked and perplexed. How can the regime kill its own people? How can this murderous president sign people's death warrants? Is he going to force his entire people to flee? Will Syrians all become refugees now that the army has invaded Jisr al-Shughur in the middle of the night and swept through the surrounding villages, burning down the crops and killing all the livestock?

I switch over to news from the other cities, without leaving the computer. Homs is tense. Military reinforcements arrive in Latakia. It is midday and news is still coming in that a violent assault is taking place right now in Jisr al-Shughur. Once the army moved in, the regime must have decided to teach the army defectors a harsh lesson. I wait for news of a ceasefire. The internet is blocked now, so I can't know what is happening all around me. The internet was blocked for most of yesterday as well. More and more I have to live without the internet. In addition to blocking the internet, they also block the roads and annihilate the cities. A never-ending nightmare.

I try to transcribe an interview I had conducted with a young woman and her boyfriend who were both detained for a few hours after a demonstration in the Souq al-Hamidiyyeh, but my head isn't clear. It is now plain to see that they may resort to annihilating every Syrian city one by one before they even consider stepping down, or regime change, and for the first time I think about how they would do exactly what they are doing in Jisr al-Shughur to Damascus if it ever decided to rise up against them. Today for the first time I realize how hard it is to talk about any other scenario than that of devastation. It is now plain to see that the president is not going to step down without a fight and the people will not go back to the pre-15 March period. The people no longer want the regime at all, even as the regime sets the sights of its war machine on its own people. There has been too much bloodshed now.

The number of people killed in Latakia rises to sixteen. The regime still insists that it is combating armed gangs. But the story of the troops who managed to escape along with the refugees to the Turkish border betrays the regime narrative. The soldier Taha Alloush showed his military identification on camera and declared that people would have killed them if they refused to carry out the orders to kill civilians. This was something we had started hearing on a daily basis on television and from the people we meet. Four soldiers who had fled from al-Rastan testified the same thing in no uncertain terms to a French news agency. Taha Alloush talked about the operation that cleansed the city of al-Rastan, a city of 50,000 in the governorate of Homs. He said he escaped from the army three days later, having thought that he and his friends were going to confront armed gangs, but discovering instead that the people were unarmed and simple folk. Muhammad Marwan Khalaf was also called up to a unit in Idlib, near the Turkish border and he is still struck dumb by the horror of this war against unarmed people. This young recruit attested to a French newspaper, "When they started to open fire on the people, I threw down my rifle and ran away." He specified that this massacre of 20 to 25 people took place on 7 June; this bloodshot and wide-eyed army runaway also attested that he and his friends had considered rebelling but they thought better of the idea because their lives would have been in danger. "They put snipers up in high places," he added. "Police officers were in civilian clothes, and when the soldiers refused to shoot the protestors, they were killed." Walid Khalaf attested to the dangers of disobeying orders by saying, "Before us there were six people who wanted to go AWOL, and our superiors killed them." Along with fifteen other armed friends, this recruit chose to run rather than invade Homs last Thursday. "I knew," he said, "that if we entered the city we were going to kill a large number of people." That news was reported by a French news agency and al-Arabiya, and I can confirm the names of the people and their families.

The news stops here. I change the channel and follow news of the bombing in Jisr al-Shughur and the conditions of the refugees in the Turkish town of Yayladağı, where Syrian refugee camps have been set up. Now I hear Muslim clerics with long beards from Lebanon and I am afraid of their presence, as one of them venomously calls on the Syrian regime to stop the massacres. I shudder at the sight. I have been terrified for days now, ever since Shaykh al-ʿArʿur went on one of the satellite networks with his sectarian talk. It makes no difference and there's nothing strange about what's happening. The fundamentalist Islamists are scary and what al-ʿArʿur is doing is no doubt going to do more harm to the Syrian uprising than if he were to stand side by side with us. The Syrian regime says that the people going out to demonstrate are fundamentalist Islamists and these media images will only confirm their story.

I think I need to go out for a little bit. I have been sitting at home for three days. I go out to do one thing for the 'Syrian Women in Support of the Uprising' initiative, to meet a young man from the coordination committees, and then come right home. My appetite is growing. We are waiting. We have to make arrangements with doctors about ambulances for the wounded on Fridays. One of the nurses told me they would never let them use ambulances to take the wounded to the hospital, that they were killing the wounded as well and that a number of the wounded had died outside the hospitals because the security forces would not let them inside.

Helicopters continue bombing to the east of Maʿarat al-Nuʿman, in Wadi al-Daif, as tanks arrive in the area. Refugees flee through the farms and the regime chases them down and kills them at will. Most of them come from families that have been ripped apart;

mostly there is only one man left with the women of the family as the young men stay behind to protect their homes. The women and children are in a state of panic and fear and most of the men in the camps are old. All the survivors deny the presence or entry of any armed people from outside.

The incursions into the cities take place without any warning and they target houses indiscriminately. Some of the nearby villages, anticipating being engulfed in the fighting, start to flee in the direction of the camps where they expect large numbers of refugees to arrive tomorrow. The army takes control of Jisr al-Shughur; they discover a mass grave there and everything is burned – the security headquarters, the communications tower, commercial shops. Everything is burned. The city is completely empty.

13 June 2011

We haven't had an hour's peace for two days. At night. During the day. In the afternoon. In the shower. In the toilet. All these noises, all the time: cars honking furiously, as sports cars and a bunch of bullhorns park in the middle of Arnous Square nearby my house, guys and girls wearing white shirts emblazoned with a picture of the president, chanting out loud, singing through the bullhorns an anthem that prattles on about their love for the president. Night and day these processions move along the streets of al-Hamra and al-Shaalan and al-Rawdeh, as the young men and women calmly march. A simple comparison between these and the demonstrations calling for the departure of the president infuriates me – the young men and women in the demonstrations don't ride in cars and they have no bullhorns other than their throats, they barely assemble for a few minutes before human monsters storm out to swallow them up in cars and stamp on them and bloody them up in the streets. No more than a few minutes and their demonstration is over. In the beginning I would say that half the street was with the president. Now I am certain he doesn't enjoy more than 30% support, and most of that comes from the frightened minorities.

We no longer live safely in our own homes. Everything could fall apart. The streets have become stages for chaos and regime spectacle. Any regime supporter can show up with a tape recorder and a megaphone and camp out under my window, chanting for days on end and nobody, no matter who they are, would ever dare to tell them, "Shut up, we're trying to sleep!" They would not shut up in any case, and then those monsters would sprout up from the earth and attack whoever spoke out. That is exactly what happened to our neighbour who asked one of them to lower his voice because his son was studying for his baccalaureate exam. One minute the man is standing there, talking calmly, and the next moment he winds up under those men's feet. They stamped all over him as if walking on top of people was an everyday occurrence. The neighbours saved him and the scene turned into a brawl that didn't end until the police showed up. They took the neighbour away with them, and I don't know how the story ended.

I can't breathe. My lungs hurt. My skin has become rough and just being outside hurts. I follow news of death from home. I can't move. I try to reach the besieged cities but tanks confront me. I try to see the people who got out from under the siege but I worry they might be subjected to the same security surveillance as I am. I am as powerless as an old wooden chair, abandoned in a forest long forgotten by summer tourists. I hear news of two hundred soldiers joining ranks with the defecting lieutenant colonel. It is announced on television. They say there are four officers among them and that they are protecting civilians now, helping them to escape safely. "We're not doing anything," he says, "we're simply delaying the arrival of the army until the people manage to get away with their lives." Pictures start coming out in quick succession of a man who went blind when a grenade exploded right in front of him at a demonstration. There was a funeral for someone who was wounded when he reached the Turkish border and who died as soon as he crossed over, as if it were fated for him to die on foreign soil, but that foreign soil cradled his torments and his death while his own country made him homeless and cast him out. The last time I tried to go out into the street, for a women's demonstration, the security forces were gunning for me.

What am I going to do? My daughter is far away from me, my mother is far away from me, I am forbidden from going to my own village and my own city. I can't do anything. I am suspended in the air. All I do now is translate people's agonies into words through my interviews and meetings with those escaping massacres and prisons.

Testimony of Two Demonstrating Sweethearts
During a meeting with a young man and woman who both got arrested during the al-Hamidiyyeh demonstration on the second

Friday, 25 March, the young man said, "She was filming the demonstration when a group of young men carrying flags and pictures of the president assaulted her" – she is his girlfriend – "turning those flags into truncheons and beating her up. They were a crew from the Student Union, and they took her away, right in front of me. Then twelve of them grabbed me and dragged me along after them. Everyone around me tried to help but they got beaten up, too."

The girl said, "One of them fondled my chest, harassing me outright, and said, 'You want freedom, you whore, you Jewess?!' I told them, 'I'm an Alawite.'"

The young man continued talking about his girlfriend: "I started looking all over for her. They let me go but arrested her, so I asked an officer what was going to happen to her. He said, 'We're going to teach every last one of you dogs a lesson,' then pulled me along and threw me on a bus with her. They started hitting us in the face and on top of our heads. When we reached the military security branch in Kafr Sousseh, they were still beating us even as we got off the bus. She went into solitary."

The young woman cut him off: "Two of them dragged me along with them."

Then the young man continued: "We went inside. The prisoners who were captured at the demonstrations came from al-Merjeh and al-Bohsa and al-Hamidiyyeh. There were three boys under the age of eighteen, two elderly men and a doctor from al-Mujtahid hospital. One of the prisoners started shivering. The doctor told them, 'Because of the blows to his head, this man has sustained a concussion.'"

The young man was taken away, thrown in jail, and his only crime was having seen his girlfriend getting beaten up and wanting to help her. He wasn't even *at* the demonstration!

The young man said: "They threw us down on the ground, walked on top of me, stamped on all of us. We were pounded for a long time. Then they made us crouch as if we were sitting on chairs but the only thing supporting us was our toes, there was nothing but air underneath us. The entire weight of our bodies was centred on our toes, and at that point our toes started digging into flesh. They were beating us the whole time and when they learned that I was the one who had hit a security agent, they took me into a solitary room and hit me with electric prods. I passed out. They woke me up. The doctor told them I was unable to talk. They wanted me to say that one of the demonstrators was chanting in support of Israel, that he had been holding up a picture of Ariel Sharon during the demonstration and that there had been sectarian slogans. They threatened to rape my girlfriend if I refused. At that moment I told the interrogator, 'I was brought here because I saw her getting beaten up, so beware, if a single one of you so much as lays a finger on her, just try me, you'll see what happens! They were interrogating her at that very moment. They didn't let us drink any water. Palestinians in particular were subjected to additional beating. The officers placed their boots on our necks and demanded that we amend our statements however they wanted them; all the while we were beaten and stepped on. A lot of young men lost their facial features because of the intensity of the beating and the swelling. They kept moving back and forth between her and me, telling me, 'We're going to let you go, but she stays here'. They would take me out and bring me back into the cell, talking about a conspiracy and fear of the Salafis if the regime were to fall."

The girl says, "I could hear my boyfriend being whipped."

He pushes back by saying, "Well, they wanted me to scream loud enough for her to hear me. While he was beating me he would say, 'Scream! Scream!' Some of the agents took pity on me ..."

The girl interjects here: "The beating went on for five hours and the interrogator was making fun of me, about how young I was, sarcastically provoking me, 'You want freedom, huh?' The security forces were crowded all around me, so I looked up at them all and then said to him, 'What do you think?'"

The young man continues, "While we were being beaten someone came into the cell and shouted, 'Beating is forbidden!' Just then somebody else came in to beat us. An elegant and handsome young man from the Republican Palace showed up and told us, 'I'm here to listen to the demonstrators' demands'. None of the prisoners responded and the security agent barked, 'Speak up, you animals!' Another minute passed, and everyone was silent until the security agent repeated, 'Speak up, you bastards!' This guy had his face split open, dripping with blood, and he rose to his feet to tell him, 'Sir, nobody beat us. We have no demands'. Then he sat down."

The young man who told me that story was friendlier than his girlfriend – she pulsed with rage the whole time, while he was more sarcastic and droll.

Today al-Arabiya enters Jisr al-Shughur, reporting that there are armed men killing security forces and that the protestors and the regime had reached a turning point. Something odd is going on. I start to worry there is going to be international coverage of what the regime is up to. It was only after the regime allowed the news media inside Jisr al-Shughur that they brought up the issue of mass graves. I always knew it was a ridiculous fabrication because during the first two months I followed the demonstrations and listened to everything the state media said in order to compare it to what I witnessed on the ground. Besides, a trustworthy officer told me that the ones found in the mass grave were actually men from Dar'a who the security forces had brought there, tearing apart their bodies and throwing them into a pit, before claiming armed gangs were killing people. The second mass grave was not filled with security forces but prisoners who had been executed and whose bodies the security forces had refused to hand over to their families. The danger now is that the regime is pushing hard on the media, opening up whenever they want to leak some news. Syrian blood is being spilled amid the media circus orchestrated by the regime, amid the strategies of foreign policy and the balance of power. Still, the burning and destruction of Jisr al-Shughur continues apace and they only allow Syrian television to enter and film in order to say that the armed gangs are the ones carrying out the burning and destruction and killing. Today passes without any arrests, the city is empty of its inhabitants and the army bombards the hills where the residents have fled, as some of their relatives are killed along the way.

....

Now, in the middle of the afternoon, I return from the streets of Damascus, the city that is polluted with people. How can a city be polluted with people? I feel a sudden disgust and my stomach spasms start up again. The streets are crowded and sports cars carry flags and giant pictures of the president. We haven't been able to get a good night's sleep for days now because of this obnoxious presence of the president's partisans. But are they really partisans? Earlier today I saw public employees forced out of government offices in droves heading for the al-Mezzeh neighbourhood where the regime and its supporters decided to unfurl the largest flag of all time. They continue hammering away with the propaganda that they are strong, forcing the employees and workers to come out and making it seem like they are all regime supporters. Anyone who refused to come out would be subject to punishment and prosecution.

I wove through a few streets, passed by a few government buildings. It was all the same: the roads were almost completely clogged, suffocating crowdedness and a burning sun. I was coming back from a café outside the *Palais de Justice* when I ran into a girlfriend of mine. Her husband had been detained and she was waiting there for him to be released; she had been arrested before and now she was wanted for further questioning – it was something like madness. We sat at a table waiting for some news with two lawyers who defended prisoners; one of them had been arrested previously for defending prisoners. He was telling me about the difficulties he faced in defending them and about their financial straits when his phone rang. He looked me in the eyes. We were sitting in a coffee shop entirely filled with men, with the exception of my girlfriend and me. I was smoking, as usual, which had become as normal as breathing for me. He looked at me and then at the men all around who were watching me. 'Just let me take this call, and then I'll tell you the story of M.' He said that so mysteriously that I started getting excited to hear the story of M. The place was gloomy and because I love colours so much I felt out of place. He wrapped up his conversation and I immediately asked, 'What's M's story?' He smiled and told me:

"Two and a half months ago, that is, just after the start of the protest movement in Syria, M., who is from al-Hujayra, a suburb of Damascus, smashes a chisel against a bust of the president, lopping off his ear and shouting for him to step down. He would have finished the job if some street vendors hadn't stopped him. You know, almost everybody knows those guys are security agents and that the security apparatus sends out street vendors among the people in order to monitor their activities. So the merchants pounce, grabbing him and then detaining him at one of the security stations. He was mercilessly beaten there until he lost his mind. Now he has a personality disorder. His father couldn't find anyone to defend him until he met me, and I gladly took on the case. In prison he was subjected to vicious beatings despite his condition. We tried to file a suit arguing that the security services were to blame for his medical condition, and after some effort we managed to secure his release, but there was another charge in store for him. He had violated public decency, as they call it. He had taken off all his clothes in prison and called for the fall of the regime, which was considered an indecent act that injured public morality!"

That is the story of M. who cut off the ear of the president.

I said goodbye to the two lawyers and my girlfriend, who had gone inside the *Palais de Justice* in order to find out some news about her husband. Every day she would go there and wait. Another girlfriend passed along news about the lawyer who was going to give us the names of the prisoners and their families so we would be able to find out their financial circumstances and offer them monetary support now that we had followed her suggestion and set up our "Syrian Women in Support of the Uprising" initiative. I had to walk through a few different neighbourhoods on my way to see the public employees who had come out of the government buildings in order to participate in a pro-regime march, but she wasn't home. In spite of the suffocating heat I was feeling confident because I had started working with the young men and women of the uprising ever since the foundation of the initiative. I chose fieldwork, meeting with the coordination committees of the revolution in order to support them directly and act alongside them.

Women and girls of all different ages started meeting ten days ago in order to come up with a program that would unite the uprising. As far as we were concerned the priority was getting more involved with the demonstrators on the ground. I was getting tired of the gatherings of well-known figures from the opposition. I believed that what they were doing wasn't moving things forward or back or really helping at all; maybe it was creating an illusion. As far as I was concerned, it was more important to go out with the young people in order to extend the uprising as much support and strength as possible.

Our first step was to place doctors wherever demonstrations were happening, which meant we had to come to an agreement with courageous and trustworthy doctors who would be placed in those areas the day before. That was no simple task, because as soon as the security services discovered a doctor treating the wounded, they would arrest and torture him immediately. In addition, we would provide bandages and first aid materials, which allowed me to meet some young doctors who were working to set up the Damascus doctors' coordination committee to help out with the uprising.

The second step was to create a support fund for the uprising, to collect donations on behalf of prisoners and their families, on behalf of the young men and women who were forced to quit their jobs and go into hiding and live underground in order to work on behalf of the uprising. Those were our first projects and my first experience working with them. I tenaciously met with a number of people and learned where the political mobilization in Syria was headed. Syria truly was boiling. People were coming together and trying to do something, affinity groups were formed, the opposition pieced itself together, everybody wanted to chip in to the process of change. Even now, though, they still haven't formed a strong unified current, I know that everyone is doing something. That's a good sign.

Tomorrow will be a busy day. I am going to meet with a number of the coordination committees in Damascus and the suburbs. That in itself will be a prelude to more serious work on the ground. Now it is the evening of 15 June, and after meeting with a secular youth group, I come home to wait for my daughter. She is returning from a long journey and I feel extra scared for her, but when she arrives she makes fun of my concern, telling me how happy she was in Baniyas and how she feels much more nervous in Damascus. I sit down on the balcony. There is a total lunar eclipse tonight. I smoke and talk with my daughter. The night sky is perfectly blue, and the eclipse turns red before becoming full. My heart still hurts and I still feel like the tanks occupying the cities and annihilating the people are never going to let up. The tanks are heading for al-Bukamal and Dayr al-Zur. Ma'arat al-Nu'man is emptied of its people and more than 8,500 Syrian refugees are fleeing their homes in villages and cities. Who does this to his own people? Our murderous president. Has the sweep of History ever witnessed this sort of killing? I cannot be sure, maybe not since the days of Tamerlane. I must go back to the history books in order to find out more about the most infamous butchers and horrendous massacres that have been carried out in this region.

Now they are not only invading the cities, they have also occupied our hearing and our sight. Our hearing with voices that never cease chanting through bullhorns every day, *Our Spirit, Our Blood, We'll Sacrifice for You O Bashar!* Our sight on al-Hamra and al-Salihiyyeh, the two venerable streets in the heart of Damascus that have become a deadly joke, as security forces are deployed as clothing merchants, corn-on-the-cob hawkers, purveyors of everything imaginable, a ridiculous situation. The vendors lay out their wares on the sidewalks and people crowd around. The number of people swells because the goods are cheap. The security services deploy their men out on the streets; they are everywhere. The owners of elegant and old-fashioned shops on those two venerable streets stand with their arms folded across their chests.

The people of Ma'arat al-Nu'man run away as the army inches

its way forward. Jisr al-Shughur is a ghost town and people are fleeing. Hama is demonstrating once again. The border with Jordan is opened today after being closed for two months. Two hundred metres: the length of the flag unfurled by regime supporters. All along the Turkish border refugees call for the fall of the regime. The refugees are shouting on the television screens: *We asked for a little bit of freedom, they killed half the Syrian people!* The revolutionaries decide to name this Friday after Shaykh Saleh al-'Ali, the rebel who refused a French proposal to establish an Alawite state and who remained committed to Syrian unity. Today another officer, Captain Ibrahim Munayyer, also defected, "because we swore to point our weapons at the face of the enemy and not at our own people." He announced his defection, citing the following reasons: army involvement in invading secure cities in order to kill civilians and intimidate the people and army involvement in providing cover for the *shabbiha*. Today there is a call to convene a national salvation conference. The women of Dar'a go out to demonstrate in spite of the siege, repeating: *Anyone who kills his own people is a traitor!* The people of Hama tear down a statue of the president and throw it down on the ground. Statues are falling in the cities. Statue after statue.

16 June 2011

It was a gray morning. My nightmare came back, and from three until nine a.m. I tried to fight off that horrifying dream. I decided to take a break from listening to these stories and go out where the demonstrations were happening. I must calm down a little bit. Yesterday during a meeting with one of the young people from the coordination committee I met a film director who told me about his time in prison and how the worst thing to happen to him wasn't the torture he himself endured but rather seeing an old man and his three children tortured. They would take one of them away to be tortured, disappearing with him for hours while the other brothers and the father waited. When they returned, he would be unconscious, his body mutilated as blood oozed out of him. This poor old man and his children would wait for him to wake up, crying all day and all night as they watched their torments pile up on top each other. The second thing that was especially hard for the young director was how they made them walk all over each other. The prison corridor was packed with prisoners who paved it like cobblestones. They would force other prisoners to walk all over them. The director found that really difficult for him to do, but anyone who didn't walk over the prisoners would be beaten and fall down on top of them, which hurt even worse. It got so bad that one of the prisoners splayed out in the hallway implored him, 'I'm begging you, just walk on top of me, it's easier than to have you crash down on us'.

In the nightmare I see myself walking through a fountain of blood. There are elderly people, deformed bodies, and colours like brass. I am not sure whether that was a nightmare or my recollection of what I was hearing every day, but it made me bolt up in bed at three a.m. to wait for the approaching dawn. My daily routine is to wake up at four, but everything changed when the uprising began. My sleep has become conditional on sleeping pills, and when I resist by not taking them, I can only sleep for maybe an hour before I wake up, falling back asleep for a little while only to awaken again right away. My days are long. It is important to schedule some meetings in order to get the women's association up and running in a serious manner. I had been thinking we should institutionalize our efforts in order to be effective on the ground. I got word that the Islamists were quite active on the ground and that their financial strength was quite formidable but that meant very little to me.

I have three meetings this morning with young people from the coordination committees, with the young women who will take over responsibility for the fund in support of the uprising. Then I have a meeting with the young physician who is going to set up a doctor's coordination committee, which points up our need to unify the efforts of all the doctors in order to make a common coordination committee; they are the ones who will be depended upon to treat the wounded and save whoever can be saved in the besieged cities, neighbourhoods and suburbs. Despite the fact that any doctor who helps or treats demonstrators faces nothing less than the punishment of imprisonment or death, both male and female doctors volunteer in large numbers. They need to be connected with the women's group. The most important demands the coordination committees make is for the creation of a support fund that can secure medical supplies and care for the prisoners and their families, and the launching of popular mutual aid campaigns. What this means is that we are working to establish civil society institutions as quickly as possible in order to join the uprising and support it in a serious way. I am more afraid than anything of not being able to carry out the work we have been asked to do.

I come home and nearly collapse from exhaustion. Without even washing my face, I get right into bed. Additional sorrow washes over me. My heart is black, and news from my family hurts me more than anything. Yesterday in Jableh a schoolteacher scolded my niece in front of all her friends, telling her she and a lot of other teachers from Jableh were going to come after her and come after me, that I had to start reforming myself and that there wasn't a single Alawite in all of Jableh as insolent as me, that I was a traitor, a whore, that I was this and I was that…and that all the Alawites had disowned me. The phone threats have abated somewhat. It has been ten days since the senior officer stopped following me.

17 June 2011

....

Shaykh Saleh al-ʿAli Friday

Some residents of Jisr al-Shughur return home. There are instances of rape, assault and beating. An entire family is killed. In Hama they unfurl a humongous flag as part of a movement opposing the flag the regime brought out yesterday. Syrian cities continue their demonstrations. 29 people are killed on this Friday; eight of them and one police officer are in Homs. It is the fourth month in which demonstrators are going out and the regime's killing and arrests do not slacken. In Damascus they are coming out in huge numbers and there is a demonstration in Aleppo. Darʿa, the besieged and gutted city is going out to demonstrate. The lying regime media still says it's fighting terrorism and armed gangs. The dying doesn't stop. Fighting between Syrian regime supporters and its opponents reaches Lebanon. Six people are killed and scores are wounded. Once again the regime sends Lebanon a message: as long as Syria isn't safe neither will they be. Each Friday more Syrians go out than the Friday before and more blood is spilled. The number of refugees exceeds ten thousand and today the army is trying to stem their exodus to Turkey after besieging the villages that lead there. Apparently the regime has decided to surround them and even prevent them from leaving their homes. But coming back is out of the question because there is such awful news about those who do come back getting killed and having their families tortured. *Where will the Syrians go?* I fret. They appear in refugee camps on satellite channels and declare there were no armed gangs and that it was the army who did all the killing, that they would not come back until the collapse and fall of the regime. Some refugees could not get across the border and are living out in the wild, sleeping under trees; they face a catastrophic situation with inhumane conditions. I think about children getting tucked in under the open sky. I notice their weary eyes as they gaze into the camera. My head is going to explode from this news. I need to take a sleeping pill just to shut my eyes.

....

Today we learn that the president is going to make a speech tomorrow. I don't expect him to say anything important. As far as I am concerned he is nothing but a murderer and needs to be tried as such.

Every day that passes in this place makes me feel like my skin is turning into scales. The phone threats have started up again and the senior officer summons me one more time. He is curt with me, which tells me they knew what I have been up to. I thought that remaining silent and not publishing articles would make me invisible, I thought I was through with them, but apparently something has happened, something I do not understand, as though word got out about the 'Syrian Women in Support of the Syrian Uprising' initiative or that I had been meeting and working with the coordination committees. One thing is certain: they have informers. It is inconceivable that they would track me with this level of precision. I voice my concerns to the young men and ask them to be more cautious. I really feel like the young men and women are in danger, to the point that I meet with one woman coordinating the group in our 'Syrian Women in Support of the Uprising' initiative just to tell her I can not meet with them anymore, for their own protection. I am more than just disappointed. There are supposed to be three meetings but nothing ever comes of them.

I think once again about how much passion is necessary in order to carry out actions like these in such troubled times. I am dissatisfied. I really don't feel like I can work at such a slow collective pace. The meetings continue but the outcome is unsatisfying. I know a number of women think me impatient, but the truth of the matter is that I am fed up. I knew that time is no longer on our side and that the people going out to demand their freedom move more quickly than the sluggish movement of the elite. I am convinced that the morality based on religious foundations that had existed for centuries, not only here but all over the world, must be recreated with theories of morality based on a different concept, one which the people were demonstrably fond of. The essence of the Syrian uprising is moral first and foremost.

Returning to the details of reality...Today I concluded that the security services were not going to just leave me alone, they were following me outright. Actually, the senior officer seemed to be the only one who believed that my stand on the uprising was directed against him personally as an Alawite. My patience with him was starting to run out. He told me he knew each and every person I met with. I thought he was lying but they have intelligence indicating I kept silent only in order to work in secret. I don't think they have any more details than that. Or maybe they know something about our night-time meetings with women in support of the uprising. I believe that my involvement with any group at this point would put them in danger.

I can't write.

I can't work on the ground with the young people from the coordination committees.

I can't do anything.

All I can do is hurt now.

I know that my breaths are numbered, each inhalation is numbered. My movements. My steps. Everything is numbered and watched. There's a prison inside me. They won't have to arrest me. That much is certain. But they will drive me to madness, they would have known that I won't be able to go on like this, they would have wanted to tell me they were even monitoring the air I breathe. I thought about going underground once and for all but the existence of my daughter held me back. It would be hard for her to go into hiding with me.

Today Angelina Jolie appears on television, visiting the Syrian refugees. My heart skips a beat. Syrians are now displaced persons; celebrities adorn themselves with them. Turkish politicians kiss Syrian babies in photo-ops as the filthy game of politics extends further and further.

I hear there is a national council being formed to confront the regime, presenting itself as a representative of political forces inside the country as well as abroad. As the army reinforces its presence along the Turkish border, the village of Khirbet al-Jouz is surrounded and its people are hunted down and detained for helping the refugees from Jisr al-Shughur. Still, army defections continue, only this time it is in the naval forces where the officer Mahmoud Habib appears to announce his defection; Sergeant Ismail al-Shaykh Salih from the air force *mukhabarat* proclaims his defection as well. My day ends with a young man appearing on al-Jazeera as a representative of the local coordination committees. I feel a small satisfaction. At least something good is happening today.

···

A lifeless mind.

A lifeless heart.

It's time for all of you to get out of here so I can start dancing to music once again, my only life amidst this oblivion.

I want to reclaim my passion for words, for the rhythm of Arabic letters, how I thrill at the letter "Jeem" as it plunges into a deep resting place, the letter "Alif" as it soars through an endless space, the breaking "Ya" as it rises toward forming the whispered whys and y's, the letter "Noon" in its tender womb.

I want to regain the warmth in my fingertips as they flutter like reeds in the wind, sniping words and painting images upon images in a world made of air. The world I belong to. I want to return to my passion for abstaining from the realistic details of human life, to get back to disdaining appointments and interviews and meetings and the ringing of telephones, back to my own private conversation that unites me with a cup of coffee.

I want to reclaim my ability to obliterate real circumstances. I want one night of deep sleep without a fiery needle piercing my heart and ricocheting out of my eyes like an echo. I want the luxury of choosing the faces I will lavishly bestow upon my intimate life. Just like that, to put it simply, I want to go back to my solitude that is crowded with novel characters. They're all waiting for me there, somewhere in my mind that is sick with them, that is sure with them. They're waiting for you to get out of here, you idiots. I want a few simple things, like for my eyes not to tear up every hour, or not to jump whenever I hear a loud noise, not to bolt up like a crazy woman whenever my elderly neighbour who lives alone with her old husband screams. I expect that one of them is going to pass away at any moment now. I have been a bundle of raw nerves, how could I not be, falling asleep to news of killing and waking up to the stench of bloodshed and stories of imprisonment and torture.

This morning the doorbell starts ringing early, at 5:30 a.m. In the building where I live now there is only the old people's apartment and a dentist on the ground floor. We are practically the only residents, that old woman who lives with her half-crippled husband and I. The two of them are tragically alone and I would tip-toe past their door coming from and going to the top floor where I live, because she is sure to open up and make me stand there for a long time as she talks about her loneliness and her sadness over the death of her only daughter. At first I stood there and listened, I would visit, but that meant spending half the day there and furthermore, it would mean spending my entire day in a foul mood. There is something agonizing about the life of those two elderly people, something that makes the way I think about oblivion more concrete. Two lonely old people in Damascus, with no children and hardly any relatives who ever show up. They live in a fusty apartment, which hints that they once had money; their problem was never poverty but rather that life has passed them both by, or that death has passed over them as well. This is painful for me to see. Today her husband falls down on the ground and throws up. As usual I fall asleep to news that made me wake up in pain from grinding my teeth together. The news of the refugees is saddening.

I don't know what I am supposed to do. The old man has nearly lost consciousness, the old woman raves and curses her life, their house smells fusty and the whole place is a mess. I stayed to help her for a while. I was shaking by the time I finally left. I think for a few seconds how my nerves were so badly frayed that I would start crying at the least painful sight. The old woman looked into my eyes, and my face felt redder than usual as I told her that all she had to do was call and I would be there at any hour, that I was like her own daughter. Tears streamed from her eyes as she threw herself into my arms. She was frail. I was trembling. She said, "Ahhh, my girl, if you only knew how much her death stings my heart." I said, "Auntie, God rest her soul, this is God's plan." I got up, put back her headscarf that had fallen and walked away so she wouldn't be able to see my own tears. I didn't even look back, quickly climbing the steps. There's nothing left. That's right, there's nothing in this life worth celebrating.

The images rush past my eyes, horrifying images from when Syrians started getting killed and imprisoned and mutilated and dumped in mass graves. Now there are pictures of the refugees on the screen, showing how they live. Simple folk say that they ran away from tanks that did not distinguish between young and old, between women and men. Every day they appear on television, talking about being chased as they ran away, how they left everything behind, escaping with their lives even as the Syrian army continued sending reinforcements.

The strange thing is that they forced them out of their homes and then chased after them as they fled. It wasn't enough to kill them and displace them in order to teach them a lesson. They had to follow after anyone who was still alive – this is madness.

Today the president gives his speech, which is shocking and frightening and even worse than the last two. His appearance conveys wilful ignorance. The Syrians are angry and go out to demonstrate against the speech. The president keeps saying there is a conspiracy, that there were gangs. He doesn't recognize the suffocating crisis the country is living through. From time to time he laughs and pedantically explains some bit of common knowledge. He is a cartoonish Frankenstein, reciting a stilted book report about the mechanics of organized, premeditated crime. The Syrian people answer back: Urban demonstrations in Homs and Hama, Idlib and Aleppo and a number of Syrian cities. His speech makes a mockery of Syrian blood and it spells, in brief, the continuation of the military-security solution.

Following the president's speech, state television announces the discovery of a mass grave in Jisr al-Shughur – they say it contained security forces and army soldiers. It is the third grave they show. The bodies have been dismembered and disfigured, and they are shown on screen. The people of Jisr al-Shughur and the defecting army officers say it was security agents and members of the army who carried out the killing, and who dug mass graves in order to slap the charge on armed men and confirm the official narrative: *The annihilation of the city was intended to cleanse it of these armed men.*

The madness continues and the killing continues. The regime says day after day, *Either us or this scorched earth policy and whatever remains of your remains, O Syrians.*

I am waiting for something to happen, despite my lack of confidence. I am really hoping for a miracle to save this country from perdition.

21 June 2011

....

Today there is a massive demonstration in support of the president. All public employees have been coerced to go out or they will
be fired and shamed publicly. They turn everyone who works in
government agencies into security forces and anyone who doesn't
do as they're told is kicked out. Walking through the streets I
notice the faces of the supporters, and as usual my tears precede
me. 40 years have passed, my entire life, and in spite of all the
torments I had been through, I never cried like this before. In
just a few months a woman like me finds out what a flood of tears
looks like, a few months in a life gone by, a sad life. I don't regret
what happened, the uprising has renewed my faith in ideas about
life and justice and strength. I am out in the streets searching for
something I had lost, something I imagine. I notice it in the face
of the young men and women as they ride around Damascus on
top of sports cars, carrying flags and pictures of the president. The
young ladies wear lots of makeup and are beautiful, as though they
have been invited to a party; the shiny black cars become a parade
clogging up the streets of Damascus. I step to the side and watch.
I cannot stay at home but I should go back there in order to add to
the story of what happened in Jableh. Jableh, my city, where I was
born, which is now off-limits to me. A lot of things are off-limits,
but somehow I still feel satisfaction tugging at my heart like a thin
string of happiness, like a thread made of dust.

The story of Jableh
My awesome girlfriend who volunteers to go to Jableh and bring
back stories of what happened was also from the city. Her family
lives there. Unfortunately, it is not possible for me to send her
to the Alawite villages as well because, by accident of birth, she

belongs to the Sunni community but we agreed to put out these diaries concerning what actually happened, to report the truth of the events. Our idea was to report what had taken place in the city where we grew up, which was shrouded in murky news that is hard to confirm given the dense deployment of security forces and *shabbiha* and minions of the Assad clan there. After her ten-day tour during which she conducted a number of interviews, she told me I was as good as dead to most Alawites. They consider me a traitor, whereas the people of Jableh sympathize with me and think I am on their side. What a nightmarish tragedy. What is the logic of justice and what is the logic of truth?

Here is a testimony of a young man from Jableh:

"After Bouthaina Shaaban came out with her speech full of job-related and political promises," he says, "Jableh witnessed daily demonstrations in support of the regime and we heralded the beginnings of change in Syria. The daily pro-regime marches in the streets of Jableh became inflammatory and exhausting for our spirits and our nerves. How could we *not* get annoyed when there was no human sympathy? Our first attempt began as a humane and human desire to articulate our refusal of injustice and our rejection of state media lies. We would have successfully protested on the Friday after the massacre in Dar'a by coming out of the Abu Bakr al-Siddiq Mosque if we had not been surprised to find it surrounded by fire trucks. They brutally dealt with a young man who loudly opposed the presence of security agents inside the mosque. The first Friday only got as far as an indoor sit-in even though the support and encouragement among those who were praying inside the mosque was huge.

"The next Friday we succeeded in getting out of the mosque and into the square we dubbed Freedom Square because it was the first square to witness our attempts at going out and organizing our ranks, and because it was the safest area for us to assemble. That was a big Friday with huge hordes and tons of supporters. Our slogans called for freedom and support for the people of Dar'a and Douma, focusing on slogans that would reassure our brothers and sisters in the Alawite sect and encourage them to join us in rejecting the language of blood and conflict. We kept on going out after evening prayer, there were more people every day, from all different classes – doctors and engineers, unemployed people and university students. Even women joined us, as did some of our brothers from the countryside and from neighbouring villages. Our slogans at this point didn't exceed demands for reform, the combating of corruption and calls for freedom."

I stop here to think over these details. I know what that young man means by corruption in Jableh and how the security forces and the regime *shabbiha* control the city, how some corrupt Alawite officers and businessmen were reported to have bought up the city, illegally and shockingly turning its people into tools in their hands. These are the places and streets I knew and grew up in as I changed from a little girl into a young woman, where I had so many memories. My school was in a mostly Sunni neighbourhood, but back then there weren't any problems between us. Most of my childhood friends were Sunnis and I didn't even know what the words Sunni or Alawite meant. I found out when I was a little bit older and went to high school.

The young man continues: "We kept on going out every day for two weeks without any security or army or *shabbiha* coming near us. If there was any movement on the part of the representatives at all, it seemed to be in making arrangements to deal with our employment and cost-of-living problems. They were cosmetic changes without any meaningful treatment of the issues, so we responded by calling for justice. They didn't understand that our demands weren't only concerned with jobs and the cost of living, that they were bigger than that. They were existential and had to do with freedom we hadn't felt the sensation of for 41 years, with democracy and party pluralism, with changing the constitution that deified the single Party and enthroned the dictator. We also called for equality of opportunity, for the corrupt and the thieves who plundered us and plundered our future and our aspirations to be punished, for a dignified and just life that would achieve equality of opportunity regardless of the connections or favouritism that Jableh perhaps suffers from more than any other city or province. Jableh swarms with corrupt people and is full of villas and palaces owned by those with influence, even as entire neighbourhoods and villages go without electricity or water or any chance of a decent life for them or their children, all because they don't have any influence. The corruption in Jableh reached the point where the city is the property of one or two figures who bought up most of the properties and land under other people's names in order to obfuscate and cover it up, but everybody knows all the details. Everybody knows these facts by heart.

"Our protests peaked on the Friday of Dignity, 22 April 2011, which they called Great Friday. It was the largest protest Jableh had ever seen. More than three thousand people took part, including a large number of women. One of those was the mother of the activist T.B., who is still in prison; she was carried on the people's shoulders as she chanted, *O Jableh, Where are your men, O Jableh!* Our slogans included: *One One One, Sunni and Alawite are One!* and *O Noble People of Jableh, Answer the Call of Freedom!* All our slogans always encouraged our brothers and sisters in the Alawite community to join us. When some of them did we realized full well how great the pressures and the difficulties were that surrounded their joining us. Over time our slogans evolved and we started to call boldly and clearly for the fall of the regime. On that Friday we marched through all of the neighbourhoods of Jableh with huge crowds until we reached the family home of Atef Najib. We called for him to be brought to justice for every drop of blood that was spilled in Dar'a and for him to be prosecuted for his crimes. This was the first contact we had with members of the Alawite sect who rejected our demonstrations and our slogans. They blocked our path, meeting us armed with sticks and knives along with a large number of residents, standing in the way of our right to revenge. At this point a local *shaykh* got involved and addressed the young men, urging them to go home. They retraced their steps toward the cinema roundabout near Jableh town hall, where they collectively held evening prayer in the street before dispersing. One group went home while another decided to keep demonstrating. They headed on foot to the al-Amara roundabout, chanting for freedom and the martyrs. There were no more than a hundred, maybe two hundred of them and this was the second time Alawites prevented the demonstrators from advancing, blocking their way to the roundabout with fire trucks that began spraying the demonstrators with water as neighbourhood residents joined in pelting the demonstrators with rocks and vegetables. Curses were exchanged and one eyewitness reported that a resident of the al-Amara neighbourhood opened fire in the air in order to frighten them after rumours spread that the demonstrators had come to the neighbourhood in order to kill them and break into their homes and capture their women. In their pro-regime demonstrations they marched through every neighbourhood and we never opposed them or bothered them. Why wouldn't they let us peacefully demonstrate with our slogans the way they do? Are the streets theirs and theirs alone? That Friday ended with tensions running high between the two sects and nasty rumours on both sides, promises and threats, and nobody knew who started those rumours or where they had come from.

"The next day there was a pro-regime march in which cars and motorcycles went all over Jableh led by a Hyundai Tucson with a big mounted machine gun for all to see. When it passed by the Corniche, some young Sunni men from the neighbourhood blocked the street with trashcans and carried sticks and hunting rifles, in preparation for any direct contact between the two sides, especially since news of an armed assault had spread throughout Jableh. The real contact between the two sects took place after the Tucson opened fire and quickly sped away, jumping the curb with terrifying speed. Eyewitnesses from the neighbourhood said that a young man from the village of Zama was wounded and the young Sunni men rushed him away for treatment. The young men joined in breaking up the clashes and moving young Alawite men to safety, far away from the tense square.

"After this dangerous incident, high-level connections were called in by some of the well-known financial and commercial residents of Jableh in order to mend what had started to unravel between the two communities through reciprocal visits, in order to calm down the situation and bring it back to the way it was before. The mediators succeeded and both sides came out together in a joint march, chanting, *Sunnis and Alawites are One*, exchanging kisses and greetings. The early signs of tension that were clear for everyone to see came to an end and along with them the story of the popular checkpoints that had been set up after rumours spread about each sect attacking the other in order to kill them and put an end to their existence. These rumours had spread like wildfire throughout Jableh and its villages after we started going out to call for freedom. To this day, neither side knows the truth or the source of those rumours. One likely explanation was that they were a security fabrication, a threat from the regime regarding what would happen if security, safety and stability were lost, especially when there had been news of young men from the villages and from the Communist Party joining our demonstrations, no longer afraid of hoisting banners that called for the fall of the regime. The fear barrier had been broken. After this dangerous incident, we thought about evacuating Freedom Square to outside the Abu Bakr al-Siddiq Mosque in order to avoid any confrontation with the other sect. Our battle isn't with the sect. The regime is our problem and we understand all too well how it seeks to hide behind the Alawite sect and exploit their fears in order to stay in power.

"The next week, Sunday afternoon to be specific, after the new governor in Latakia had been appointed, he came to see us, wishing to meet with city representatives and some of the young people of Jableh at the mosque at Freedom Square in order to hear our demands and needs. The meeting between the two sides ended two hours later with the young people announcing, *We want to topple the regime!* At this point the governor stormed out, vowing, "Now I'll show you all." The very same day the city witnessed a substantial deployment of security forces and the army as well as a large number of regime *shabbiha* dressed in civilian clothes but who were distinguished by their tennis shoes and, of course, armed to the teeth with weapons and ammunition. Two hours after the meeting was over, public safety in Jableh was divided on a sectarian basis, with dirt barricades set up in all the Sunni neighbourhoods, particularly in all the 'zones of disturbance', as they called them. The partition started outside the Teachers' Union and extended all the way to Jableh Stadium. Large trucks set up dirt and sand barricades at the entrance to the city and the entrances to the well-known neighbourhoods (al-'Azza, al-Dariba, al-Jirkis, al-Saliba, al-Fayd); snipers were stationed on top of government buildings, giving them free rein to look down on the streets and easily watch all the action, destroying any green space in order to expose the area for them, like the Jableh cemetery, which had most of its famous ancient green trees chopped down at the root.

"The activity in the city that day was abnormal – suddenly a substantial and intimidating security presence on a calm and natural day where nothing seemed to indicate the need for such forces in a small city like Jableh. In less than two and a half hours, without any warning or alert, Jableh started to hear the heavy gunfire of a chaotic attack. For many hours throughout the day, shooting continued to blanket the city, forcing people to hide wherever they were, in stores, for example, to avoid being hit by bullets. They didn't know the reasons for all that gunfire, or who the targets were. A premeditated massacre befell the people of Jableh, with brutality and fury never before seen in its modest history. Nine young men were killed and many others were wounded. They prevented ambulances from arriving, which they might have targeted anyway. We were able to get some of the wounded out of there and into the neighbourhood mosque in order to treat them and prevent the theft of their organs by the regime *shabbiha* at the national hospital, as had happened with a young man from the Al Jum'a family. He had been assisted by K.Q. in his own responsibility as a member of the People's Council. Only the young man came out with his neck slit all the way down to his stomach, in spite of the fact that his original injury was to the foot. We depended upon doctors who hadn't been taken away for arrest and torture on the charge of aiding and abetting criminals and terrorists and infiltrators. It was obvious that the regime *shabbiha* were using very sophisticated weaponry and a kind of explosive ammunition that either killed people or completely incapacitated them. We were trying to help one guy who had been hit in the head by sniper fire, it was unreal to see his brains spill out like that. At that point we used the imam's cap to scoop his brains back inside his head. It was a sight I'll never, ever forget. Most of the martyrs had to be buried in secret and far away. Before allowing anyone to recover and bury the bodies, security required people to sign a form stating that the ones who killed them were armed men and saboteurs. Only a limited number of family members were allowed to be in the presence of the security agents.

"After the massacre, Jableh became a ghost town. Nobody dared leave their house for fear of a sniper's bullet and most of the inhabitants resorted to replacing the doors on their houses, which had always been wooden and open, with only a cloth curtain separating the inside from the outside. Now most doors were impenetrable black iron out of fear of another massacre like the last one. We had to limit ourselves to night-time demonstrations, some of which were 'flying' and some of which were very crowded. Women participated along with us but we reduced the scope of our actions to very narrow limits in order to evade the eyes of the security, which had noticeably infiltrated us in Jableh despite its small size and narrow spaces. The scope of the infiltration was horrible. It was awful; none of us trusted anyone else. That's the only plausible explanation for the huge number of arrests the city has been subjected to up until now, on all kinds of charges, despite the fact that they had been releasing well-known criminals accused of smuggling and drug use ever since the first spark of the Syrian revolution. Day in, day out Jableh continued to live on rumours and predictions and every day it expected another onslaught, another massacre. To get ready, we all came up with new ways of self-defence, one of which we called 'the eggplant', which was like an explosive stick of dynamite that made a booming sound but wouldn't kill anyone. People say the residents of the al-Dariba neighbourhood evacuated the women and children from their houses for fear of the impending unannounced raids. Now, by going out to demonstrate and calling for the fall of the regime, we were playing our part in a game that was becoming a turf war."

I can imagine a turf war in Jableh. It's a small city and I know those poor alleyways the young man referred to. I want to transmit the news neutrally, but this is hard. I try to imagine the scenes, preoccupied by all the city's nooks and crannies. I love it now even more. I continue with the young man's testimony:

"The first day Jableh started calling out *Allahu Akbar* from inside the houses, the security and the *shabbiha* began treating people brutally. The security response was awful and very violent. They targeted everything they could find that moved and the city fell asleep that night to the sounds of gunfire and dynamite until the small hours. Unfortunately it resulted in the martyrdom of the young man, Ahmad al-Attall.

"The third incursion into the city was on 5 June, 2011. When news started to spread about the arrest of H., who had been wanted for some time by the security forces on the charge of murder and who went by the name of 'The Prince of Jableh'. There were a lot of stories about the scandal over his propositioning his secretary. Some sympathized with him after the massacre of Jableh, in which the people saw his courage and bravery defending the city and its people, exposing himself to mortal danger on more than one occasion. But before that massacre the people were all disgusted by him and his machismo. They found it strange to see him walking around with his pump action weapons so conspicuously. As rumour of his arrest spread, some guys who were close to him or at least sympathetic hurried off with light weapons, including 'eggplants' and hunting rifles. There were only about ten of them, and at 6:30 in the evening they clashed with security forces at the *shari'a* school that had been converted into security headquarters. I heard gunfire and the sounds of 'eggplants' and this adventurism resulted in death of three of them. Tensions flared high in Jableh into the evening and the security forces and the *shabbiha* wouldn't shut up about this failed attempt. They intended to terrorize the Sunni neighbourhoods with the sound of heavy and violent gunfire, which continued throughout the night with the thunderous sounds of Jeeps and Mercedes cruising the streets. Jableh is a small city, more or less cut off from the outside world. Its only trade is with the inhabitants of neighbouring villages. It has no other livelihood. The city is an epicentre of poverty. Education is limited. Most of the representatives from there and the surrounding villages, along with Atef Najib, were able to buy up most of the properties and houses under assumed names that were used as a front. A new class of businessmen appeared – call them the *nouveau riche* – overshadowing the original and historically well-known merchants, a completely different class known for its tight relationships with people in the regime and for working on its behalf. Now Jableh follows the rules of cat-and-mouse; turf wars to tire out the *shabbiha*, to distract them so the demonstrators can get out, even if only for a few minutes on Friday to call for the fall of the regime. That's why they seem so starved for any piece of news, especially since the bounty of the internet is unavailable in Jableh. TV is the only source of news and information."

Here ends the story of Jableh, the city Atef Najib hails from; a relative of the president, he is the one responsible for the arrest and torture of the children of Dar'a. We sons and daughters of that city know the influence of Atef Najib as well as everything else the young men say about his corruption, wealth and tyranny but it never once occurred to me that the oppression and ruination this criminal from my city carried out against the people's dignity might ignite the Syrian uprising.

The murderers and I are from the same city.

Some of their blood flows in mine.

Some of my relatives are theirs, people who embrace murder and bloodshed. I am weighed down with a heavy burden in the face of all this death.

23 June 2011

....

Today I meet up with a few young women from the coordination committees. We are going to record a video of Alawite women who are against the regime of Bashar al-Assad. Our aim is to affirm national unity among different sects and sectors of Syrian society.

The whole thing seems pretty funny to all of us, as we get together in the tiny apartment of a young woman in her early twenties who would go out with the demonstrators. We sit there laughing, drinking coffee and smoking cigarettes while we wait for everyone to arrive. We write on placards in order to videotape them – homemade video recordings, a sit-in at home. We are going to post it online because we can't demonstrate in public. One of the placards reads: *We're in hiding because we're scared we won't make it back to our children.* All the girlfriends I meet there are eager and excited. I am happier than I could have ever imagined being. Their faces bring me some joy after I have been so tense and nervous all the time. We start filming, doing several takes of reading a statement: *We, the women of the Syrian coast, announce our repudiation of the regime's crimes and that we stand side by side with the people's uprising.* A young man videotapes us and we never stop commenting on how he is alone with us there. Watching the girls, I feel a green sapling sprouting from my heart. I love them all so much. My heartbeats become regular once again. All my negative feelings towards everyone disappear. However much my soul has been liberated from negative feelings, I owe this to the uprising itself.

When we are finished shooting, we all make our way home cautiously. Before leaving the place I smell the mysterious odour of human bodies. We all notice how much we sweat during the filming; the room was pungent with our odours. Suddenly I remember my mother's face when we were young, as she would check my sisters and me to make sure we were clean before we could leave the steamy bathroom. These giggling girls exude the smell of family, for a moment it seems to me like the smell of exhaustion, like the smell of a cave. I leave the house in better spirits.

Night has fallen when I open the door to my house. Today I feel a fleeting happiness. Having met with so many groups in order to coordinate among them, I am thinking about all the actions I want to do with them before my time runs out. Four consecutive meetings in a single day and what a magnificent outcome.

I place my head on my pillow, satisfied. It takes so little to make me feel happy. I am exasperated by this blind existence. Returning home from a jam-packed day and night of activism and activities, I wonder what murderers think about during the moment in which they shoot unarmed young men in the chest. I think about that moment, which is like oblivion; I think about the thousands of Syrians who go hungry while my stomach is full, of those who are homeless while my home is warm; I think about the prisoners I saw by chance from underneath the blindfold when I went in for questioning the third time. I am not even sure it was questioning; it should be called kidnapping. A different senior officer later tells me, during a phone conversation in which he tries to drag me over to the side of the murderers, that he never knew about the matter of my summons, that the whole thing happened informally and that there was no official order for my detention or anything against me, that the security forces weren't behind the rumours and articles on the internet or in the leaflets against me that were distributed in the coastal region, that it was my group in the opposition who was mistreating me and maligning my reputation. He will say a lot of things: that I had never been subjected to injustice and that it would be ungrateful of me to deny that, that I was their daughter and that I have to protect them the same way they protect me. I'll respond to him with a kind of calm that will seem strange to me later on: I don't have to feel my skin being scorched in order to scream, I have seen and heard enough to want to protect the sect from you. Don't play with me like that.

That's right, on the day of my third kidnapping I saw from

underneath the black blindfold how they threw prisoners down on the ground. I thought it was some kind of a courtyard, because light shone in and I could see their backs under a ray of light, as shoes trampled all over them. I saw some of them jump up from where they were when they got hit with a whip. I heard their screams, sharp screams like a whistle that have still not left my ears. For some reason I noticed that the feet stamping on their small young backs were not wearing military boots but cheap athletic shoes. And for a split-second I could see the back of one young man as he tried to get up: he was half-naked and I saw red whip welts on his flesh.

Today I can clearly remember the third kidnapping. It was different somehow; clearly the senior officer had something personal against me. He wanted to put my eyes out, in his understanding. He wanted me to feel afraid of him, which was something I took care not to do as I had done the last two times. Men used to come, put the blindfold on and take me away but this time I refused to go with them, telling them I wouldn't go and before the words could even finish coming out of my mouth one of their fists roughly squeezed my elbow. My fingers were tingling. It was nine o'clock in the morning, and my daughter, who usually doesn't wake up until one o'clock in the afternoon, asked from her bedroom, in an annoyed voice, "What's up, Mama?" I told her, "Nothing, Mama. I'm going out with some friends and I'll be right back." Then I left with them silently. Every time there was just one concern that would overtake me and make me tremble: What if I didn't come back? What would happen to my daughter?

The officer was harassing me. I panicked even more when he mentioned my daughter and nauseating things in the same breath. Just thinking about it makes me want to throw up. If time allowed me to see that man again, I wouldn't think twice about killing him. That's another thing I'll never forgive them for. They made me know what it feels like to think about ending someone else's life. It was only in those moments, but on my way home I would start shaking just at the thought of killing him one day. I tried to feel the desire to kill in those moments when he was harassing me. I also decided I was going to leave the country no matter what the consequences. I started having flashbacks to things the al-Assad clan and their relatives would do to young girls. My memory takes me back to the late eighties when we were young college students in Latakia and how afraid we all were of speeding black cars and the men who drove them. We all knew they belonged to the *shabbiha* of the al-Assad family, if not one of them personally. We girls felt indescribable horror after the death of one of our college friends, a very beautiful young woman who people say had been harassed by one of Jamil al-Assad's sons. She stopped coming to university when he began stalking her, but we were all shocked by the news of her death. Her cold corpse was discarded after she had been raped and disfigured. The incident passed but we were all terrified and spent days afterward without leaving our houses. Any young woman who refused the sexual advance of an interested boy from the al-Assad clan could wind up with the same fate. The more I thought about this and my young daughter, the more I thought about how I was going to kill him before I ever let him insult my dignity.

Now I remember all the details as I catch up on what has happened today and write down what the murderers did: six hundred Syrian refugees are on the move towards the Turkish border from fear of a military action. Armoured cars are deployed five hundred metres from the border. Syrian forces have moved into the village of Manbij after invading the village of Khirbet al-Jouz. Five students are killed at Damascus University; wounded students are still at al-Muwasat hospital. There is a general strike in several districts of Homs and Hama, in Dar'a and al-Ma'damiya, in Dayr al-Zur and Latakia; in al-Qamishli dozens of shops go on strike. They also go on strike at the central prison in al-Hassakeh. Syrian television broadcasts the funeral of 26 martyrs from the army and the security forces. I feel some consolation; what is happening to me is nothing compared to the crimes against thee people. O, gloomy feelings that live within a human being are what make me rise up. We always feel consoled when we see misfortunes that are greater than our own. That's a fact of life, but a gloomy one.

24 June 2011

. . . .

The Fall of Regime Legitimacy Friday

Fifteen people dead, most of them in the suburbs of Damascus, the Union of Syrian Revolution Coordination Committees announces them in Barzeh and al-Kisweh as well as in Homs and Hama. Tens of thousands pour out into the streets in Homs, Aleppo, Dayr al-Zur, Damascus, al-Qamishli and Dar'a. A banner in al-Zabadani appears on television, which reads, *Germs and Rats of the World, Unite!* making fun of Bashar al-Assad who described the demonstrators as germs in one of his speeches. The zone of protests expands and grows as the people announce their rejection of Bashar al-Assad's speech. The will was strong, the will for regime change. *No Legitimacy for Anyone who kills the People; No to Dialogue with Murderers* – those are the slogans held up by the demonstrators.

In Dayr al-Zur the demonstrators come out chanting for freedom and championing the other Syrian cities. They recite poems and sing songs. The popular protest movement is reaching a fever pitch and the demonstrations are spreading. I start to think that the army is going to carry out a military strike against Dayr al-Zur, as had taken place in Dar'a and in Baniyas. I think about this city from my childhood. I had lived with my family in al-Tabqa, a city on the Euphrates. I know what the Euphrates looks like. That river bathed my soul. I know al-Raqqa and Dayr al-Zur and I remember the bends of the river that connects the cities through which the river flows. They sparked in me an inchoate longing for a lost joy. That's why I am afraid for Dayr al-Zur, which I know is not going to give in to the brutality of the regime as it rises up and its people shout to demand their freedom.

One hundred and one days. European sanctions expand as far as

Tehran, sanctions and new pressures on the regime but I doubt they are going to have any effect. Today four representatives are added to the sanctions list: Dhu al-Himma Shalish, Riyad Shalish and two businessmen who were partners with Maher al-Assad. And four companies: two that were owned by Rami Makhlouf, the Hamsho International Group and the Military Housing Establishment.

The new dividing line within the opposition movement regards the call for a dialogue session. The regime approves of such a meeting, as it wants to announce, *Yes, that's right, we have an opposition here, and it says whatever it wants. The people we are fighting are those armed gangs.* I know from the start that those behind this meeting have the best intentions; the disagreement I have with my friend who sent me an invitation to this meeting is over tactics and timing. I tell him the regime wants to exploit certain names in the opposition in order to forward their interests. He says that he wants to pursue the most peaceful way possible to democratic transition in Syria. I think he's scared, the famous fear among the minorities. So I do not participate in the meeting. I was sure that the so-called reforms Bashar al-Assad had talked about are fake, nothing but a façade and an opportunity to kill some time in order to go behind the back of the protest movement and pounce upon the demonstrators with an iron fist. I am also upset by the phone conversations this friend of mine had with Bouthaina Shaaban and Faruq al-Shar'a.

I believe that the idea of presenting a political alternative to the regime through establishing an opposition political bloc does not have to take place with the agreement and under the auspices of the regime itself, even if mine may seem to be an extreme and inflexible position. But I am not at all interested in the political game plan or this dress rehearsal between some parts of the opposition and the regime. I am pessimistic, one hundred percent certain that it will not amount to much of anything, to say nothing of the fact that the absence of activism and political mobilization makes the idea of democratic deliberation and difference of opinion among various wings of the opposition very difficult. Like everyone else, I carefully follow what they are saying and it seems to me that some symbols of the opposition now bear the mark of authoritarianism that had been planted over many decades of arbitrary rule.

25 June 2011

....

Today the phone threats start up again in an awful way. I am terrified to be so closely monitored. The strange thing is that I am starting to become convinced that what the senior officer is doing violates all boundaries. A single nod makes me shut my Facebook account. Less than fifteen minutes after posting a comment about how the Makhlouf family had sold the free trade zone to Kuwaiti investors I get a phone call from him, telling me, *Close your account or else I'll come bomb your building with artillery that will erase you from the face of the earth.*

I close the account, thinking about what I should do next – now even writing on Facebook is forbidden? I am embarrassing them. I know I have been making them nervous and I think that what the crazy officer is doing to me is a sort of revenge against those in the opposition who belong to the Alawite community. Shall I stop watching Syrians get killed and fall silent? Am I going to give up the revolution of the poor and the marginalized? That would drive me to madness. I will not just sit by and watch everything going on all around me: killing and intimidation, imprisonment and disappearing and urban annihilation. How can a person remain neutral in moments like these? How can I be so far from the daily torment I see everywhere I go? All these thoughts make me an even more nervous creature. So they will not come into contact with my extreme anxiety I steer clear of my friends, focusing instead on transcribing the interviews I had conducted.

Today I am working on the story of a young Alawite man from a village outside of Jableh who requested extreme secrecy and discretion regarding his identity, not only before the fall of the regime but even after as well. Before we even began our interview he asked me, "Do you actually think that after the fall of Bashar al-Assad you'll be able to just go back to your normal life on the coast? If so, you're mistaken. Everyone thinks you're a traitor and it's going to be years before you can go back there safely." His words horrified me and I scarcely needed any more horror after living outside of society and convention and the norm for this long. I feel horror though, as this is the first time I have ever been targeted by an entire sect, or at least by most of them, since I know a lot of activists in the uprising who belong to the Alawite sect.

The Story of the Alawite Young Man

"In a village near Jableh they waged a campaign against the people of Jableh. Before that there hadn't been bullets or any substantial military deployment. The governor was going to meet with the people of Jableh and we in the Alawite villages heard that he had even met with demonstrators who insulted and chastised him, that they were nothing but a bunch of thugs who had beaten up the driver of the head of this region and smashed his car. Those turned out to be rumours spread by guys from the Ba'th Party and security forces. On the day of the massacre in Jableh, 25 March 2011, there was calm in the city and for three days I had not heard any news or any gunfire.

At 4:15 we heard the sound of heavy gunfire near our village. I went out and saw armed men opening fire into the air, so we ran to get weapons from the village and then blocked the international road facing in their direction. We heard rumours every day being spread by the Ba'thists and the security forces to the effect that the Sunnis of Jableh were going to attack us and that we had to get ready. The people of the villages got scared and took up arms. A man from the *mukhabarat* showed up and shouted at the people of the village, asking them to go home. The gunfire continued and the people went back to the village. Some of them stayed behind to guard the entrances and exits of the village with guns. Every half hour, a car would pass by with armed men shooting at the committees that were protecting the village. They were firing indiscriminately and one man from our village was wounded. That night they captured one of the armed men and said he was one of the wanted people. We believed he was one of the Sunnis who wanted to kill the demonstrators but it turned out he was from a small village near al-Qardaha and that he was a well-known weapons smuggler. During this time, while bullets rained down on the roads, leaflets were distributed accusing you of being a collaborator, inciting people to kill you."

He fell silent and stared into my eyes. As I tried to ignore his talking about what the security forces had done to me, I felt a searing line slowly creeping along my back.

The young man continued: "It's a strange coincidence for the leaflets to be handed out under such conditions. The security services in the coastal region in particular have a criminal and vengeful mentality. They were furious. They seemed to have some kind of vengeance against you, just like the Christians have against Judas!"

He stared into my eyes as he said this, then apologized and continued, "I'm sorry, but I was there the day they handed out the leaflets stirring people up to kill you."

I remained silent, I didn't want him to notice my trembling fingers, which I hid inside the notebook.

He went on: "The next day rumours got started about weapons that were found in Jableh, about operations that had been planned to exterminate the Alawites, how the army had moved into Jableh, killed all the armed men and discovered their weapons cache. Jableh was a closed city night and day, most of the Alawites had left and we were forbidden from going down into the city. We were frightened by the heavy daily gunfire, which would start at ten o'clock at night and end at three in the morning. It was happening in the al-Fayd neighbourhood. Then the people of Jableh started to demonstrate and things escalated. We heard that the Sunnis were demonstrating, cursing Imam Ali bin Abi Talib and the president.

Even though some of the Sunni and Alawite notables were trying to staunch the crisis, the escalation was an obvious consequence of the rumours. Alawite and Sunni clerics walked arm in arm in a joint procession against sectarianism and arrived together at the al-Hasan Mosque in the al-Amara neighbourhood. A delegation from the Sunni community went to a mourning ceremony in the villages of Zama and Harf Matwar, and the *imam* from the Sunni mosque went along as part of the mourning delegation. People from both communities were trying to mitigate sectarian strife but the next day rumours would spread that stirred it back up again, like making up stories about Sunni men deflowering Alawite women and then spreading them among the Alawite villages. Of course nobody knew who was actually behind the rumours; they would materialize like ghosts, then become unimpeachable.

Rumours were the main source of information for many Alawites because the internet had been blocked for the most part inside of Jableh, and al-Dunya station and Syrian television were the only other news sources. Obviously someone wanted to ratchet up the sectarian tension, and within two days of the massacre people had become convinced that the army presence was necessary in order to protect the Alawites from the Sunnis. Even some of the Sunnis were convinced by that narrative. During that time, supporters of the Assad family were present in Jableh and making daily visits. We heard rumours that the demonstrators were hitting the army with dynamite and small arms and that the tension between the Alawites and the Sunnis was intermittent, but the spread of rumours wouldn't stop.

The demonstrators started going out every day and all we heard about their demonstrations was how they wanted to attack and curse the Alawites, how they were calling for them to be killed. The security forces and the Ba'thists kept distributing leaflets in the villages along with the names of people from Jableh who were wanted. The leaflets said they were armed men and they included both their names and their mothers' names. The security forces passed out leaflets in which they claimed to have captured three Israeli officers, explaining that this was the reason why the army had moved in and opened fire. Then a wild rumour that frightened the Alawites spread, saying there were ten Sunni militiamen with heavy weaponry heading for the Alawite-majority Jableh suburbs. Alawite shopkeepers would close up their stores in fear at four or five in the afternoon even as two Alawite notables then opened their own shops and went back to work. The Sunni stores were all closed, and from then on it became a tradition for Alawites to boycott Sunni businesses, and Alawites who wanted to shop in Sunni stores became afraid of the other Alawites."

The young man stopped talking.

I remember Jableh and I remember the Sunni-majority square. We never thought about the fact that they were Sunnis. We bought from them anyway. The people of the village had all the purchasing power. What united those businessmen with the Alawites was mutual interest and need. I never dreamed that things would become this strained between them.

The young man continued: "After these incidents the number of armed Alawites grew, suddenly you would see weapons in the villages. When the security forces saw Alawites carrying weapons, they would look the other way. Meanwhile the security forces would expose Sunni men, including doctors and other upright and honest people just for making humanitarian contributions to those who were wounded during the demonstrations. One time they handed out leaflets with the name of a dead man, but for the Alawites these names had become killers and armed men and criminals who wanted to slaughter them, as the security forces and the Ba'thists and the *shabbiha* claimed in their flyers. They would put the names of real criminals alongside respectable people. They were dead-set on drumming up slander and sectarian strife between Sunnis and Alawites by smearing the reputation of Alawite women. This heightened the fear among the people of the Alawite villages. This one time they spread a rumour in the villages that a porno film of a Sunni man with Alawite women was being circulated among the demonstrators. The incitement reached the most horrible and filthiest point you could imagine. There's something else I forgot to mention. Before the Jableh massacre, a man from the al-Assad family came to the village of Bustan al-Basha and started handing out weapons to people for free, but there was a catch. He would take their IDs. In the village of Damsarkho outside Latakia, the same guy showed up and asked people if they needed weapons, but the people kicked him out."

The young man stopped here as I finish writing down what he said. It's time for my meeting with one of the guys from the coordination committees.

We have to organize something for the uprising support fund, which is supposed to be made available to the young people of the coordination committees. Connecting this fund directly to the young people is going to require some precision. I noticed how slow the movement was in keeping up with the movement of people on the street, ordinary people, most of whom had no education or training at all but who came out in defence of their dignity to demand their freedom. And so most of the time I would grumble about that slowness, but I didn't look at things that way for long. It is imperative to start mobilizing immediately in support of the people.

Last week I met one of the important young men involved in the coordination committees. He expressed concern that this project was going to go the way of so many other ideas they had discussed which ended in failure. With great determination he said, "We want real support, everybody says they're going to support us, but we haven't seen a cent. Real financial support would cover three main causes: monitoring the conditions of prisoners and their families, paying doctors and organizing the demonstrations." In that young man's eyes I saw determination and eagerness that pained me more than it brought me joy. That's right, I saw vigour and movement and action in his eyes whereas I had seen lethargy and bureaucracy and foot-dragging among some personalities in the opposition, both women and men alike. So in my meeting with the other guy today I seized the opportunity to put him in touch with a group of young women active in organizing the support fund. We called one of the women. I left the young man and went to see her right away. She concurred with what I had to say so I put her in touch with the guy. After our meeting we agreed she would be in direct contact with them without going through any other group, not even the women in support of the uprising. That was the only way to hurry up the assistance for the people.

I knew I needed to act fast and put the different groups I knew in touch with one another. At least they would know about each other, even if that contact didn't lead to anything. But I had confidence in many of those men and women, and after saying goodbye to that woman who was going to follow up on the matter of the support fund, I went straight home. On the way I felt like my skin was grimy, that a layer of the blazing sun had settled on top of my pores. I wanted to take a nice, long hot bath, to soften my joints and get ready for my daughter's anger at me for being out all day.

26 June 2011

. . . .

I am supposed to meet with a young man from the coordination committees in order to discuss a statement they are about to release regarding the dialogue session at the Semiramsis Hotel. They want to announce their opposition to it but I have a different recommendation even though my personal opinion is that those young people are right. I am trying to foster more open-mindedness among all the different factions, something I go back and forth over inside myself, something I am trying to ignore. The young man was moderate, saying, "Let's wait and see, we have a meeting today and then we'll decide whether or not we're going to put out the statement." I plead with him to consider postponing the meeting.

At this point I am getting ready to start a new phase. The rumours that the security spread about me have even reached the opposition, and one of my intellectual friends wrote to me, "By God, I'm so mad at you. Come back, shut up, and quit doing all these horrible things." At the time I didn't understand what he meant. I had met with him in order to discuss a national coordination body and I wanted everyone to know that I wasn't about to join any group or council, that I preferred to remain an independent writer. My thinking was that the critical intellectual is more important than the idea of lining up within a social movement. I know I will be among the first to criticize whatever group takes over the reins of power in Syria following the fall of the regime, because the process of democratic transition will require a conscience and witnesses of truth. Still, the statement produced by the Semiramsis conference was pretty good, and what it called for matched up with the ideas of those people going out in the demonstrations. I was satisfied, despite my certainty that the concession made by the regime in allowing this sort of conference did not happen without Syrian blood being spilled. It was a step back by the regime with the intention of taking two steps forward. Even so, I kept silent.

I was also silent about the home movie we had shot. It took a long time before it appeared under the title, *The Free Virgin Women of the Syrian Coast*, which infuriated me. I called the girl from the coordination committees who had been in charge and I tried to find out from her why they had called it *The Free Virgin Women...* with its Islamic cultural and linguistic connotations. Why couldn't they have just called us 'The Free Women'? Talking openly over the phone was difficult. She told me we would meet soon. I called her again to tell her I would not be able to meet. She was an activist in the uprising who planned the demonstrations. She always seemed worn-out and talked very little. We'd meet again some other time. This is why I said I must remain silent – a lot of mistakes are going to be made but we have to move past them. We can point them out and criticize them later.

27 June 2011

....

Outside the *Palais de Justice* I wait for the judge to show up. I have to get my daughter permission to travel. Here, we are still governed by unbelievable laws that prevent a mother from leaving the country with her daughter without her father's permission if she is under the age of 18. I have always lived alone with my daughter and now I need the consent of her father, who has never been her guardian, not for a single day.

To tell the truth, I am not in the mood to feel any more injustice on top of the injustices I have been seeing on a daily basis. It pisses me off! Sure, I'd be happy to elaborate on this perpetual anger: I have to wait for a piece of paper from my daughter's father before I can go to the judge in order to get his approval, and from there I have to go all the way back to Emigration and Passports in order for them to certify that her father has agreed before they give me a permission slip. These personal status laws, which I always rail against, violate me. I cannot escape what violates me. These are not issues that only have something to do with injustices against others; they are things that concern me directly. They always make me think about how to deal with the anger in my soul at what is happening all around me, how to think about turning this anger into words, words that are scattered by the wind most of the time, and which inspire the distaste of so many people. But that in itself makes me feel like I am OK. Being satisfied with what is happening all around me would make me feel like I was not OK, especially since I live in a soundless atmosphere; that's right, intellectuals live in a frozen environment, the world has passed them by. And the mobilization that has taken place in Syria, what spurred people into the street, was not the writers or the poets or the intellectuals.

Until now the intellectuals have not risen to the level of courage we see in the street. With very few exceptions writers have remained on the sidelines, panicked and afraid. I never expected that those who stood by, neutral, would then direct their arrows and their rancour at the people who are with the uprising. Sometimes a human being thinks himself so important that he is willing to condemn others around him. I expected this from many people and simply ignored it; this was just one more injustice atop all the other injustices we face here.

The funny thing is that the *shari'a* judge at the court tells me I need renewed consent from my daughter's father, that the old one has expired, which means I will have to come to court a fifth time and await more paperwork. As several women line up behind me I tell the low-key judge, "But I'm her mother, isn't it obvious?" Looking up at me indifferently, he says, "Ma'am, these are laws, not a game." He turns his head and addresses the women standing right behind me. I storm out of the *Palais de Justice*. I am almost broke, waiting for a payment to arrive for the translation of one of my novels into Italian, so my exasperation is even worse. In that moment I take shelter in thinking about the people being killed and arrested and disappeared every day. I think about them in order to suppress my rage, telling myself, *Girl, people are dying for their freedom, and you aren't bearing this on behalf of your thoughts alone, people are putting their lives on the line for their freedom, and you can't even handle what's happening!* I always beat myself up just to go on living.

My daughter is at home waiting for me, and I hurry online to find out what has been reported about the dialogue session that the regime is trying to use to its advantage. For the first time ever a conference is broadcast live on state television. It is intended to play up the fragmentation of the opposition. What the authorities are doing is far from innocent. They are distorting the opposition men and women on the one hand, and welcoming them on the other. Beating some and trying to drag others into line. I know some of those people who are meeting with officers, but my real fear is of an officer who is a relative of the president, whose image is always being given a face-lift by the intellectuals. But he will smash them and break their ranks. Besides, there are no longer any unblemished names in the opposition. I express my concerns to some of my friends who met with him: This officer and Bashar al-Assad are one and the same. Bashar al-Assad is a murderer, how could you let him get so close to you?

28 June 2011

. . . .

Today...heavy gunfire in Jabal al-Zawiya and several demonstrations call for the fall of the regime even as the arrest campaign continues.

The opposition delegation's meeting in Moscow concludes with their asking for Russian intervention. Moscow says that Russia is a friend of the Syrian people and those in the opposition argue the justice of their cause and ask Moscow to stand side by side with them in convincing Bashar al-Assad to step down.

Today I go with one of the young men from the coordination committees to meet a female political prisoner. It was a quick visit. The young woman wears a *hijab*, is friendly and well-mannered and talks about her arrest with an unusual calm. Agreeing that she and I would meet again, I say goodbye to the guy, heading for a meeting with another young man from the coordination committees. I want to document the genesis of the committees and how young Syrians organize themselves in order to continue the uprising, and, from there, how the revolutionary coordination committees are formed on the ground.

The meeting takes place at my house, the safest place for us to talk. We had met once before in a café, I think we were watched by the security forces. I make food for us to share, I trust this young man. I always told him and one other guy that I was like their mother. For the most part this is to make them feel at ease, but the sentiment is real. When we are done eating I start the interview.

The young man, who would be arrested twice, says: "Before the mobilization started in the Arab world and before the revolution in Tunisia, we had a bunch of cultural and social and development projects with a number of intellectuals. Young people would meet with older intellectuals. After the mobilization in Tunisia, but before the fall of Ben Ali, we became optimistic and held a sit-in outside the Tunisian Embassy in support of the Tunisian revolution. We were repressed and kicked out by the security forces. When the mobilization broke out in Egypt we were sure Syria's turn was coming. The ceiling over our conversations started to rise: Could we start demonstrating and sitting-in in Syria? On February 3, we sat in against the only two telecom companies in the country, Syriatel and MTN. The sit-in was scheduled for three in the afternoon, but when we showed up at the al-Rawdeh café it was packed with security agents. Outside the café there was a substantial security presence as well so we tried to reschedule the sit-in but some of us were detained. Then we started preparing for an even bigger mobilization. We never thought it would be like this, though. After Egypt and Libya the groups got bigger and young men started getting more interested in public affairs. Guys who had been apolitical before poured out into the mobilization, especially after the fall of Mubarak and the regime atrocities in Libya.

On 14 February about ten or twelve young men and women got together. We were from all different ethnicities and sects and nationalist orientations. A larger gathering had been planned for 15 March and we were nervous. The question was: Will the Syrian people come out into the street? We had decided to go out cautiously on 15 March, thinking that all we needed to do was nudge the street in order for it to mobilize and even if that didn't happen we would do whatever we could to make it move. We got the idea for mobilization from a bunch of Facebook pages like 'We are all Khalid Said' in Egypt, pages with some connection to social, economic and employment demands being made by citizens. Those pages would throw light on the negative effects of emergency laws and political authoritarianism, on Article 8 of the constitution and the Ba'thist monopoly over the levers of power and chairs in the universities. On an education page that exposed malfeasance in the educational system, especially the universities, we would publish stories on corruption; to give one example, there was a page on hypocrisy in Syria. The point was to identify the people who had a vested interest in the regime.

"On 15 March we were blown away by how many people came out to demonstrate, which meant there was no need to mobilize and rally them. The people were ready. They came out of the Umayyad Mosque in the heart of Damascus. There were five young men who animated the demonstrations. Then there was the story about the children of Dar'a on 18 March. We had started a sit-in in Damascus. From the beginning the notion of having the demonstrations in the squares, along the lines of the model of Tahrir Square in Cairo, was on our minds. We tried demonstrating in the squares of Damascus but with the security presence and military checkpoints, we couldn't make it happen there."

I remember those actions. I would tell myself there had to be someone behind them. I would go out during the actions in order to monitor the street. Back then the mobilization really was quite weak.

The young man adds: "The signs came from Dar'a, and the mobilization was begun. Even though the street was ready, we were all isolated islands. We hadn't yet fully processed the movement of the street because we had no political, local or even security expertise. It wasn't only the fact that we had major security obstacles to face; they were brutal with us. On Saturday 19 March people died in Dar'a. A group of us was looking into possible ways of protesting in support of Dar'a. Simple demonstrations were going out into the street. On the morning of Monday, 20 March, a demonstration went out in al-Baramkeh chanting against the regime that was dispersed with force and violence. We had carried out a strike outside the Interior Ministry on 16 March. During the week we started getting ready for Friday.

The Egyptian model had affected us subconsciously although that wasn't the only reason we thought about using the mosque. We faced a lot of difficulties, including the heavy security deployment in Damascus, which made gathering outside the mosque impossible. We were well known to the security forces, pretty much all of us. We tried going out to demonstrate as secularists on more than one occasion, but without any religious content we failed, so we had to direct the protest movement from inside the mosque, because there was a social assemblage already there that the regime couldn't repress. We figured that if we chanted this time then the masses would let us lead them. We believed that the people really did reject the regime because they had gone out before us, and that if we stood up and chanted the people would support us. Honestly most of us were young leftists and secularists, but we were through with our hang-ups about Islam or our fear of it.

On 26 March we took cameras inside the mosque and came out chanting in support of Dar'a and freedom and the martyrs, decrying all acts of repression. There was more than one demonstration in Damascus. That in itself was a sign of a major popular mobilization against the regime. That day, we came out of the Umayyad Mosque. Some people headed for al-Merjeh while others went toward al-Baramkeh and the demonstration in al-Mezzeh. That meant we weren't alone, and we confirmed beyond any shadow of a doubt that the popular mobilization had begun to boil and wasn't going to stop. There's one other point I'd like to make. In Damascus we would go out without any organization. Because of the extreme repression, security forces started choking the streets of Damascus, the protest movement withdrew to the suburbs. Security started taking IDs from anyone who wanted to go inside the Umayyad Mosque. We searched for other venues and tried using the al-Rifa'i Mosque in Kafr Sousseh but soon there was a sizable security barricade there as well."

As the young man talks, I remember going to the Umayyad Mosque. I talk to him about the heavy security presence that had surrounded not only the mosque but also the entire neighbourhood, from Bab Touma to Bab al-Hamidiyyeh.

He agrees with me and goes on: "Given blood relations and historical ties with the people of Dar'a, the al-Maydan district came out with us. Al-Maydan is mostly inhabited by people from Hawran and the people of al-Qaboun also mobilized in part because of their ties of blood and kinship with Dar'a. If anything, it was more about tribal and kinship ties than Islam. The al-Rifa'i Mosque was under siege so we started to look for other ones to use. At first, the preacher at the al-Rifa'i Mosque wouldn't cooperate with us. He was more inclined to stand with the regime. In al-Maydan the demonstrators came out without any intervention on our part. We started to follow their lead. The preacher in the al-Maydan Mosque was cooperative with us. Douma and Baniyas were both invaded by the army; then both places started to mobilize and we started to feel that the zone of protest was expanding. The general atmosphere became livelier and we started getting ready for something new. We felt like the uprising had really begun.

We were increasingly in touch with young men abroad, including through the 'The Syrian Revolution' page, eventually naming the Fridays together. We needed connections. At first 'The Syrian Revolution' page had been naming Fridays without consulting us. As a group inside the country, we opposed this and started to get involved in naming Fridays. After the zone of protest started to expand, the actions grew larger and we felt added pressure from the greater responsibility. At this point the mobilization started to delegate responsibilities. We got to know one another through the demonstrations and the Friday meetings, everyone came in a group. We were young women and men working all the time, and when the security pressure got too intense the young men would get together on their own and the girls would meet by themselves, for social and security reasons. We started being in touch with each other on the ground and on Facebook through these groups we already knew. Our communication was at a high level, everyone met with a group, and we federated each group with another. This happened more often on Friday when we were able to join science students with medical students as the arts and education and economics all staged sit-ins in the quad. After the uprising had been underway for a little more than a month, we started making plans to liberate the squares because that was Evacuation Day and we wanted to take advantage of the symbolism of the day in order to expand the zone of protests.

Our first mistake: We had been leading the movement in groups. We hadn't yet shifted to coordination committees. Second mistake: They wanted people to come from the outskirts of the city, particularly from Douma and Harasta and al-Tall, in order to sit-in at the squares. We managed to shoot down any other ideas. One of our guys made a special visit to Douma, where he delivered an oral invitation for the people of Douma and Harasta and Jawbar and al-Tall and Arbeen and Zamalka to come to the sit-in at Umawiyeen Square, and that's what actually ended up happening. The security forces carried out a massacre in which eleven or twelve people were killed, and they started cruelly closing the streets of Damascus and its suburbs. A lot of checkpoints sprang up between the suburbs and Damascus. That was a strategic blunder. At this point we felt we needed more discipline in the movement and to organize the sit-ins better. Needs we hadn't noticed before started to come into focus: material needs among families of the martyrs and prisoners, medical needs and assistance. Once these groups were federated together and discussions and conversations had begun, the most active and faithful elements distinguished themselves. Each and every one of us started to work on our own specialty. We came to realize that our clash with the regime had multiple fronts but at the same time the regime was becoming more violent and brutal, just as we started falling into the hands of the security forces. One person would get arrested, another would get killed, a third would disappear...and so on and so forth.

"Once the groups were federated, we sorted people out on the basis of activism and ability to serve the movement. With all the security pressure we tried to organize ourselves into tight circles. Around the beginning of May, the term 'coordination committees' starting rising to the surface. A month and a half had passed since the outbreak of the protests and the tasks of the coordination committees were distributed according to various issues: politics, media, organization, medicine. We started learning that in the bloody protest areas like Douma and Dar'a and Homs and Baniyas there wasn't any time for culture and art and so the focus of our activities had to be on humanitarian support and politics. Soon we had an organized group of young men and women working on art design and posters, graphics and communications, media pages and websites; there were others who didn't understand politics but were able to get people to come out to demonstrate, guys with media connections; lots of other guys had political consciousness and worked on statements that we published. At the same time we began to have real debates when we went out into the streets, because the entire street wasn't cut from the same cloth – like in the mobilization in Douma, which was led by the Socialist Union, who are Arab nationalists, and on the other side there were a lot of young Islamists with an Islamic way of thinking, but the former weren't particularly partisan and the latter weren't fundamentalists or extremists.

"No matter what, we knew that the mobilization came first on the popular level and attempts were made to pull the mobilization forward for the benefit of all sides. After much debate we concluded that pulling the mobilization in any one direction signalled the victory of the regime and the end of the popular mobilization, a distortion of it. We entered into discussions with them. The young men were open-minded and understanding, regardless of whether they were nationalists or Islamists or leftists. The beautiful thing was that everyone realized that the mobilization had a democratic platform, not just in Syria but across the entire Arab world.

Some guys tried pulling the mobilization on the ground in one direction, saddling it with ideological baggage, but through marathon discussion sessions we managed to arrive through consensus at the truth that replacing Ba'thist ideology with another simply wouldn't help anyone. The mobilization would lose its popular momentum and it would open up questions of the Islamists intimidating minorities in real life, the scarecrow the regime uses to really frighten people. At the same time it would open up a gap separating the secularists from the Islamists from the liberals. We came to the conclusion that the most important thing was for us to work together on the ground in a non-ideological way, that we wouldn't propose any ideological angle. The notion was that the Islamists weren't partisan in general.

Once the popular mobilization had reached an advanced stage we thought it best to divide the committees into specialties and each group of young people would work within that specialization. The political committee was responsible for negotiating among the coordination committees, for unifying the political vision and formulating the ideas behind the public statements, which would in turn be handed over to the media committee that drew up its final form. The media committee working inside the country had about fourteen young men from all the various governorates, including those who worked in the media field. They were responsible for delivering news to the satellite channels and the news agencies through a network of friends who became correspondents on the ground. We started meeting people who had the desire to report the news in the absence of any functioning media.

At the same time, for security reasons, we put into place four spokespeople for the local coordination committees abroad – Omar Idilbi, Rami Nakhleh a.k.a. Muladh Umran, Mohammad al-Abdallah and Hozan Ibrahim – who wouldn't speak without first coordinating with those inside the country. Inside the organizing committee there was a group of young men who were capable of mobilizing on the ground because they had a large number of contacts and who were able to organize demonstrations in Damascus and the suburbs. The cultural and artistic committee was a group of web designers and programmers as well as musicians and artists. We had a game plan with them, each one worked in his or her own field and then the media committee would get it published in the media.

Our strategy relied upon satirizing the regime – *Don't Call me a Jackass, I'm an Infiltrator* – and, along the same lines as the posters put up by the regime – *I'm an Optimist, I'm a Pessimist, I'm with the Law*. We waged a parallel campaign on Facebook – *I'm a Pessimist...We Love You* or *I'm with the Law, But Where is it, Exactly?* or *My Way is Your Way, But the Tank's in the Middle of the Road*. We played on more than one angle. Now we have more than one group designing posters for the revolution – a visual culture with a peaceful revolutionary character. We also have people working on consciousness-raising, who take the pulse of certain targeted segments of Syrian society and find out the orientations of the street. Some of us agreed to fan out every Thursday until we all assemble wherever the demonstrations were set to happen. Our guys would go out and try to control the slogans in the demonstrations, in order to ensure things remain peaceful and civil. There was a female human rights activist who worked with us a lot; her job was to link up the coordination committees with friends in every city. We couldn't use our phones because of the security surveillance, the patchy communications and the iron security fist. At least as far as Damascus was concerned, we had to rely on verbal contact.

"We had to come up with ways of staying in touch with the other cities through communications channels that the internet would have provided ordinarily. The human rights activist was the one who put coordination committees in Damascus in touch with the provinces. We managed to find a way of working together in order to come up with a unified political vision. In the end what helped us the most was the revolutionary atmosphere in the Arab world and our democratic vision. There were other groups of young people working on the ground, but because of the communications obstacles and the security crackdown we weren't able to be in touch with them consistently. They all coordinated with another group and launched another Facebook page, 'The Union of Local Coordination Committees.' We collaborate with them. We work together collectively and there are no dividing lines between the two projects. Currently we are working to unify the coordination committees completely all over Syria, under the name, 'The Federation of Local Coordination Committees'. On the ground we have no disagreements and we are making every effort to convene a meeting within the next ten days in order to come out with a single framework unifying the local coordination committees and the union of coordination committees."

....

My head is swimming with all the political mobilization that is now taking place. Popular committees are revitalizing civil society, new coordination committees are announced, young men and women are getting together to form federations and affinity groups – the kind of political mobilization Syria hasn't seen for nearly half a century. History will later record these days as exceptional. There is no horizon beckoning me. I am stultified by insomnia and consumed with all the details of the past few months of my life. There is a rift between me and my daughter, a psychological boycott between me and my family – it's unimaginable just how distant they have become – a break between me and my childhood friends, between me and my entire environment in the village, between me and my sect. I never thought such a day would come.

My sect is being persecuted for the third time in history. The first time was when the Alawites were subjected to slaughter and massacres. The second time was when the al-Assad regime in Syria was labelled an Alawite regime, which was historically inaccurate. The third time is now, as they are subjected to a misinformation campaign by state media, the security services and some of those who benefit from the regime, by making the Alawites line up behind the regime and defend it. All this despite the fact that they would turn them into human shields if their path ever got too narrow and they had no option in front of them but to kill the people from their own community and force them into a civil war with the other sects. My girlfriend and I were getting ready to visit a young woman who had been arrested. My friend asks me, as usual, "Why are you so depressed?" I look at her with the expression she used to give me for years; she smiles, because she knows that her question is the same thing I would always ask her. We used to sit together for a long time in silence, without speaking. Ever since the uprising broke out we have become even more silent.

The young woman is an engineer in her thirties. She has been arrested twice, the first time on 16 March when she remained in jail for sixteen days. I find this bit of information odd and tell her I was at the same sit-in but did not see her there. She smiles and says, "Who saw anybody?" We all laugh because she is right. We barely had time to assemble outside the Interior Ministry to demand the release of the prisoners when the security forces pounced and dispersed us with beatings and detentions and stampings. The second time she got arrested was in an ambush the security forces had set up for her. She and a group of young people had been preparing a food convoy to break the army and security siege of Dar'a. Security agents would arrest anyone who helped the people of Dar'a, even killing doctors and emergency workers. They seized one of the young men who had been helping her, then called her from his cell phone and pretended to be him. She fell into their trap and the security forces captured her in the middle of the street. She was screaming and people tried to save her but the security forces responded savagely. She managed to shout her name out loud so that people would know who it was being arrested.

She says: "They wanted me to put my thumbprint on a statement but I refused, and they threatened to go get the lieutenant colonel, who came and demanded that I give my thumbprint, but still I refused. He told me, 'We have two ways of doing things here: the human way and the animal way. Your choice.' In that moment I stared back at him with strength and defiance, I didn't blink. They beat me hard and I screamed loudly. The beating and kicking continued. I didn't budge so they started beating my face. Then he shouted at me, 'Down on the ground!' He wanted me to fall down. I remained standing, and he started pulling my head out from under my *hijab*, so I said, 'God alone is sufficient for us, and He is the best disposer of affairs.' He responded, 'The Ba'th Party above all else.' He punched me square in the face and blood gushed from my nose. Then he started cursing me with filthy, slanderous, vulgar and cheap insults, cursing Dar'a and its people. When he threatened to rape me I signed the papers finally and then went inside the cell. They brought me out one more time and said, 'The lieutenant colonel orders you take off your hijab.' I refused defiantly at first, but eventually took it off. One of them was kind and said, 'Let her go into solitary. She can take off her hijab there.' And that's what happened.

They left me there overnight. I slept deeply. It was very cold and there wasn't even a blanket on the ground. They woke me up early the next morning. A female prison guard came and asked why I wouldn't eat anything, saying that if I didn't eat the lieutenant colonel was going to torture me. I was scared. She brought an orange and I ate it. Some of them pretended to be nice. They waged all kinds of awful psychological warfare. For example, they would call me by the name of the female prison guard and when I would tell them my real name they wouldn't listen and just say, 'No, you're so-and-so,' and at that point I feared they were going to keep me hidden forever. I started telling all the prisoners in there with me my real name so that some news might eventually reach my family. I was held there from Monday to Friday, and then they moved me to a better cell. Other prisoners took care of me when they could.

On Saturday they transported us to political security, where there were young men walking around with shackles on their hands binding them to one another. Their crime was delivering food to besieged Dar'a. When we went inside the political security branch they took our stuff and insulted us, the security agents were rough and vulgar, whereas the officers were nicer. I was sent into a solitary cell. It was filthy and crawling with cockroaches but I was too tired to feel anything and fell asleep with all the bugs.

They woke me up in the afternoon and took me to the office of a major who was nice. He tried talking to me about the opposition even though I told him I wasn't in the opposition. He apologized for my being in jail and said he wished there didn't have to be any female prisoners at all. He told me I had to eat, that I should not refuse food, because in the evening I was going to open my Facebook page for them. In the evening I opened my Facebook page.

I would go out into the prison courtyard without eating anything, but some agents from the political security were sympathetic towards me and one of them gave me an orange. I couldn't eat the filthy prison food. One of them was an Alawite from the coast, he was very nice and brought his own food and forced me to eat. We had human conversations and one time he told me, 'You put yourself in this situation.' I told him, 'So have you.' When I told him I felt lonely in there, he said he did too.

"Then a different kind of pressure started. They wanted to take my statement again and started interrogating me. There was an officer who was constantly screaming, he seemed very angry and impolite. I would answer him curtly. The whole time they kept bringing others and comparing what I said with what they had said, they talked about treason and a food convoy that was headed for Dar'a, but I insisted I was only trying to provide humanitarian assistance. On that day I cried from the cold. I was hurting from the cold and they took my statement again in which I affirmed to them that I hadn't intended to be in touch with the media and that all I wanted was to deliver humanitarian assistance and put out a statement about the siege of Dar'a.

The next day they took me to the *Palais de Justice*, but the case didn't stop there and we went to the lodging house in Kafr Sousseh, which was where unclaimed foreign workers, Filipinas and Ethiopians and others were taken. It was inhuman, and I couldn't believe such a place existed in Syria. The people's circumstances were horrendous; the conditions were harsh, some female servants had been there for a year or even two because they couldn't find anyone to cover their travel costs. One of the servants was silent; she wouldn't talk and looked like a frightened animal; she was feral. A woman in the next room wanted to kill herself; in another room there was a woman who had lost her mind. One servant told me about the horrifying things the people she used to work for would do, awful things I can't even talk about. Another woman approached me. I had a sandwich and she asked me for half so I gave it to her. She then broke that half in half and gave it to another woman, who broke that into even smaller pieces and started handing them out to the other women. There were more than 30 women in a single cell. The room was small and we were crammed on top of each other.

The next day we went to the *Palais de Justice*, where the judge questioned me while I was bound in chains along with the other young people, like common criminals. As we waited for a while in the dock at the *Palais de Justice*, I noticed my brother was locked up there as well. He shouted my name and I shouted back his. We saw each other before we were both taken away. I don't know anything more about him."

This story was told to me by a woman, an engineer from an educated and wealthy family, her body was slender, her skin was as soft as a baby's, her voice only barely came out and she was always laughing. After she had finished her story I couldn't believe such a delicate young woman had ever been in prison. When I said goodbye to her I felt like I was suffocating. After we left, I asked my friend who was driving the car to pull over so I could go on alone. She stopped the car and I got out. The sun was blazing and I felt like I was about to collapse in the middle of the street. I decided I had to stop meeting female and male prisoners, and that I needed to be alone for a few days. My soul was clenched. A taxi pulled up and as I got in I thought about how many people were fated to die between morning and afternoon in this land. I was getting ready to leave the country and I was more than a little afraid of not being able to return.

In the evening I attended a mourning ceremony. How could I walk through those neighbourhoods? How was I able to confront the madness all around me? I would avoid looking directly into people's eyes, I was afraid of eyes. I wasn't afraid of talking, only eyes confounded me.

The house where I went to pay my respects was right in front of me and the mother of the young martyr was standing at the end of the hallway that leads directly to the front door. There were three of us and I wanted to avoid any confrontation. I didn't want to look into that mother's eyes. I didn't want to cry either. Who ever said that language isn't impotent? I didn't dare look into her eyes, and even though I wanted to tell her, *We are all your children*, I kept silent. As a mother I understand just how ridiculous it would have been for me to say something like that. I remained silent and sat there for a while. The silence was solemn until a woman got up and started talking about the martyr. The women all ululated and I felt a knot in my heart. The women all talked about the martyr and another woman commented on it all. They were all talking about him as if he were still alive. I had spent my days listening to the stories of prisoners and meeting with people who had just got out of jail, following the news of bloodshed and people who were killed, running through the streets from place to place. My blood was turning into vapour, it really felt like my skin was a cover for continuous evaporation. Trying to look that silent, dignified mother in the face, I could see red rings around her eyes. Suddenly my daughter's face appeared right there in front of me. As the mother turned to stare right back at me, I gazed into her eyes. It was only a moment, no more than a fleeting second, but it was enough for us to share that piercing sadness. Round crystal balls scattered in an existential void out in front of me, that lovesickness nobody will ever know, but which I noticed in the eyes of that 50-year-old mother. I felt like my throat was about to cave in, like I was a cloud of fumes set to explode.

I ran out of the gathering, out into the street. My girlfriend caught up with me and asked, "What's the matter?" At that point I burst into tears, crying out loud. I could hear the sound of my own crying, which I never heard from the cool and collected mother. The voice of the bereaved mother who had lost her son a few days ago in last Friday's demonstration sprang from my throat. I knew, my entire being was certain, that she would be able to guess why a panicked woman like me might have run out of there. I sat down sobbing. She must have known that I saw my daughter's face in her son's. The rules were for us not to stay at mourning ceremonies for more than five minutes as a precaution against raids by the security forces, who broke up such occasions on a regular basis. Thus my girlfriend took my hand and turned me around. As we walked down the street, she told me, "I think you need a nice long rest." I had heard so many stories about sons dying in front of their fathers, about a young man's head rolling down dead in front of his family and siblings, his blood and guts going everywhere and his brains spilling out of his head that was separated from his body as his skull came to rest between his legs. Women whose children were killed right in front of them. Houses ruined and demolished and burned as their owners watched. And most important of all,

I had heard women tell unending stories about how Syrians had been helping one another, as if they were one big family, against the practices of the security forces and the *shabbiha*. Stories I will come back to one day.

. . . .

This morning I sit down to write up what I recorded about Hama, while I wait for the coming afternoon, which has become like a curfew in Damascus. A young woman from Hama told me the story of a female doctor. A man brought seven bodies to the morgue in order to store them there until they could be buried. This doctor said the man seemed half-crazy as he tried to convince her there was nowhere else to store the bodies until the burial. Thinking he was deranged, she told him she only had enough space for two bodies, which was the truth. The man left, and the doctor would later find out he was telling the truth and that there were dead people without anyone to bury them or to protect them until they could be buried.

I write down the testimony of a journalist who stayed in Hama for a few days. He was in hiding and we met in his safe house:

"As soon as I arrived in the city I saw twenty thousand demonstrators chanting, *Peaceful, Peaceful, No Salafis and No Infiltrators, We are all Syrians*, chanting for freedom, *We're Muslims, We're Alawites, We're Christians*. I saw women riding in a big car that trailed behind a demonstration. My girlfriend was at the demonstration with me, and we saw women demonstrating everywhere, out on the balconies and in the streets, every particle in the air was demonstrating in Hama. It was obvious we weren't from around there. Someone came up and asked if I spoke Arabic. They thought I was a foreigner. We were afraid of getting arrested so we walked right in the middle of everything. At the head of every group there was a small truck with a loudspeaker. We climbed up on the Suzuki and started filming. The people were cooperative and nice to us. We were really afraid of the security forces. We didn't know at the time that Hama was a city that had been liberated from them.

That was the first time in my life I felt such feelings, the feeling of freedom. After filming for about half an hour, we wanted to leave. It was just my girlfriend and I. Starting to leave, we grew more certain that we were about to be arrested. I held my friend's hand as we walked in a group and got in a taxi. We told the driver, 'Take us anywhere.' He took us to the al-Hadir neighbourhood, near the Umar Ibn al-Khattab Mosque. Our friends came to pick us up.

"The next day we met with the doctor and did a television interview with her. She told me how she was treated when they arrested her and put her in with the whores, insulting and cursing her and how the people guarded the al-Hawrani hospital by forming a human shield around the building so that the security forces couldn't get in and take away the wounded. Then we met a woman whose husband and son were killed in 1982. She wouldn't let us film her, so we only recorded her voice.

She said, 'In 1982 I was at home with my husband. I didn't know what was happening inside the city. Everyone was a prisoner in their homes. On 2 February the security forces invaded my home. My husband was holding a radio, listening to the news. He wanted the whole world to know what was happening in Hama. The security forces used the radio to beat my husband over the head until they killed him right there in front of me. My son was twelve. The officer said, 'Kill him.' I threw myself at the officer's feet, begging him to let my son live. On the officer's jacket pocket I could see the words, 'Death Squad.' They killed my son in front of me and I stayed in the house with my two small daughters and my youngest son. The officer and the security forces stayed for about two weeks. Every two hours they would raid the house with a new patrol, not just my house but everyone's. They would beat people up in their own homes. The electricity was disconnected and there was no water. People were starving.

They would come to inquire about the girls, pulling them out of the houses either to rape them or kill them. Sometimes the girls would be raped and then killed. Some girls would pour gasoline all over themselves so they could set themselves on fire before the troops and the officers would be able to come and rape them. There was a beautiful pregnant woman, the officers raped her and then set her on fire. There weren't any men around, in one week anywhere between thirty and forty thousand people were killed in Hama. I lived in a wooden house. The whole neighbourhood was made of wood. They set the whole neighbourhood on fire and we started throwing ourselves from the balconies. I lived on the third floor and threw my five-month-old son and myself from the building. Some women tossed out their furniture. Before that the army and the security had mined the buildings in order to destroy the al-Kaylani neighbourhood, which was one of the most beautiful neighbourhoods in the Middle East.'"

After an emotional pause, this journalist friend continues. As he tells me about the incident according to the mother he had met in Hama, I feel as if I am inside that mother's heart. I think about the horror that envelops me whenever I recall the officer threatening to rape my daughter. He didn't come right out and say it but he hinted at it. When I think about that mother, a salty sting washes over my eyes and I feel like I am on the verge of exploding, but I ask him to go on.

He says: "I went up to the building the woman had directed me to, and I saw a demonstration. I stood where the mines she had told me about had been placed in order to bomb the al-Kaylani neighbourhood in 1982. Right now in Hama there is neither electricity nor water, including in the al-Kaylaniyya neighbourhood that had once been a mass grave where they buried the people from the Hama massacre under their own homes, which had been destroyed by the bombs of Hafiz al-Assad and Rifaat al-Assad.

"Anyone who travels to Hama will feel as though they are entering a giant wound. That was the first time I had ever visited the city. Fate had brought me there in order to investigate atrocities; the city itself was one big atrocity. There wasn't anyone in Hama who hadn't lost somebody. They had all lost fathers or mothers or uncles. All the details of Hama have something to do with death and murder. I lived inside that atrocity for four days. I saw Hama heading in the opposite direction. We stayed there from 29 June until 2 July. Every single day there were demonstrations against the regime, even the children were coming out to say, *The People Want to Topple the Regime!* It was there that I met the leadership of the blocs and the coordination committees. The people were protecting them. On Thursday, 30 June, I met the leadership of the Liberal Bloc of Hama, and we agreed to broadcast live from Hama. They were prepared for anything, and they were working to make a national flag that was 2,900 metres long. They printed the words, *Get Out* or *The People Want to Topple the Regime*, on umbrellas and hats. They worked together to bring the demonstrators water. They were simple, ordinary young people. They didn't have any extremist religious views and I saw secularists among them. That's what I saw with my own two eyes.

We asked to meet with some religious *shaykhs* but they refused. Not a single *shaykh* agreed to talk about Hama. They all said, 'We don't represent Hama, the people represent Hama, the Syrian state media would just exploit us.' The Liberal Bloc of Hama was a group of people who had wide influence on the ground, a lot like the coordination committees, but they had no connection with them. When the uprising broke out in Hama, only 300 people went out to demonstrate. Their demands were similar to those of all the other Syrian cities. They went out three or four times and were arrested and tortured. Before the Friday of The Children of Freedom they went out in large numbers and the leadership on the ground were distinguished and the young people were active. On the Friday of The Children of Freedom there was a massacre and according to what the young people in Hama told me, about 120 people were killed. In the media they only reported about 60 or 70. It was the army and the security forces that killed them. They planned an ambush for them; the demonstrators were drawing closer to the riot police who were holding shields in front of their faces. As the demonstrators got closer, they moved aside the shields and all of a sudden, armed men appeared opening fire on the demonstrators. That happened more than once. A woman told me there was an officer who picked a little boy up by his hair, high enough to look him in the face, and then shot him and threw him back down on the ground.

"On the Friday of The Children of Freedom they moved into the neighbourhoods and broke into the houses, arresting people and beating them up. From that day forward all of Hama came out to demonstrate. About half a million demonstrators went out, and they forced Muhammad al-Muflih, head of the military security branch to step down. A new governor had to be appointed and until 2 July, Hama remained an independent city. When news was reported that Hisham Bakhtiar had gone to Hama twelve days before, the people of Hama knew something was being prepared for them, something the regime calls the military solution. The people of Hama knew all too well what that meant.

"People had been coming out to demonstrate without the security getting near them. Then this governor of Hama was forced to resign, and Muhammad al-Muflih was restored to his position in the security forces. Get Out Friday was the governor's last day. The people of Hama told me that on 25 June, a delegation of Alawite *shaykhs* came, this time under the auspices of Hisham Bakhtiar. The authorities came up with this in order to make it seem as though there was sectarian strife in Hama. The Alawite *shaykhs* went to see the Sunni *shaykhs* in Hama and told them, 'We are brothers, and there's no need for us to fight with one another.' A Christian man who had been part of the other delegation from Hama told us that the whole thing was made up, because both delegations were close to the security forces and the Christians. He added, 'I withdrew because attempts were being made to exaggerate the issue and impose the sectarian issue from above. On the popular level nobody knew this was happening.' The demonstrations continued."

I know how the security forces work. Once the demonstrations are over they kill both Alawites and Sunnis. Then Alawite and Sunni *shaykhs* appear in order to declare to the public that what was happening was sectarian strife. So I wasn't surprised by what my journalist friend said about the matter, when he continued:

"I saw with my own eyes a man speaking into the microphone among the hordes of demonstrators: *I'm an Alawite and I'm against this regime, sectarianism isn't the issue, the regime wants to drum up sectarian strife.* The people would repeat in unison: *One, One, One, the Syrian People are One!* The people in Hama were organized. To me, life there seemed beautiful and awesome, with no security forces and no police. The people were the traffic police, they were the ones who cleaned up the squares and the streets when the demonstration of half a million men was over. The people were cleaning up the square as if it were their own home. They were carrying around the flags of independence as well as the current flag of Syria. They wrote a huge banner that read, *Thank you Turkey, Thank you France.*

One man told us about the massacres in Hama in 1982: 'I come out to demonstrate so that my children won't have to live through the humiliation and orphanhood that we all experienced. My father was killed in '82.' We were in a car cruising around the streets of Hama and one of the young men who was protecting us proceeded to tell us, 'Hafiz al-Assad killed my dad and my grandpa and my uncle. There's a neighbourhood in Hama called 'The Widows', they named it that after '82 when they killed all the men there, they didn't spare a single one.' Women from 'The Widows' neighbourhood told us a lot of stories. The neighbourhood is located south of the municipal stadium. When we went to the cemetery, I saw a lot of open graves, the people of Hama told us how they used to dig their graves before every Friday and wait. We filmed the graves and on the night of Get Out Friday I went to the family house of one of the martyrs. They didn't agree to talk to me at first, they feared for their children who were still alive. We went to see another family of three siblings, the elder brother died in February '82 and the second died on 3 June 2011. We filmed the only surviving brother along the Orontes River. He had gone out demonstrating on Get Out Friday and told us he no longer has any trouble with death, seriously, anyone who goes to Hama will have to march in a funeral procession, a funeral heading in the opposite direction, towards the future, not towards the cemetery.

All the people we met had lived through two massacres, Hama had lived through three: 1964, 1982, 2011. One of them was crying as he told us, 'In '82 I was coming back to Hama from Aleppo by car when we got stopped at a security checkpoint. The security forces said that everyone from Hama had to get out. The driver was from Homs and he handed over his ID at the checkpoint instead of mine. The Hamwi guy who was sitting in the backseat got out and they immediately shot him in the head and killed him. He fell down on a pile of bodies. That's how I was saved.'

He was crying as he told us about the incident. His wife was listening from the other room, frightened because her entire family had been killed right in front of her in '82. For the first time in my life I felt as though I was living in the Syria of the future, the free Syria that knew no fear. During the four days I spent in Hama, demonstrators were coming out every few minutes in spite of the massive memory of death the city had experienced. While we were sitting up on the citadel I told my friend, 'Hama is grieving. I never dreamt I would experience a city like this. There's great sadness all over, but Hama has given me strength.'"

The testimony of the young journalist who worked with the coordination committees comes to an end. When the day is done, I try to record the events of that Friday, but instead I listen to a song by Ibrahim al-Qashoush, who the security forces had slaughtered, slitting his throat and dumping him into the Orontes. I wanted to hear his voice after this news about liberated Hama. Is there anything more barbaric? A young singer sings out against Bashar al-Assad and his family and they slaughter him, they slit open his throat. Here are the words of his song:

O Bashar, you aren't one of us, just take Maher and get out of
     here, you have no legitimacy left…Yalla, get out, O Bashar
O Bashar you're such a liar, beating us with that speech of yours,
     when freedom's knocking on the door…Yalla, get out, O
     Bashar
O Maher you're such a coward, and an agent of the Americans,
     the Syrian people will not be insulted…Yalla, get out, O Bashar
O Bashar screw you, and whoever likes you, I swear you're too
     disgusting to look at…Yalla, get out, O Bashar
O Bashar there's something going on, and blood is on your
     hands in Hama, forgiveness is not in the cards…Yalla, get out,
     O Bashar
Every once in a while another criminal, Shalish and Maher and
     Rami, they stole away all my siblings and uncles…Yalla, get
     out, O Bashar
O Bashar, you're an infiltrator, you bludgeon us with the Ba'th
     Party, go and learn how to pronounce the letter S…Yalla, get
     out, O Bashar!

1 July 2011

Get Out Friday

Ambulance sirens wail from time to time under my house that looks out on the intersection of al-Hamra and al-Shaalan streets and the al-Rawdeh neighbourhood. The streets are empty, the sun is blazing. I watch this Friday on the internet and on television. Like every Friday, I sit and wait for sadness. How can a person wait for sadness? We don't just live it here, we wait for sadness and death and prison. Sadness and death and prison have all become a part of our diaries, like water and the air we breathe.

When I heard the ambulance sirens I tried to figure out in which direction they were going. The news coming out of Barzeh is that people have been wounded and killed there; there is heavy gunfire in the al-Maydan neighbourhood, where people have gone inside three different mosques. With every siren wail, my knees buckle. I think about the blood streaming through the streets of Damascus and about the faces of the demonstrators out in the sun. I remember how at the start of the protest movement I had gone to Jableh in secret, without my family knowing about it, dressed in a disguise: a long dress, black sunglasses and a headscarf. With the help of my girlfriend I managed to get inside the old neighbourhoods in Jableh that were on the brink of death. Death on all sides, from all the shooting. If they had got their hands on me, most of the Alawites in the demonstrators' neighbourhoods might have killed me; if the Sunni fundamentalists knew I was there, they might have done the same thing. If the security forces and the Ba'thists got wind of my presence they would have launched a military campaign against the neighbourhood, claiming there was an armed gang there. But I walked in like a visiting relative with a fake ID. My name alone was guarantee of a problem, after I had been marked for death and leaflets against me had been handed out in my city and my village.

My friend got me into one of the fishermen's houses, where the poor man couldn't furnish his clean-smelling, one-room house with anything more than an old shabby couch. There were blankets and bedding and sheets piled on top of each other extending as far as the metal door that let out a sharp creak when it was opened. The man told me what the security forces and some Ba'thists had done at Jableh port and what the *shabbiha* had done to them. It was a long conversation that required several pages. One day I'll give it its own folder. After sitting there with him for two hours, I was upset when I left. How could a human being dare to take a cut from those poor people who can barely eke out a living from the sea? How could they take a cut from what kept their empty stomachs alive? The man was in his forties and had three children, who were out playing in the street. His wife was veiled. He was basically illiterate, but he went out for the demonstrations. He told me, "We want them to leave us alone so we can live our lives, nothing more than that."

This is the people's revolution of dignity. This is the uprising of a brutalized people who wish to liberate themselves from their humiliation. That's how the uprising in Syria broke out. I saw it among the people I first interviewed, before I was prevented from moving between the Syrian cities and before the security services and the *shabbiha* and the Ba'thists placed a bounty on my head wherever I went.

Now I get back to remembering that day. I hear about two people who are killed in Homs. The bloodshed is starting back up again even as we sit here. My energy flags on Friday. I don't meet with anyone, I think about answering the call of the young men and women who have been questioned about me by the security forces but any action I take along with them will be in the spotlight. There had been one last warning. My case had truly come down from the office of the senior officer who told me he was going to transfer my file to the security services and leave it to the grunts to take care of me. That's literally what he said, and after that things were different. Apparently he had actually done it. A number of friends started calling me and asking me to be careful. I took some comfort in the fact that the regime didn't want to implicate itself any more by detaining intellectuals as part of whatever scheme it was going to hatch next. But I was nervous about getting arrested at the airport. I was intent on getting my daughter as far away from here as possible and on running away from the senior officer who would not stop harassing me, which seemed like the craziest thing I could do. I wanted to find a safe haven in a calm place far away from everything that was happening around me. My life had been ripped open and had reached the point of no return. There at that shadowy point, where I found myself floating in a current of discomfort, I decided to leave the country as soon as possible.

I return to the television. Demonstrations are getting started in Syrian cities and towns and rural areas. In Hama alone half a million demonstrators come out. Nine people have been killed today so far. Numbers have become a game, turning into engineering problems. The three people killed in this city are crossword puzzle trivia: two in that one, one person is killed in another. It's as if these numbers don't mean souls and human beings with names. My heart hurts and I feel nauseous. This feeling always comes on Fridays when the demonstrators are going out, but lately, with all the daily killing, I get sick to my stomach, which has to be evacuated of everything inside. As soon as I have thrown up, I open the refrigerator to eat some more, continuing to keep track of what is happening four months on from the outbreak of the uprising. I think about what has happened, what is happening and what is going to happen. The uprising isn't going to stop. The organization of the local coordination committees and the Federation of Coordination Committees take intelligent steps that reflect a deep consciousness among the young people in organizing an uprising, rising to the occasion and guaranteeing its persistence.

3 July 2011

....

I have to get ready to go back to my former home. There's no longer
any pressing reason for me to stay in this downtown apartment
that costs half my monthly income, and which everybody knows
about anyway. I don't have to stay in hiding anymore, since it's
now clear to me that they are not going to arrest me. Intimidation
and smearing my reputation and frightening me – that is all they
are going to do. What else could those trips I had to take have
meant, the trips I called 'Visits to Hell'. They were not visits, maybe
'Snapshots of Hell' would be more like it, but they were enough to
sow hell in my heart.

The second time they came to my house there were only two
men instead of three. I had stopped writing and I was trying to
reorganize these diaries, trying to recall all the details, but they
kept escaping me. The two men were exceedingly polite and I
thought it strange that they didn't look anything like the security
forces and the *shabbiha* that had taken me the first time. They
calmly knocked on the door and politely asked me to get dressed.
I refused and tried to find out what they wanted, but one of them
just shook his head and pointed outside. The second confidently
stated, "Madame, we're going to stay here at the door until you
get dressed." He had said 'Madame' with a funny accent, it made
me want to laugh, and then turned his back. I could see a pistol
at his waist, shoved between his belt and his wine-coloured shirt.
Flashing the gun spoke more than words, but the other one said,
"The boss is waiting for you."

I knew what was going to happen, but the idea of going back
to that shadowy dungeon and seeing the young men's mutilated
bodies terrified me. I wished they would just arrest me and throw
me in with the other prisoners so I could be through with this

nightmare, but I knew in that moment that they weren't going to do that. It would be hard for them if it ever got out that there was an opposition in prison consisting of well-known personalities from the Alawite community. In addition to covering up this issue, it was clear that the officer held a personal vendetta against me. Blind rage – I understand the reason for it and I understand the communal loyalty it stems from. I heard from a relative of Hafiz al-Assad that when he seized power after the military coup in 1970, he imported German officers to train his security services based on their expertise. I know that this officer who takes pleasure in torturing me was the apt pupil of one of those German officers at the time. I thought about how smart Hafiz al-Assad was to employ loyalty-building strategies that would turn his sect into loyal killers who would fight to the death for him and his family. It never once occurred to the father president that his entire sect might not always stand with them. Nevertheless, he managed to create an army of murderers among the ranks of his security apparatus. So much of the information I have about that family and other families seems like the stuff of novels and fictional stories; it was all so strange and scandalously mired in injustice.

I had gone out to al-Rawdeh Street with the two security agents when the man put the blindfold over my eyes. As I tried to figure out where we were headed, the car looped around a few times, driving in a circle and returning to the same spot. Just then I told myself we must still be in the al-Jisr al-Abyad neighbourhood; some people had told me that's where the senior officer's office was located. But how could this giant prison so crammed with people be right in the middle of downtown Damascus? I thought perhaps I was mistaken and we were heading towards the Kafr Sousseh roundabout, where all the security branches were located, but I couldn't be certain where I was exactly. The blindfold was tight around my eyes, and the man held my hands and placed them behind my back, politely saying, "Madame, don't move your hands."

I was in the same office as the last time but this wasn't the same senior officer. Even though I didn't recognize his rank I knew he couldn't have been as senior because of the harshness in his eyes. Here's something I noticed in recent years whenever I was summoned by security: the higher ranking the officer, the nicer they would be; the lower their rank, the more brutal. I thought they must have sent me this lower-ranking officer in order to torture me and I was truly indifferent in front of him. I played my game of turning the details into a novel, staring back at him in order to seem more courageous, but the man didn't do anything. Three other men came in. They were enormous, staring daggers all over me and they threw onto the ground a young man who was completely naked except for underwear splotched with blood. His body resembled the mutilated bodies of those young men I had seen last time, only he was whimpering. The officer told me, 'This young man says you help him organize demonstrations.' I looked at the young man and calmly replied, "That's not true. The demonstrations don't need organizers. The people go out without any organization."

The officer drew near me, staring into my eyes, but I didn't flinch. I stared right back at him. I stubbornly refused to blink. He hissed, 'I swear to God I'll flay your skin from off your bones, you bitch.' He gestured at the men and the enormous guys came over to me. I was like a rag doll in their hands. One of them tore off my jacket and I was left there in a see-through shirt that barely covered my chest. Still staring at me, he said, 'Well, Madame, what do you say we start getting undressed?' I didn't respond. I kept staring at him with the same cruel stare. The truth of the matter is that I was panicking and I started to feel paralysis creeping up from the soles of my feet, into my heart. I tried not to look at the young whimpering man's body.

The officer told me, 'He also says he's your boyfriend!' I started to tremble, but I kept staring back at him in the same way. My eyes started to burn. In reality, I was already very shaky even before I came. I was having bizarre spells. I would be wracked by crying fits in the middle of the night, as the images of dead bodies broadcast on television seeped into my dreams, cackling. My daughter with her throat slit from ear to ear and bathed in strange colours flickered in front of my eyes as I awoke. Every bit of news was about murder. It was enough to shake me deep down inside. The sight of a tank would send a tremor through my nerves, the sight of a military roadblock and those truncheons and human masses pouncing on people and beating them.

I couldn't take it, and so when he stripped me half-naked from the waist up, my body started to convulse. I gathered that the colour of my face had drained to blue, and I felt my teeth start to chatter. I continued staring at him. My body was beyond the non-negotiable red line; I had such a direct and clear relationship with it that I hadn't even known about prior to that moment. I am the master of my self, the owner of my body, my body is made for love alone and only love can make it obey, anything else and it will be a silent, unmovable stone. As those two men held me and squeezed my back, the thought of my body being violated made me shudder. He stared into my eyes. At this point I detached from my game of imagination; it was too much for me to go on playing. I could hear the beating of my own heart, and I felt like there were ropes entangling my head. He drew closer to me and I was ready to bite him if he came any closer. He nodded at the two men and, as one of them got closer, I screamed. I felt as though a sharp knife had cleaved my head in two. It was only a few moments, the two men backed away, and I simply fell down on top of that young whimpering man's body. I crashed into him and he let out a loud yelp I won't forget as long as I live. It was the last thing I heard before my head split in two and I blacked out.

When I came to, the senior officer was there and the officer who had initially received me was gone. I was lying on a couch, fully dressed, and I could smell blood. When I was finally able to see myself clearly in the mirror, later on at home, I would discover the young man's blood all over my neck. The senior officer said, 'See how harsh they can be with a delicate girl like you!' He glared at me scornfully. I shut my eyes, my headache was killing me and it still felt like there was a knife splitting my head in two. He said, 'Let your admirers come and see what a tough girl you are!' Then he let out a resounding laugh.

I was groggy. I didn't know what was happening but he suddenly picked me up. The earth was spinning all around me and I fell down again. Then I heard him shouting at them to take me home. His shoes passed right by my eyes as I lay there on the ground. I'll never forget that moment. It's seared in my mind. His shoes were shiny and hip, but they were flat. I noticed the curvature of his feet as his shoes clipped the tip of my nose on his way out. At that moment I closed my eyes and wept.

I recall that hellish visit as I get ready to move home. My daughter is upset. I was aware of how difficult this was for her, but returning to her grandfather's house was out of the question. The Alawites who treated me like a traitor would never leave her alone, and in Baniyas, where her father lives, the situation was even worse. The Syrian security forces and its websites were urging people to kill me for the crime of inciting people to kill a sniper, this would only expose her to greater hardships. I didn't say anything about her anger, I tried to make things easier for her but my body was worn-out, to the point that while I was packing my bags to go home, I started chronically passing out. This wasn't easy for me to deal with, especially since my mother was sick and I couldn't visit to see if she was all right. I shut off my phone and used a new one so they wouldn't be able to find me. I had cut all my connections, but that was impossible for my daughter. My plan was to go into hiding and work with the young men and women until the regime fell. That was impossible with her around. There was no way to hide when she was with me, and there was no way for me to just leave her to an uncertain destiny. I was at the point of no return but I could not go forward; I was standing there like a silent stone. The idea of leaving the country was the spitting image of my own death. Even though the idea persisted and would soon become a reality, just thinking I was ever going to leave Damascus made me anxious.

Today I sit down to transcribe some testimonies I recorded from my friends, as I try to postpone carrying out my decision to leave Syria.

Stories from Latakia

"On the day of the 26 March massacre in Latakia, my brother and I were coming back at night from the shop where we work. We have to pass through the al-Saliba neighbourhood to get home. Some guys at a checkpoint told us to turn around because there was a demonstration up ahead. We couldn't tell if they were from the army or military security because they all wear the same clothes more or less. The demonstration wasn't that far away from us, but at night and from that distance nothing seemed clear. We changed our course as they told us to do, but my brother and I were curious and tried to get closer, hanging out on a street corner not too far from the demonstration. The demonstrators weren't carrying any weapons. They were chanting, *Peaceful! Peaceful!* and calling for freedom. The army and the security forces asked the demonstrators to go back, they pushed them away five hundred metres or so. There was a huge army presence and along with the security forces, they formed two continuous roadblocks. When the demonstrators had backed away a little bit, the row of army personnel was suddenly forced down on the ground, twenty soldiers in all, while the second row remained standing. We were stunned to see heavy gunfire directed at the demonstrators, as if they were game and the soldiers were at a shooting range. I saw more than 50 demonstrators get hit. Some were killed and others were wounded; I couldn't tell which were which. They took the wounded away in trucks and took the dead to some unknown location. They couldn't see my brother or I. We were in the darkness at the corner. If they had seen us they would have killed us. The cars that took away the dead were Suzukis, and they sped off fast. Then the fire trucks came and their fire cannons sprayed around where the killing had taken place, clearing away the blood. Within an hour the street was back to normal. It seemed weird that the gunfire would be direct, at close range, and aimed at the head and chest."

I finish transcribing the incident and think about how the demonstrators had been betrayed. Betrayal was the cornerstone of the Syrian regime's dealings with its own people. They asked them to back away 500 metres while the murderers were protected by a first row of security forces and then they opened fire. How shameful. How despicable to kill unarmed and peaceful people in such a cowardly manner. As I transcribed the stories about the uprising, I also draw strength from them.

Story #2
"During the first demonstrations in Latakia, Alawites came out alongside Sunnis. At the Umar Ibn Khattab Mosque on Antakya Street, there were hundreds of us committed to nonviolent

demonstrations and we refused to let even a single demonstrator carry a rock. We chanted, *Peacefully, Peacefully, No Alawites and No Sunnis!* Some figures from the Alawite community were in the lead and at the Shaykh Daher statue we were met by the *shabbiha* who started cursing us and pelting us with rocks. Up until that point there had not been any direct contact. During that time somebody informed a group in the al-Saliba neighbourhood and in al-Skantouri that the Alawites were killing Sunnis. I think it was one of the *shabbiha*, or one of their helpers in al-Saliba. At that point, a group of thugs from the al-Saliba and al-Skantouri neighbourhoods showed up and ransacked the stores. There was heavy gunfire. Four people died, and for your information, neither the police nor the security forces ever came near the people, who continued chanting, *Freedom, Freedom*, until some giants with bulging muscles showed up. We all knew they were *shabbiha* and that they were the ones who opened fire. That was before the four demonstrators were killed, when the al-Saliba and al-Skantouri group took out their knives and started stabbing the police with them. I saw with my own eyes how those knives scraped off flesh.

"The sectarian tension seemed very high in Baniyas, Jableh and Latakia. The *shabbiha* would stir things up by going to Sunni neighbourhoods and shouting sectarian slurs as they passed through. They found willing ears among some people while others responded in kind with sectarian slogans of their own, which all took place while the men from al-Skantouri and the Palestinian camp of al-Ramel and the al-Saliba neighbourhood would use their knives to attack anyone they saw, without distinguishing between security forces and demonstrators. I can assure you that the situation was not sectarian at the beginning of the protest movement, because I saw with my own eyes a man named Ayyub from the Alawite community stand up to address the demonstrators, 'I'm an Alawite and I'm participating in the demonstrations. I'm against the regime; they forced me from my home for many years. We are a single nation.'"

The man's testimony ends here, and I know deep down what these words mean, because this was one of scores of testimonies that I collected about the participation of some ordinary Alawites at the beginning of the protest movement and how they were brutally repressed by the regime and its supporters.

Story #3

My neighbour, a volunteer in the security forces, told me about this incident.

He says: "During the siege of Jisr al-Shughur, the bombardment was violent, things got all confused and I no longer knew what I was supposed to do. Suddenly I was all alone amidst the rubble and I started running, trying to hide my identity. I was sure that if the people captured me they were going to kill me. I believed the armed gangs actually existed and that they wanted to slaughter and kill us all. I entered one of the alleyways and tried to disappear down one of the paths. I saw a man and I hid who I was from him, but the man knew I wasn't from around there. He had a beard and dust all over him, and he was holding a bag in his hand. I later discovered that he was delivering some food to his family. I stood there before him, weaponless. I was wounded in the foot and limping. The man approached me and asked, 'Are you with security?' I said yes, and waited there to die. He calmly said, 'Come with me.' I followed him inside his house. There was a spare room where he cleaned my wounds, put on some bandages and then looked at me, saying, 'We aren't animals, and I know you're not a killer.' He left the room and came back a little later with another man. The two of them talked amongst themselves, saying that if I stayed there people might take revenge on me, that even though it was unlikely, I wouldn't be safe there. 'What do you think about crossing the border pretending to be my cousin?' I was speechless as he handed me his ID and said, 'Use this to cross over until things are safe for you, you can send it back to me later.' I didn't know what to say. First he saves me and now he wants me to save myself while he stays behind in Jisr al-Shughur. He told me he'd join up with me in a few days, and he gave me his phone number so I could call him. They took me to a secure location but I never crossed the border. I gave him back his cousin's ID and thanked him. When I got home to Latakia, they asked me what had happened to me, and I told them simply that I blacked out and suddenly found myself someplace I didn't recognize."

The man in the story left his house and disappeared. His neighbours no longer see him. The neighbours say he was killed but I know he's hiding out for fear that the security forces are going to kill him. He told me as much:

"I won't participate anymore in what's happening, those people were kind to me and saved my life, despite the fact that the man who gave me his cousin's ID was with the Muslim Brotherhood."

Story #4

"A man from the military security in Latakia came and told the Alawites in the al-Hammam neighbourhood near Basnada that the Sunnis had attacked their daughters at the Qaninas School, and so the people rose up and attacked the school, frightened and in a panic. There was a big commotion as tens of cars showed up and surrounded the school. The people took sticks and savagely attacked the school. The girls screamed and the teaching staff fled, but not a single Sunni was inside the school. After hours of recrimination and shouting and beating with sticks between the people and the teachers, the people came back with their daughters, and one of the girls' relatives came back after taking his daughter home, his blood still boiling in anger, and told the security agent who had been in touch with the group of *shabbiha* at the entrance to the neighbourhood, 'It isn't true, there was no reason to frighten the people.' The security forces and the *shabbiha* surrounded him and shouted at the man, 'Go home before I have all of you arrested!'"

Story #5

"A citizen of Latakia was coming home from his fiancée's house when he got stopped by a military checkpoint and told to get out of the taxi. Although he swore to them on his highest honour that he hadn't taken part in any demonstration, they became furious with him, beat him violently and cursed him anyway, telling him, 'You don't love the president, you dog!' He replied angrily, 'I don't love injustice, but I swear to God that I was just going to my fiancée's house.' They threw him down on the ground and stamped on him. They beat him in middle of the street and then arrested him. In prison they tortured him violently until he confessed to them what they wanted him to say. He is still incarcerated today."

Story #6
"In al-Haffeh, Abd al-Qadir al-Sousi 'the Sunni', a man who was known for his open-mindedness, moral rectitude and good relationships with a number of Alawites, was killed and his corpse was dumped in the Alawite village of al-Zubar. When his body was found, Alawite *shaykhs* and Sunni *shaykhs* got together and disavowed the act. In spite of the incident there was no sectarian conflict. A resident of al-Haffeh confirmed that the *shabbiha* had killed him and dumped his body in the Alawite village in order to provoke the people to start fighting each other. The *shabbiha* were killing people and the ordinary people were still licking their wounds when a number of sectarian troubles took place after the discovery of the death of al-Sousi. The people of al-Zubar village got together and went to al-Haffeh and told the people there, 'We are not responsible for the death of this man. If you have any proof that we killed him, bring it forward now and hold us to account.' But the matter ended there. That doesn't mean there weren't individual acts of revenge, as when security forces or ordinary people from both sects were killed."

Story #7
"A man went into one of the neighbourhoods and said, 'There's an infiltrator here!' The people would run off after him to chase down this supposed infiltrator and hand him over to the security. On another day and in another neighbourhood the same infiltrator appeared and they captured him again. But because the Alawite neighbourhoods were so close together, somebody noticed that they had captured the same person. One of the men told the head of the security detention centre sarcastically, 'Uncle, change your infiltrator every once in a while if you want the people to believe you!'"

I stop writing down what the security forces were doing in Latakia to stir up sectarian conflict. My friend supplying me with information said he had dozens more stories about what they did in the city.

"They were breaking down people's sympathy and building up walls of hatred," he tells me. "The security and the *shabbiha* both, they worked hard at that."

His testimony stops with that sentence. I think about how my compiling all these conversations and testimonies is no substitute for redoubling my efforts in the street. Just now I wish I had not written in the newspaper about what I had seen, and I wish I were able to move around with greater freedom, not to be directly in the spotlight. But on the other hand I also think: Somebody has to smash the narrative of this criminal regime with the truth of the revolution. This is a revolution and not a sectarian war, and my voice as a writer and a journalist must come out in support of the uprising, no matter what the cost.

. . . .

Today I hear more news about the arrest of a young activist in the uprising, the young man I had been coordinating with and whom I saw on a regular basis. I feel boundless pain, because I knew the young men of the uprising, quite a few of them. I have seen morality and their humane spirits, their determination and their patience amidst the difficult circumstances they were going through.

This is the young man who had sent me a warning just days before the security forces started asking about me. Apparently the senior officer's warning that he was going to leave me to his underlings in security had come to pass. This leads me to the conclusion that he was acting on his own. That doesn't really matter anymore because this young man who left his work and his university education and committed himself to working for the uprising and coordinating demonstrations needed constant support. I have been worried about him lately, him more than others. He is a noble young man. I find myself sobbing in the street. I feel a maternal instinct towards him. I am very concerned about him, but I simply say, "He'll get out in a few days, no doubt they have nothing on him. Especially seeing as he wasn't arrested at a demonstration."

I go to a mourning ceremony in Harasta with two young girlfriends. They tell me there would be a few military checkpoints, nothing too scary, people coming and going. I put on a headscarf until we are past the checkpoint. There are no expressions of sadness at the mourning ceremony, which is the strangest thing about mourning sessions for martyrs who have fallen in Syrian cities. They always turn into demonstrations. People are gathered together in mourning, chanting for the fall of the regime. I withdraw to a distant corner as the weeping continues. I don't know whether I am sad for the young people who are killed and who fall like birds or whether I am happy to discover that I belong to such a strong, free and proud people. I don't budge from where I stand. The people chant. I greet all of the women and embrace them. I have been going to mourning ceremonies in secret, without wanting anyone to know I am there. Two young men help me out. I am supposed to write stories about the martyrs' mothers, but time is not on my side.

At the end of the evening I return home, my eyes burning and my heart racing. The bouts of sharp ringing that spread from the base of my head to settle in my ears return, and as I climb the stairs I start to feel dizzy again. My head is like a swing. I have been smoking like a madwoman, but I simply must keep watching the videos that one of the young men had sent me showing how the martyrs' bodies were returned with their stomachs split open, stitched up in a strange way. The young man who sent them said, "It's really awful, they steal organs from the young men before killing them, maybe while they were still being tortured. There are testimonies from their families." I wrote to tell him I could meet with the families of those martyrs, and he asked me to wait a while because they were scared. I continued watching the videos. There truly was something peculiar going on.

The martyrs' bodies were stitched up in such a way that proved they had undergone some kind of an operation. I wasn't sure whether the families ever verified that their children's organs had been stolen before burying them. I sent the video to a group of friends in Europe and the Arab world so they could follow up on the matter, and I stop working on that issue just before falling asleep on the couch. It isn't enough for them to kill people; they were buying and selling their bodies. Oh my God, how can we live alongside these murderers? How can they walk freely among us? My shaking fits start up again as I think about the bodies of my young adolescent friends and the criminal scalpels of the security forces cutting them to shreds.

....

News of the killing increases by the day. There are many stories of people disappearing and being kidnapped, about the torture of children, stories about prisoners. I sit down to transcribe the testimonies of young men who are barely twenty years old. I record them as they are, in colloquial dialect, because I find this to be fresher than writing them in modern standard Arabic. A female journalist recorded them for me.

The First Testimony

"One time when I was little, they brought a file and told me to write my name and sign. 'What is it?' I asked them. They told me it was for the Ba'th Party, and when I asked them what that meant and why I should sign, they beat me up. We learned we couldn't say anything against the regime. Take the Lord's name in vain, just don't curse the regime. You couldn't go complain, there was nothing you could do. We got older and I went to the army. In the army I learned what a joke we were living. I was one of those planting landmines along the front. And when everything happened on the Day of Return, I was shocked: Where were the mines I put there? I used to tell my friends, don't get close to the mines; turns out there weren't any. How can that be?

"I served in the army. It was awful. When I first started out, the commanding officer at the barracks came out and said, 'Pigs on one side, humans on the other!' The drill was, I'm not serving a homeland, I'm serving one person. Corruption was everywhere, it was shameless. It was always like anyone with connections could get time off. It took seven months before I got leave. There were other people who never showed up.

"I got tortured in prison while I was still in the army. The first time, they needed to get a presidential convoy through and we were moving people out of the way. This old woman walks by and I tell her, '*Yalla* Auntie, move along.' The station chief comes over and beats that 70-year-old woman with a stick. I ask him, 'Sir, why would you treat an old woman like that?' He says, 'None of your business, jackass.' So I tell him, 'When his Excellency the President comes by I'm going to tell him and he'll stop the convoy.' They pulled me out and took me somewhere called the security office. They beat me a lot. I was strapped to a chair while two of them stood over me, beating my chest nonstop. Even Guantanamo would have been better. They put me on the ground and told the guys, 'The one who gets the most hair off his body gets a cigarette'... so they attacked me and started plucking. There was one guy in there with me who had got drunk and cursed the president...before my very eyes they shoved the whip up so far up his ass that when they pulled it out he threw up flesh...he couldn't walk and they broke every bone in his body. Meanwhile, we had all been taken out to the bathroom.

"I got to try 'the tire.' I took 235 lashes on my feet and 250 cracks before the stick splintered on my body. After that I spent a month unable to stand on my feet. I couldn't walk. They took me to the military hospital and I couldn't stand up for an entire month.

"This isn't to boast about how brave I am or how bad I had it. I came forward to complain about the prison guards because the law gives us the right. Later the prison guard came to me and said, 'I'm an officer at the presidential palace, you can't touch me.'

"The second time I was arrested I was still in the army. It was around the time Imad Mughniyeh died. I asked the officer, 'How come everyone wanted by the Americans here ends up dead? Why is that?' He told me to shut up and sent me to jail. That place was unreal. Every time you enter a room there are whips coming at you right and left. They say it's to purify you. I got to try the wooden tire a lot. I was held there for ten days, never allowed to sleep, never allowed to lie down, never even allowed to talk. You had to be naked in there. There was a guard called Issa, who I'll never forget for the rest of my life. He'd say to me, 'You. Come on.' And he'd start beating just to hurt you. He'd come in through the main prison door bellowing, and whenever we heard his voice we all had to turn our heads to the wall. You could never let that guy see anyone wearing clothes. Would you need anything more than that to be against this regime?

"Then came all the Arab revolutions we had been dreaming about. I would say, 'When are we going to smell someone setting himself on fire so that we'll get out into the streets?' Sometimes we'd ask jokingly, 'Does anybody smell burning? I'm just saying.'

"I was arrested on 30 June. The Faculty of Economics demonstration was happening. It was the last day of finals and we were all hopeful that the students were going to mobilize. We demonstrated outside the faculty. It was the peak of defiance because the security could see us but we wanted to demonstrate and raise the banner of freedom despite them. I didn't stay there for long, and when they started attacking everybody fled. I crouched down outside the Faculty of Arts, shouting at my friends. Some people had run away a little before the demonstration, and I was yelling at them to come back. 'Why did you all run away, we weren't that many in the first place, now look what happened, they're turning everything upside down.' I was spotted by security, I mean, the Patriotic Union of Syrian Students as they call themselves. The Union even had popular committees. I know for a fact that it's the Union of *Syrian* Students. Not the Union of Bashar's Students.

"They caught us. My head still aches from the truncheons, the beatings and the curses. What a disaster. They would divide us according to al-'Ar'ur. 'You're all al-'Ar'ur followers, you're all such-and-such.' Five of us were taken to the al-Qanawat station. There was so much killing. They put my friend on the ground and started in on him. Then they brought us over to wipe up his blood with our bare hands. He's a medical student. He left the country and is never coming back. They beat another one a lot just because he's from Hama.

"We were transferred to criminal security. How can I describe for you the horror, the beasts, the heroes? I mean, what is heroism? Is it, like, to beat up some defenceless guy with a blindfold over his eyes and smash his head against the wall? Is it heroic to throw down insults on my mother? They brought us in. One of us happened to be gay, just imagine what was in store...

"There was all kinds of torture. And they had this game called 'electricity' they would play with us whenever we were coming or going. They held it to my friend's neck. He was paralyzed for five minutes. There was interrogation every few minutes, first thing in the morning, at mid-morning, in the afternoon, before and after we ate. Just so you would confess you were at the demonstration.

"I was kept at criminal security for six days, and then they transferred me to political security. The situation was worse there. They took my friends downstairs and I had no idea what they were doing to them, but we could hear their screams up above. It was like a sort of terrorism for us, so that we would confess, you know, that we were there. They brought us each in turn to see an interrogator...and before you could say anything he would greet you with a slap. We got used to being slapped like that, it became a totally normal thing.

"They would start questioning me, beating me the whole time, even though I had already told them I wasn't at the demonstration, that I'm a Druze from Suwayda and we don't have anything but pro-regime demonstrations.

"They brought us to the *Palais de Justice*. We were supposed to spend the night there, but then they sent us to court and we were released straight away. We have a trial on 20 August."

A Second Testimony

"With the outbreak of the events, everything exploded in Dar'a. The events really hit us hard. The idea of a revolt against this regime had been brewing for years. We were all involved in politics and human rights but there was never the space or enough freedom for you to work on it the right way. There are always immediate causes and more distant ones. Dar'a was the immediate cause while the distant ones are well known: Syria, the current situation, the state of tyranny, miserable circumstances and widespread corruption.

"When the events broke out we started building a network and making phone calls and getting in touch with other young people who were involved. We pushed aside what some now call 'the Islamic character of this revolution.' We all worked together, young people well known in their fields; intellectuals and others who were concerned. We mobilized on Facebook, through art and writing. We tried to forge relationships during that period. Of course, Fridays were the day people went out demonstrating. Some regions were easier to mobilize than others. Damascus was an unlikely spot because it was encircled. We had the option of the Umayyad Mosque. We weren't Islamists; I wouldn't even set foot inside a mosque. It just didn't seem like a good idea for me to be going inside a mosque. So we searched for another place, but in the end we were forced to use a mosque because it was the only place that many people were allowed to congregate.

"There was a group working out of Douma who we started coordinating with, and then there was a call for a demonstration in Douma. Some friends and I went and met inside the mosque. It was plain to see that there were a lot of security agents present, foreign faces, they obviously weren't from Douma. The prayer ended quickly, as if the *imam* knew what was happening, he rushed through his sermon. We all went out onto the balcony and saw more than two thousand soldiers – not just peacekeepers, they were fully armed with Kalashnikovs and pistols, and there were two convoys around the garden where the mosque was located.

"Rows stretching out behind them were all *shabbiha*, in addition to the *shabbiha* already inside the mosque. That was the moment of truth – either you come out and don't disappoint the people who are expecting you, or you give it all up and run away because the security forces and weapons are too terrifying. You only have two choices: do the right thing and mobilize the people they way you have come there to do, or run away. We got together and some of us locked arms and started chanting the first slogan, the second slogan, *God, Syria, Freedom, That's It!*, *The Syrian People Won't be Humiliated!*, that's all. Because the *shabbiha* had already organized themselves inside the mosque, they started beating us from behind. They attacked us from the staircase. There were 70 of us outside and some people still hadn't made it out. Others were waiting for us outside. They formed a perimeter to prevent anyone from getting inside the mosque. It was the Great Mosque in Douma and there are other smaller mosques all around there. People were coming to the square outside the Great Mosque in order to start a demonstration.

"They started hitting people with tasers and all kinds of chains, wooden sticks and truncheons. They started beating us from both sides, from behind and from the front. There was only one way out. I remember I tried to get away but the stairs were too far and I couldn't make it. One of them hit me on the head and I fell down. Next thing I know there are ten guys on top of me. One of them squeezes my head and starts pounding me, something like five batons appeared in the blink of an eye. They broke my teeth. It was a savage beating. They threw me out on the street and whenever I tried to get up, one of them would kick me in the chest. They crushed me on the ground. I tried to get away. There were ten of them. Of course not all of them could get to me at once, so they start spitting on me from afar, so much blame and spite, I have no idea where that came from.

The *shabbiha* took me to the security and peacekeeping forces who were standing off to the side. They put me next to the detention buses and started to beat us before throwing us inside. The bus was like a red container on the inside from all the blood. People were so bloodied up it was hard to recognize them. They were all blood. I killed my phone, switched off my SIM card and handed them my mobile. I was in bad shape, I couldn't breath. I was in a lot of pain. The bus could hold maybe 21 people. We must have been about 30. 73 of us were taken to the security branch. Some people had nothing to do with it. They just rounded them up from inside their shops. The arrests were random like that. They were recording us there at the front of the mosque, anyone who went inside was videotaped. Then they would just wait for that person to come back out again.

"The bus was all red. The windows were blood red. We were piled on top of each other. They shut the curtains and took us to the security branch. At the al-Khatib station, there's something called 'reception'. They'll all be standing there on both sides, right and left, and as soon as you enter they start beating you from both sides. I was in really bad shape when I got off the bus, my stomach and my chest. I had been hit a lot in the chest. I couldn't go any further and just fell down. Three guys rush over and start beating me, 'Come on, get up!' I couldn't walk. I wasn't all right. Two guys picked me up, counted to three and then threw me down on the stairs, hard. I make it as far as the entrance. They start clomping on me as soon as I get inside the room. The reception room was big, seven by five metres, the ceiling was made out of tin, not cement. It wasn't a very old room, and it obviously had been painted recently. I'm a painter myself. I could tell. The paint smelled fresh. They must have painted the walls every two days because of the blood that got smeared all over them. When we first went inside the walls were white. Four hours later they were all red.

They started taking names and whipping people with big twisted handcuffs. 'Your full name!' 'Who's this?!' 'Who's that?!' Naturally I got hit more than most because I'm from Masyaf. That's another thing. I'm from Masyaf. Without even asking what my sect is, I get it even worse. After like an hour and a half, an ambulance finally arrives, and of course the EMTs are all security officers, but they're also doctors and nurses. Male and female nurses were rough with us. They showed no mercy.

The worst thing about it was how their treatment methods didn't adhere to any health care norms I'd ever heard of. They'd stitch up a wound with a regular old sewing needle, stitching and making incisions without sterilization. They wouldn't give you antibiotics even if you were very badly injured. For run-of-the-mill injuries they wouldn't give you anything at all. Not even painkillers. Someone had a nervous breakdown and they just left him there off to the side, spasming. He didn't have any visible wounds on his body, but then he started vomiting a lot of blood. Somebody else had been shot. They left him there for three hours before coming to take him to the hospital. My eye was in pretty bad shape and I was losing a lot of blood. Then they'd come and decide who they were going to take to the hospital. Some people nearby pointed at me, saying I needed to go. My chest was so badly beaten I was having trouble breathing. I could hear the sound of my laboured breath. Those people near me got scared and said I was definitely going to die, that I was in really bad shape. It went on like that for seven hours before they finally took me to the hospital.

My Christian friend was in really bad shape as well and he also needed medical attention. They came to put him on the bus but then brought him back because his name wasn't on the list, even though I could see that it was and told the officer as much. 'None of your business,' he said and then smacked me. Later I found out they didn't take him because he was Christian, because he would have exposed their lie.

"They unloaded us in the square outside the al-Mujtahid hospital. They had emptied the square and security was lined up blocking cars from getting to the ambulance entrance. The first one would step out and they took him away, then the second, then the third.

"Then came my turn. They brought a wheelchair for me, sat me down, and five armed security agents escorted me. One of them held people away, a second pushed me along with another in front of me, shouting at people to stay back, that I was armed, that I had killed five security agents, that I was a sniper. It became an inside joke between me and my friends that I was 'the sniper who killed five security agents.' They wheeled me around the hospital just to let people spit on me, saying 'May God curse you, infidel!' 'Infiltrator!' 'Salafi!' I couldn't even lift my hand to tell them they were wrong. When their charade finally came to an end, I deduced why they hadn't brought my Christian friend. Someone might have known that, as usual, 'the Salafi turns out to be a Christian'!

"We entered a private family room with cloth curtains where I laid down on the bed as the beatings continued, only more lightly now. 'Come on then!' The orderly arrives to take my chart, my name. As if I am any ordinary patient, they take my father's name, my mother's name. The officer walks over and tears up the piece of paper. They wanted to turn me into a number instead of a name, so they wrote down John Doe. At this point I had to respond: 'I have a name, here's my ID, look, I'm a Syrian Arab, a citizen just like you, I won't let you or anyone else say I don't have a name.' I got slapped. 'You may talk like that outside, but not in here!' There was no mercy. They could have helped me get out of bed. It was a kind of punishment, they would try to dislocate my shoulder or hit me. They took me to have an X-ray and an MRI. When the eye doctor saw me he told me my eye was pulverized and that I would never be able to see out of it again.

The doctors were a security front. They didn't show any mercy. They treated me as though I were a sniper or a criminal. I couldn't see out of one eye and I didn't know what the point would have been for him to lie to me by saying I wasn't going to be able to see out of it ever again. They wrote me a prescription for some medicine but before we got back on the bus they took it away and tore it up. 'You want medicine you son of a...' I'm a bastard. I don't deserve medicine.

"They took us back to the security branch. There were more people there who looked just like us, some even worse off. There were people from Douma, from al-Hamidiyyeh, from al-Tall, from Dar al-Umawi. We go inside the room and the senior security officer tells me to cover my face when we leave the prison cell and that I am not allowed to see anyone, not the interrogator, not the torturer, not even the path. Once my eyes are covered, he asks, 'What's your name? Your father's name? Your father's Muslim Brotherhood,' he tells me, 'and you're with the armed Jund al-Sham organization.' I start laughing because we had absolutely no connection to religion whatsoever. I tell him, 'Excuse me, if you're accusing me, I'd be glad to respond, but if you're informing me of something, then I simply must plead ignorance.' 'You don't have any rights,' he tells me. I tell him about my father's regular glass of *araq* and how I'm not a believer. At this point, he gets insulted. He tells me to go back, and naturally I was beaten the whole way. Back in the cell they interrogated me like five times. Every time there was whipping and bastinado, their most famous weapons, of course, used with extreme violence. It was the worst. I sit there, a board flat on my back, and they ask me questions. As soon as the question is posed, they start beating my feet with an iron pipe, hard enough to break them. The wounds are still there, some of them have started to bruise. My eye's still black and blue, my teeth are broken, my chest still hurts.

"After five interrogation sessions I admitted I was at the demonstration. 'Why didn't you say so at first?' they ask me. 'You never gave me the chance, from the moment you picked me up you started beating me, you never asked, you just kept beating me, you ask me why, I'm telling you I was at the demonstration, you never gave me the chance, just kept beating me nonstop!'

"Then they left us there like that for another day. Of course the food was nasty. We went on a hunger strike anyway.

"The next day the lectures started. I like to call it 'the intellectual *shabbiha*', those jingoistic lectures we've had to sit through ever since first grade. *His Excellency the president and the homeland and you are the future.* As soon as we went inside everything changed. Suddenly we were traitors, dogs, little boys, brats. In there, it had been just the opposite: *You are the children of the homeland, the children of this land. You are all beloved human beings. There may be some dogs among you. We know who they are, and they aren't going to get away from us. May God preserve his Excellency, the president, and keep him with us. Because he's such a great human being he's going to let you go, there's been an amnesty. Come on then, guys, with our blood, with our spirit, we'll sacrifice for you, O Bashar!* Naturally, we were all coerced – anyone who didn't chant was beaten. I had a problem, though. I couldn't even chant because they had beaten me so badly. They started saying, 'Come on guys, we're your brothers, we only beat you to teach you a lesson.' Then the intellectual lecture begins: all the accomplishments, the democracy that was on the way, the economic liberalization, the sacrifices. 'Just be patient with us and you'll see what we're working on.' They couldn't sleep through the night, as if we were behind them and our demonstrations wouldn't stop troubling them. And when he spoke, whenever he mentioned the name Bashar al-Assad he would raise his voice for us to cheer...but nobody did, so he would stab his finger at us. 'Come on, do it, do it!'

"When he found out I was from Masyaf he really got pissed. I could tell how angry he was from his sarcasm. They deal with you in sectarian terms. 'You're from Masyaf? So you're an Alawite, what's the matter with you, you jackass?!' They didn't treat us like people, more like sects.

"They ask my Christian friend – by the way, I'm sorry, we call him the Christian but he has a name and I'd shout it out to you – 'How did you know about the demonstration?' From *al-Akhbar* newspaper, he says. 'Whose paper is that?' they ask. 'Hizballah.' 'Well I'll be damned, a Christian in Douma comes out with Sunnis and a group of Shi'a, what religion is your God, anyway?'

"After the lecture, they brought us all together and made us sign two pieces of paper with a fingerprint. *Everyone signs this, and it is the intention of everyone who does to no longer participate in any action or to take part in any demonstrations.* We were forced to sign. If you asked what the white piece of paper was, they beat you. *It's your job to sign!* We did and got back on the buses where we were forced to chant. They were all assembled in Douma waiting for us. Afterwards we learned they had formed a delegation in order to go and speak with the president. On the day we were arrested there was a massacre in which fifteen people were killed. There were two snipers, gunfire. The next day when we went out for the funeral. There was a heavy sadness, a black city, a three-day strike. When we reached the square, they unloaded us from three buses so there wouldn't be commotion in the city. They unloaded us and took off right away. As we got off, we watched the bus drive off behind us, and we gathered together to form a demonstration, all of us bloody and broken. *With our blood, with our spirit, we'll redeem you, O martyr! God, Syria, Freedom, That's It!* we shouted in response to those who forced us to repeat their slogans. There wasn't any security. The place was completely empty. There was another funeral the next day.

"The next day my friend came to see me. He had been crying. I thought it was because he believed the Alawites had beaten me up for being sectarian. I told him I wished he wouldn't talk to me like that. It wasn't the Alawites who beat me up. It was the authorities. Then he clarified that he was actually crying because the ones who beat me up were his cousins."

That is the end of the testimonies I made sure to pass along in colloquial speech. I felt they would be truer that way than if they I translated them into modern standard Arabic. I have abridged this final testimony to stand in place of scores of similar ones, and written it in modern standard Arabic. It was completed through correspondence.

There is a strange mood spreading among Syrians. Someone cries when his relatives beat up a friend. It was a kind of counter-mood that created all this violence in the first place.

A Final Prisoner's Testimony

"I was arrested at a demonstration in Arnous Square on 19 May 2011, and held in jail for six days. During the demonstration we carried banners and chanted for an end to the siege of Dar'a, shouting, *No to Sectarianism!* and *Spilling Syrian Blood is Forbidden!* We repeated the Syrian national anthem. Just as they grabbed me I was in the middle of reciting...*venerable souls and a glorious past...*

"The first people to grab me were dressed in civilian clothes, all those itinerant merchants in the market were actually security forces. They grabbed us, beat us up and kicked us. They shoved us into one of the stores and cursed us.

"The shopkeepers were terrified as the security agents shouted, *Thief! Thief!* One shopkeeper helped out by hiding a girl in a fitting room. We were hit violently and furiously. A security unit arrived with the officer who started cursing us. Then they put us on a bus, hitting us the whole time with tasers and iron chains. We arrived at the security branch in al-Maysat, where they also beat us badly. We were blindfolded. If we fell down on the ground they beat us even more, stamping on us until we reached the interrogation room. In the interrogation there were simple questions about how well we knew certain people. Then they would hoist up our legs and violently bastinado us on the soles of our feet. The whole time they frightened us and cursed us. We were blindfolded the whole time. Blindfolded and with my hands tied, they took us downstairs. I walked through the darkness with someone behind me until I ran into a wall and fell down on the ground. They had been giggling all along because they knew I was about to run into it. Then their laughter rang out and they stamped on me.

It was the same deal when I came out from interrogation: beating and kicking and electric prods. We were also blindfolded while we were being taken from one security branch to another. The new branch was on Baghdad Street in the middle of Damascus, but I only learned this later. The same mechanism upon going into interrogation: beating and kicking and curses. There was a young man there with long hair. 'Are you a faggot or what?' they demanded, laughing and making fun of him. They started making him really uncomfortable. We were a source of mirth for them. Even though there were doctors and writers and intellectuals among us, they wouldn't stop insulting us, beating us and kicking us. They stripped us completely naked inside the branch, then put our clothes back on and transferred us to a cell with drug and arms smugglers. They were nice to us for a little while. Then the interrogation began. There were political activists and ex-prisoners in there with us. It was a psychological war, they told us we'd never get out of there, and when we used the word 'reform', they'd beat us even more savagely. I was blindfolded while an officer questioned me. I told them I was a high school student, that I was at the demonstration by coincidence and that I only went out with them because I heard people reciting the national anthem. They beat me even more because they knew I wasn't telling the truth. They wanted to know who had invited me to demonstrate but I didn't give them any names.

They made me lie down on the ground with my hands tied behind my back, my legs bent at a 90 degree angle, and they bastinadoed the soles of my feet, then they placed a tire around them. The interrogator asked me about the political parties in Syria and I pretended not to know anything; I played dumb. He asked me about Facebook and I denied knowing anything about it. After being tortured, I was sent back to the cell. The officer told the prison guard, 'Take him back.' I thought they were going to use electricity. They marvelled at the fact that we were all leftists and secularists. They thought everyone who went out to demonstrate had to be a Salafi.

"My second interrogation was in the hallway. I was kneeling there with my eyes closed. This interrogator was less bright and he actually believed my story. I could hear other people screaming under torture in the adjacent rooms. There were three old men from Douma in there with us. One old man wanted to hand over his son because he was going to march in a funeral. People thought they had to give up their children in order to protect them. When the father handed over his son they arrested him as well. They smashed his son's head against the wall and made him look at his father coming back from violent, utterly brutal torture. Not all the interrogators were Alawites but when they shouted at us, they all spoke with an Alawite accent. Talk in the security branch was sectarian. They all said we must not go out and support the fundamentalist Salafis. They were very annoyed by the demonstration we had in Arnous Square, in the centre of Damascus. People from all different sects had come together alongside secularists.

They made us all sign testimonies, but I hadn't signed mine yet. We knew we were about to be released. They gave us back our cell phones, blindfolded us and we left. While we were leaving we were subjected to the same carnival of beating and kicking and insults. In the bus we remained blindfolded with our hands bound as well, our heads on the floor as we were subjected to the same beating. They started messing with our nerves in the bus, sharply turning corners in to knock us onto the floor. They all laughed as we tumbled down and stood back up again, over and over. When the bus stopped, one of them loaded a Russian Kalashnikov, saying loudly, 'Sir, do we kill them all at once?' We were terrified and they all laughed, saying, 'Get out, you motherfuckers.' As we were leaving they beat us again with unparalleled brutality. At the Kafr Sousseh branch there was a torturer who would hit us with a kind of sadistic pleasure, savagely beating us and then laughing. With each blow he would let slip a little giggle, spinning around in place, then coming back to beat us and laughing out loud all over again. He flayed us with a whip that was like the head of a snake."

8 July 2011

....

Say No to Dialogue Friday

The French ambassador enters Hama and visits a hospital in order to make sure the wounded are receiving treatment. The American ambassador visits Hama as well, and the Syrian Foreign Ministry releases a statement voicing its distress over the visit, declaring that what the ambassador has done is contrary to diplomatic protocol. Syrian television says the ambassador met with *agents provocateurs* in Hama and incited them to violence, while an American spokesman says the Syrian authorities were informed of the ambassador's visit to Hama. The Americans say they support the Syrian people in their transition to democracy. It appears that the regime has failed to find a military or a political solution and has failed to garner the approval of the great powers.

Today there are sixteen dead and scores wounded, some of them in Damascus. Washington decries the response of the Syrian authorities to the ambassador's visit even as hundreds of thousands of Syrians pour out into the city squares. Say No to Dialogue Friday affirms that the demonstrators do not want 'dialogue'. Richard Ford drives around among the protestors. The domestic opposition and the opposition abroad agree there will be no dialogue. Hama is the epicentre of the protest movement.

Sitting there, I pack up my suitcases with everything I want to take with me.

Images of Syrians on television and others on YouTube rush by like a raging flood, shouting full-throated and resounding in a single voice: *The People Want to Topple the Regime!* I sit down to transcribe a recording I received from one of my friends who is a correspondent for Radio Monte Carlo and France 24 and who was with other journalists along the Syrian–Turkish border. Hoda Ibrahim: I mention her name without fear, in contrast with all my other witnesses who remain anonymous in the darkness. I acquired a testimony from her about the time she spent in the refugee camp, and from a young man of the uprising from Jisr al-Shughur, who I'll call M. She spoke with him over the phone while he was up at the Syrian–Turkish border so he could use the Turkish internet.

The Story of Jisr al-Shughur
M. says, "We were going out to huge demonstrations in Jisr al-Shughur, approximately ten thousand people. There were only about 300 security forces. They let us demonstrate because they knew if there were any more martyrs, the demonstrations would only get bigger and then they wouldn't be able to control the area.

While we were demonstrating outside a state security branch in Freedom Square and the post office, a man named Bassem al-Masri was killed. During his funeral, security opened fire on the people in Freedom Square. The people were just chanting slogans and the security requested army backup, which came from Idlib in the form of additional troops from both the security services and the army. When the army reached Jisr al-Shughur they believed they were going to find armed fighters, but they discovered this was a lie.

At the time we were fifteen thousand demonstrators without any weapons. The security forces gave the order to open fire. They were standing behind the army. A number of soldiers fled into the fields while others turned around and opened fire on the security forces. There was a clash between the security and the army, and as the fighting continued the security fled into the fields out of fear. Most of the army sided with the defection: approximately 300 or 350 soldiers. The army was stronger than the security forces and they took control of the area once the security forces had fled to Idlib. There were clashes there all the time and the people welcomed the army and the army joined them.

Along with the soldiers there were three defecting officers. They clashed with the eight security forces that were still in the post office building. Five or six defectors died as martyrs and all of the security forces were killed. The army stormed the building and then the security support forces arrived along with army reinforcements. They pounded the place with gunfire. The defectors sprayed gunfire on the state security detention centre, and the security forces inside said, 'Don't shoot, we surrender!' They handed over their weapons and not a single one of them was harmed, then the defectors went to the military security branch and demanded the security forces hand over their weapons but they refused and there was a clash and gun fighting between military security and the defectors. By the next day there were 170 defectors. We didn't know how many military security forces there were but there were a lot of them. Some of the defecting soldiers and those fleeing Hama, Latakia and Homs joined up with the defected army. The lieutenant colonel Hussein Harmoush was among them, and their numbers grew to between 700 and 800 defectors. They attacked the military security station, took it over and killed whoever was inside. There had been negotiations before that. The defectors told them, 'Come back to the people and leave the regime behind', but they refused to give up their weapons, saying they were going to demolish all of Jisr al-Shughur on top of its people's heads. The lieutenant colonel told them, 'Hand over your weapons or we're going to break into the detention centre.' By that time, the director, Abu Ya'rab, had killed fifteen security agents because they were against all the killing. Their bodies were still inside.

"The defectors broke into the security detention centre and after two days of fighting security forces from Idlib arrived and they clashed with the defecting army in a town called al-Freekeh, seven kilometres outside of Jisr al-Shughur. The defecting army had set up an ambush for the security forces and 120 men were killed. They knew the force defecting from the army in Jisr al-Shughur was large, so they sent 15,000 soldiers and 300 tanks to invade the city along three axes: the Hama axis on the al-Ghab road, the Western 'Ishtabraq' axis and the Eastern 'al-Freekeh' axis on the Aleppo road. At this point the defecting army became concerned about Jisr al-Shughur getting bombed and the risk of a lot of civilian casualties, so the defectors started moving people to the Turkish border and securing a way out for them. One reason why they didn't confront the army as it advanced into Jisr al-Shughur was that the defectors knew that what the regime was saying about armed gangs would be validated somehow if the defectors fought back. They preferred instead to withdraw out of Jisr al-Shughur to the Jabaliyyeh region, just before the Turkish border in the west."

This is the end of M.'s testimony about Jisr al-Shughur, about which we had been getting nothing but distorted news of unexplained killing and gunfire. I still have the last testimony of Hoda Ibrahim to transcribe in front of me. Hoda spent the last two weeks of June along the Turkish–Syrian border, entering Syria briefly and then returning to Antakya.

Hoda says: "I had already entered Syrian territory and was on way back to Turkey, in the village of Ayn al-Baida and the camp at Khirbet al-Jouz. There were nine camps all together. Everyone was from Jisr al-Shughur. Sixty thousand people were living there. Many of them had been forced to flee to Aleppo and other parts of the country, not only along the border. In the Khirbet al-Jouz camp there were two sections: the family section and the men's section. It was mostly men. The families had been smuggled into Turkey. Jisr al-Shughur is seven kilometres from Khirbet al-Jouz.

The young men had set up a media centre I can't reveal the location of, a farmhouse out in the middle of a field to which people risked their lives bringing news and pictures and videos on USB drives from Aleppo, Homs and Hama and from all over Syria. They were only about a kilometre from the border and could use the Turkish internet. The young men of the uprising told me that whenever there was a defection they would inflate the news of the number of defectors and say the siege of Homs and Hama had been broken in order to confuse the regime and steal as much time as possible to get the people out. This caused the regime to send fifteen thousand troops to Jisr al-Shughur. They also told me this was the wrong thing to do because it had a negative impact on the people.

According to the testimonies I heard from the people of Jisr al-Shughur, the people who remained in the city were either imprisoned or killed. They told me about one incident: eleven people on motorbikes, labourers returning home from work in Beirut, came under fire. Three of them were killed and the rest arrested. I had a conversation with one of those who had been taken and he mentioned how they were detained in a sugar factory where they were severely tortured. Everyone was talking about this sugar factory that had been turned into a giant prison for men and children and the elderly."

I stop here for a moment, shivering. The Syrian regime has turned playing fields into prisons, which is exactly what happened in Baniyas, where they turned the municipal stadium into a giant prison; it turns factories into prisons: What savagery. Someone who was released from the municipal stadium in Baniyas wrote something on Facebook describing the brutal treatment he and the people of Baniyas were subjected to there, how they were force-marched and made to walk on top of each other's bodies, stamping on them and kicking them.

Hoda continues, far away from my trembling fingers:

"One person who stayed behind in Jisr al-Shughur during those last days mentioned how the sounds of screaming and torture could be heard echoing throughout the night as far as five kilometres away. I heard a few stories from those who managed to escape the sugar factory without being killed, about people being tortured and one worker who saw two of his friends killed right in front of him. He told me the security forces disagreed with one another about killing him, and they finally let him go after killing three of his friends.

"Around 15 June a rumour got started, saying things had calmed down in Jisr al-Shughur. Some people called up those who had fled to Turkey and told them others had come back to the city now that the army had entered the villages. People talked about how the entire family of Al Qasqous believed this and came back. Every last one of them was killed, men and women and children. But another story claimed that the men and women were killed while the children of this family were arrested. In all honesty, when I got to Syria I met a lot of people who didn't know where their families were. I saw men wandering around alone, who didn't know what had happened to them. I saw women and children who didn't know the fate of their men. It was awful, like an entire world had been lost.

"The Syrians in the refugee camps were living in jail," Hoda said as I continued transcribing:

"They were forbidden from making phone calls, and I saw how fleeing death had caused people to suffer one of the worst possible outcomes; some of those who fled found refuge with their relatives in Iskenderun, and their situation was better than that of those people in the camps. Generally speaking, the Syrian–Turkish border is quite long and the refugees' circumstances varied from place to place. There were so many sad and painful stories. I met a truck driver whose eye had been injured when he got beaten up and whose truck had been torched; they warned him never to come back to Latakia. He used to work between Latakia and Jisr al-Shughur and Iskenderun. I asked him, 'Who threatened you?' 'The *shabbiha*,' he said, 'I don't know who they are, but I don't go there anymore.'"

Hoda said that the driver, Abu Ahmad, remained in the village of al-Rihaniyyeh, selling coffee at a border crossing point.

"We journalists weren't allowed to cross except when the Turks were holding press conferences there. We entered three times.

"The thing that got to me the most was the difficult road we had to cross, stretching five or seven kilometres, in order to enter Khirbet al-Jouz and Ayn al-Baida. Originally the road was only two kilometres long, but we had to loop around it in order to pass through the army checkpoints. It was hot and the road was hard and exhausting. It makes you sad to see such beautiful natural surroundings overlapping with death.

"On 19 June, after the army had moved into those villages, I saw children and women, some of whom were pregnant, walking along the same rocky mountain road. This is what really got to me: crossing this kind of a deadly road could only mean one thing: they were fleeing death or other situations where death was the least of their concerns. We watched the army through our cameras in the village of Guvecci, and noticed they were arguing and disagreeing about something. It seemed obvious that a group of them was in a constant state of disagreement. One young Syrian told me about a horrifying incident, when seven soldiers defecting from the army sought refuge in the village of Ayn al-Baida, turning to an old man for help and asking him to point them in the direction of the road to Turkey. The old man asked them to wait there for a few minutes, and when he came back with security forces, they killed some of them and arrested the rest.

"But what really caught my attention was how many women and children there were. The children were lying on the ground. I saw children wherever I went, and when they saw us they would run toward me to say they didn't want Bashar al-Assad, that they wanted the fall of the regime, and then they would start singing what they had just said. The people informed me that they had captured some of the *shabbiha* in Jisr al-Shughur, but rather than killing them, they let them go. There was someone there who had escaped from Jisr al-Shughur, arriving with iron chains on his hands; he told me terrible things about his imprisonment and torture.

When they handed out food, all the refugees in the camps turned into one big family. In that solidarity I saw a kind of bulwark against death. The water flow dried up and the heat was getting worse. When the water ran out, the camp children drank from the ponds all around them and many of them died as a result. I remember that during my first few days there they started building a camp called al-Rihaniyyeh, but you were forbidden to enter. Ten days later I went back to the camp. It was finished and full of refugees. Turkey was building three other camps, and during our stay in the village of Guvecci we could hear heavy gunfire after the tanks entered the villages. They were combing the villages with bullets. In other villages near Jisr al-Shughur such as al-Zu'iniyyeh and al-Shatouri and al-Sarminiyyeh the army would go in with security forces and snipers, and the exact same thing that happened in Jisr al-Shughur would happen there as well.

"The people told me that many had been executed at the Jisr al-Shughur school after it had been converted into a prison as well. If they couldn't find someone they were looking for, they would arrest the closest members of his family. One man shouted right in front of me in a quavering voice, 'What the Assad clan did in Jisr al-Shughur makes you think they have a personal vendetta against this city!' One young man in the Khirbet al-Jouz camp said,

'There were two young girls who stayed behind in Jisr al-Shughur, they were stripped naked and forced to walk through the streets like that.' Houses were demolished in Khirbet al-Jouz and Ayn al-Baida, livestock were slaughtered. They told me that in the village of al-Sarminiyyeh they took a child, tied his hands behind his back and brought him down into the valley; nobody ever saw him again. They told me there was international Arab silence in the face of the Assad clan's crimes, and that the idea of dialogue with the regime was out of the question.

"The refugees want the fall of the regime. Near the village of Guvecci I saw four families with nineteen children. The children in Hajji Basha would steal glances through the fence around the camp, while a child on the other side would try to communicate with the children inside, but the Turks forbade this. All the Syrians in the camps were hiding under veils, they were thirsty to know what was going on outside of the camps, which had become giant prisons."

Hoda's testimony ends here. I drown in a sadness that is hardly accidental. Bashar al-Assad and his family have turned my people into martyrs and prisoners, fugitives and refugees, prisoners of camps in foreign countries. What more can this criminal do against his own people?

9 July 2011

....

I leave in a few days.

Despite the constant calls of concern from my friends, I am certain nothing bad is going to happen to me at the airport. Yet I am really nervous about the idea of leaving Syria. I convinced myself it was only going to be temporary, a period of time that would pass and then I would come home. The important thing now is for me to save my daughter. I'll give interviews and meet with representatives from humanitarian organizations. I'll communicate to the world what's happening here. They must know that the demonstrators going out to protest are unarmed and peaceful people, and that their demands are for freedom and dignity and justice. So many thoughts run through my mind, but one thing is undeniable: I am living through one of the most difficult moments of my life.

This is the first time I put my daughter first. All I want is to find an agreeable way to make the hardships all around me end. I'll leave my heart here and float away like an empty balloon. Maybe I'll come back soon, maybe not. Leaving now, like this, brings to mind a nursing child yanked away from her mother. I have become a raging storm; I must rise above it and soothe myself. Now I need to transcribe the final testimony I collected from a frightened officer on the run. I don't want to cross the border at the airport with the tape recording in my possession. He told me the name of the neighbourhood they invaded but he trembled as he made me swear on my daughter's life not to mention it. I had understood his fear. He is married with two daughters. He went so far as to shoot himself in a town near Homs, on the edge of the desert, injuring a part of his body he wouldn't let me mention either. He told me he did that so he could go home without arousing any suspicion.

When I asked him whether the stories we were hearing about soldiers being killed were true, he asked, "Do you want to hear my story or somebody else's?"

"I want to hear yours!" I said.

He was a handsome young man from one of the coastal cities, he belonged to the Alawite sect and that was the reason for his fear. I understood his anxiety. In fact, I understood it better than anyone. They would never forgive him if they found out; they would liquidate him at once.

"We got orders to head for the neighbourhood," he said. "Orders to attack an armed gang there. The orders came directly to us. Agents from the air force *mukhabarat* station were there with us. Twenty agents and I went. As soon as we entered the neighbourhood we came under fire. There was a small room off to our left, and even though we were sneaking in under cover of darkness they were able to ambush us. I sensed something suspicious going on. It was the third time they had gone to attack the armed gangs, and suddenly we're caught in an ambush. This always seemed to happen just before Friday. It was Thursday night and we had to be back in Homs by morning to deal with the demonstrators. There was a real battle, a battle of life and death. Every member of the armed gang except for one died. Three of my comrades were killed. Their injuries were all direct hits to the head and chest. Until that moment, the task as far as I was concerned was to get rid of Salafi armed gangs that wanted to kill all Alawites, but several things happened right in front of us. We were sitting ducks for those gangs that always managed to appear and open fire on us wherever we were."

Even more importantly, he added, his veins bulging out of his neck, "Every time we captured someone from that gang the air force *mukhabarat* would take him away immediately. Except last time, one of the prisoners was right there in front of me, he was supposedly a member of the gang, but when he fell into the hands of one of the agents who pointed the barrel of his gun at him, he started crying and screaming and blathering. He peed his pants, and when the higher-ranking officer from the air force *mukhabarat*, whose name I won't reveal, showed up. He took care of him personally and, as he did, someone escorting the officer, a security agent, shot the prisoner in the head, at which point I became certain of one thing: We were just bait. How that happened, though, I have no idea. It seemed we had fallen into a trap, and after seeing our comrades killed by armed gangs we would be even more aggressive with the demonstrators the following day. The whole thing was very strange, like everything they had told us was a lie. I have no idea who the people going out for demonstrations are. We in the army are completely cut off from the outside world, but I knew for a fact the officer killed that prisoner because he was afraid of what he might say. All these things pushed me to shoot myself the following Wednesday. I waited for the gunfire to come raining down on us as we advanced, and that's what actually happened. In those moments when life and death were one and the same, while everyone else was distracted, I opened fire. I've been home now for a month and a half, and I hope this nightmare will be over before I'm forced to go back into that hell..."

As he says 'that hell', something inside of me jolts, because now someone else is uttering the same word I repeat on a daily basis.

Hell...

Hell...

After finishing up his testimony, I continue getting ready to leave.

I'll leave behind a whole raft of small issues.

I'll leave behind my anger at all the intellectuals who remain silent in the face of this killing, at their cowardice and fear.

I'll leave the door in my heart open onto death and open the door of life for my daughter. That's exactly what I am going to do: walk resolutely towards death. Leaving Syria means death and nothing else. It means shedding my skin, casting away my heart and everything I ever wanted to do.

My mind was hazy as I packed my bags, I must have folded my clothes a thousand times. Throwing away everything behind me, letting my daughter walk her own path, hiding inside the night in order to become whatever I want.

For the first time I really must not become what I don't want.

To become whatever I want – such a simple phrase, but it can limit one's life: who among us is actually what we want to be?

Writing these last words I resolve not to return to these pages until I can turn my diaries into a book. I'd never be able to do that in Syria; if I could, I would just stay. I will pack my bags and zip them up, closing along with them so many horrifying secrets I witnessed and that have happened to me. I am afraid for them to be revealed. I am afraid for my family and for my daughter. I know I am panicking, that is an accurate description of what is happening. That's the way I have been throughout the past few months. I have been alone, and more and more I realize just how very alone I have been, how even some of my friends would be willing to walk over my dead body in order to make their loved ones look better.

I don't like to talk about heroic deeds. Heroism is an illusion. Sure, I was panicked, but through that panic I learned how to cultivate a dark patch in my heart, a zone no one can reach, one that remains fixed, where not even death can penetrate. All the trials and torments, which I had once thought worthless, would make me a stronger woman; but they weren't enough to make me the kind of woman who could just calmly go on living while such shameful acts crash down on people all around her. As with every major turning point in my life, and in spite of all my panic, I was positive that if I were to travel back through time I would have done exactly the same thing, even if some serious mistakes that were made from the beginning of the uprising could have been avoided, mistakes that rendered me and what I was doing visible to so many people.

Now I can say, along with so many others:

Fire scalds. Fire purifies. Fire either reduces you to ash or burnishes you. In the days to come I expect to live in ashes or else to see my shiny new mirror.

NOTES

2   Bouthaina Shaaban is a political and media adviser to President Bashar al-Assad who became one of the chief mouthpieces of the regime during the uprising. Shaaban was the recipient of emails from a New York-based public relations guru who advised al-Assad on effective ways to handle his upcoming December 2011 interview with Barbara Walters that were subsequently hacked and leaked to the media.

7   The largest market in Syria, the Souk al-Hamidiyyeh in Damascus dates to the late Ottoman period and is named after Sultan Abdülhamid II (r. 1876–1909).

8   Derived from the Arabic word for ghost, the term *shabbiha* (s. *shabih*) is a Syrian colloquialism that refers to 1) thugs or henchmen who are considered the regime's staunchest defenders and most terrifying manifestations, willing to defend the interests and reputation of the regime against opposition by any means of violence and intimidation; and 2) organized crime syndicates that operate with relative impunity throughout the country, but particularly the "Alawite territory" of the northwest.

12   Bashar al-Assad (b. 1965) is the second child of Aniseh (née Makhlouf) and Hafiz al-Assad and the current President of the Syrian Arab Republic. His older brother Bassel (b. 1962) was the heir apparent to the presidency, but when he died in a tragic car accident in 1994 Bashar immediately cut short his ophthalmology post-graduate training in London and returned to Syria in order to be groomed for military and public service; after Hafiz al-Assad died on 10 June 2000, he acceded to the presidency in July.

13 "J'envoyais au diable les palmes des martyrs, les rayons de l'art, l'orgueil des inventeurs, l'ardeur des pillards; je retournais à l'Orient et à la sagesse première et éternelle." Rimbaud, A Season in Hell/*Une saison en enfer* & The Drunken Boat/*Le bateau ivre* trans. Louise Varèse (New York: New Directions, 2011 [1945]), 70–71. Reprinted with permission.

18 Known as Nusayris, after the eponymous founder of this esoteric Shiite sect, Abu Shu'ayb Muhammad ibn Nusayr al-'Abdi al-Bakri al-Numayri a.k.a Muhammad Ibn Nusayr (died circa 874), until the French Mandate period (1920–1946), the Alawites (also Alawis/Alaouites) are a heterodox offshoot of Shiite Islam, presently constituting approximately 10–12% of the Syrian population. The community in Syria was historically concentrated in the mountainous and coastal regions of the northwest.

21 Saadallah al-Jabiri (1893–1947) was a political notable from Aleppo who co-founded the National Bloc and twice served as Prime Minister of Syria, appointed for the first time by President Shukri al-Quwwatli in 1943. He remained involved in elite Syrian politics until his death in 1947.

21 Shukri al-Quwwatli (1892–1967) was a nationalist politician from Damascus and the first President of Syrian Arab Republic (1943–1949); he became President of Syria again in 1955 and retired from public office in 1958.

22 Kafr Qasim is a Palestinian village located just inside the Green Line in Israel that was placed under Israeli military government along with all Palestinian citizens of Israel from 1949–1966. On 29 October 1956, amid Israeli military maneuvers during the Suez crisis, Israeli border police acting under the command of the Israeli Defense Forces carried out a military strike that killed nearly fifty innocent civilians. The massacre is now officially commemorated as such in Israel. Lebanese filmmaker Burhan Alaouie directed *Kafr Qasim* (1974), a feature film based on the Kafr Qasim massacre.

29 Hafiz al-Assad (1930–2000) was born into an Alawite family in the village of Qardaha in the province of Latakia. After a military career that included flying in the air force and serving

as Minister of Defense in Ba'thist administrations following the 8 March 1963 revolution, Hafiz and a faction of supporters seized power through a "correctionist movement" in November 1970. Over the following three decades, he consolidated power in the executive branch and dramatically expanded the size of the armed forces and the security apparatus. He died in 2000 and is buried in a mausoleum in Qardaha, along with his son Bassel (d. 1994).

33   The *mukhabarat* (also *istikhbarat*) are the intelligence services or secret police. In Syria, the *mukhabarat* are divided into upwards of fifteen divisions, each under a separate personalized command. Under Hafiz al-Assad, the security apparatus ballooned into a force as numerous and more powerful than the national armed forces; manpower estimates are sketchy, but range to as many as several hundred thousand.

38   Rifaat al-Assad (b. 1937) is the younger brother of former Syrian president Hafiz al-Assad and currently resides outside of the country. In addition to heading up the internal security forces and the "Defense Brigades" (*suraya al difa'*), he is most infamous for being one of the commanding generals who oversaw the Syrian military operation against the city of Hama in February 1982 that led to the decimation of the city and the death of more than 15,000–20,000 people.

41   The Ba'th (lit. resurrection or renaissance) party is formally known as the Arab Ba'th Socialist Party (*Hizb al-ba'th al-'arabi al-ishtiraki*) and was founded in 1947 by Michel 'Aflaq and Salah al-Din Baytar, two schoolteachers at the renowned *Tajhiz* secondary school in Damascus who had studied at the Sorbonne in Paris during the 1930s. Inspired by Romantic European nationalism and pan-Arab nationalism, from the early 1960s the guiding ideological principles of the party have been Arab unity, liberty and socialism.

43   Maher al-Assad (b. 1967) is the younger brother of Bashar al-Assad, head of the Republican Guard and commander of the Fourth Armored Division of the Syrian army.

65   The Syrian Arab News Agency (SANA) is a state media organization.

73 A maternal cousin to Bashar al-Assad, Hafiz Makhlouf (b. 1975) is a colonel in the Syrian army, a senior officer at the General Security Directorate and the brother of Syrian telecom mogul Rami Makhlouf.

74 Syrian Vice-President until 2005, Abd al-Halim Khaddam (b. 1932) was forced out of the government and into exile, from where he has been attempting to direct various groups in opposition to the current regime.

80 Fawwaz al-Assad (b.1962) is the son of Hafiz al-Assad's younger brother Jamil al-Assad (1933–2004). The European Union placed sanctions on him in 2011 due to his suspected involvement in organizing and providing material support to the *shabbiha* in Syria.

81 Between the end of World War I and 1922, the Alawite territory in northwestern Syria was ruled under an autonomous administration. Attached to French Mandate Syria in 1922, the French renamed the territory *L'Etat des Alaouites* (The Alawite State) in 1925 and then the *Gouvernement de Lattakia* in 1930 before the province was formally incorporated into Syria.

82 Abu Muhammad ibn Yusuf al-Makzun al-Sinjari (d. 1240) is a minor Alawite folk hero who is said to have traveled from Iraq to Syria in the early 13th century in order to help unify the sect against local Kurdish rivals.

82 al-Husayn ibn Hamdan al-Khasibi (died circa 957–969) was a traditionist – i.e. a *muhaddith*, or transmitter of traditions or sayings of the Prophet Muhammad – as well as the main transmitter of Nusayri tradition after the death of the eponymous founder of the Nusayriyya, Muhammad ibn Nusayr (died circa 874); the Nusayris were labeled extremist Shiites (*ghulat*) who would come to be known as the 'Alawiyya or the Alawites under French Mandate rule (1920–1946).

82 The *Ikhwan al-Safa* (Brethren of Purity) are authors of an eponymous 13th century collection of letters that is an important medieval literary source and thought to have been penned by adherents to Isma'ilism, another esoteric Shiite variant. Their inclusion in Alawite sacred history may be attributable to the erroneous conflation of Isma'ilism and Nusayriyya/'Alawiyya

by Ibn Taymiyya (d. 1328) in a well-known yet highly controversial and sectarian *fatwa* (non-binding opinion) against the Nusayris.

82 Born in the town of Kufa (present-day Iraq), Abu al-Tayyib Ahmad ibn al-Husayn al-Mutanabbi (d. 965) is perhaps the most acclaimed Arab poet of all time.

105 Al-Nakba (lit. the catastrophe) Day commemorates the Palestinian catastrophe of dispossession that accompanied and resulted from the establishment of the state of Israel on 15 May 1948, and the ensuing conflict that led to the dispersion of some 700,000 Palestinians. On 15 May 2011, thousands of Palestinians and Syrians attempted to hop over fences near Majdal Shams in the northern Golan Heights and several people were killed when Israeli forces opened fire.

119 *baltajiyyeh* is derived from an Ottoman Turkish term for "axe-wielder" that refers to hired thugs; it is more commonly used in Egypt and North Africa.

178 It is common in many Mediterranean cultures for intimate family members to address each other reciprocally by the same term, so a mother (Mama) will call her son or daughter "Mama" and a father (Baba) will call his son or daughter "Baba."

179 Jamil al-Assad (1933–2004) was the third brother after Hafiz and Rifaat, who played a somewhat lesser role in politics.

190 Free Virgin Women (*al-hara'ir*) is a term that is derived from the same root as the Arabic word for freedom. The term does not appear in the Qur'an and is rarely cited in compendiums of *hadith* (Prophetic sayings), including the following attested by Ibn Maja (d. 887) in chapter 8 of his *Kitab al-nikah* (Book of Marriage): "Whosoever wishes to meet God in purity should marry a free virgin woman." However, the term appears commonly in Islamic legal and juristic writing (my thanks to Michael Cook for clarifying this). Since the outbreak of the Syrian uprising a women's group loosely affiliated with the Muslim Brotherhood has emerged, calling themselves *al-Hara'ir*.

216 Ibrahim al-Qashoush was a poet and singer from Hama who wrote and performed a number of important protest songs during the first few months of the revolution. His throat was

slit and his body was dumped into the Orontes River in Hama on 4 July 2011.

233 The Day of Return (*yawm al-'awda*) is another name for al-Nakba Day, emphasizing the persistent Palestinian collective and individual rights of return to their homes and their land.

TRANSLATOR'S AFTERWORD

When the first buds of the 'Arab spring' sprouted in Syria, there were many skeptics regarding the prospect for the country to experience peaceful political transformation. Meanwhile, ordinary Syrians rejected the baseless notion that they were somehow incapable or unworthy of the same mobilization, hopefulness and sense of possibility that was sweeping across the Middle East and North Africa. Although sporadic protests took place throughout Syria in January and February 2011, including at least one instance of a man setting himself on fire in al-Qamishli – most likely a direct echo of the iconic Tunisian Mohamed Bouazizi – it was only after several attempts to organize collective "days of rage" demonstrations in February that mass mobilizations were successfully carried out simultaneously in multiple Syrian cities on 15 March 2011.

Over the ensuing months – the first four of which Samar Yazbek evocatively documents in her riveting diaries – the Syrian people sprang into action. During these heady early days, young and old Syrian men and women from across the political spectrum demanded the rights to life, liberty and dignity, building upon previously-existing civil society institutions but also, almost miraculously, organizing themselves into new kinds of affinity groups and associations, which eventually took the form of the local coordination committees. Many activists dared to dream big, envisioning their "Syria of tomorrow" – a post-authoritarian Syria where fear of arbitrary harassment, arrest or worse would melt into the stuff of memory, and some version of direct democracy might become possible.

Syria had been ruled by a single-party regime held together by durable interlocking alliances between the army, the Ba'th Party, the state bureaucracy and – increasingly since 16 November 1970, when a clique surrounding then Defense Minister Hafiz al-Assad seized power in a relatively bloodless coup d'état or "correctionist movement" – a substantial paramilitary force encompassing some fifteen separate divisions of the security apparatus.

In the wake of his brother Bassel's untimely death in a car accident in 1994, Bashar al-Assad, an ophthalmologist then pursuing post-graduate training in London, returned to Syria. Shortly after the death of Hafiz al-Assad on 10 June 2000, Bashar somewhat awkwardly and hesitantly inherited the reins of power. Many Syrians hoped this would be a meaningful turning point in the country's political history as well as in the spheres of economy, society and culture. To a certain extent, this proved to be the case. During the first several years under Bashar al-Assad, Syria witnessed substantial economic growth, apparent political liberalization and gradual cultural opening. However, the so-called Damascus Spring of 2000– 2001 and further attempts to unify forces in the political opposition through the Damascus Declaration in late 2005 were effectively stamped out as Syria found itself traversing more and more unstable local and regional circumstances. Despite occasional proposals to shake things up including the unveiling of a five-year plan based on the principle of a Social Market Economy in 2005 and other minor adjustments, by the late 2000s it became increasingly clear that the regime would only ever condone political and economic transformation in Syria in the guise of gradual reform managed from above.

If the country was in something of an economic and political holding pattern through the late 2000s and early 2010s, Syria was plunged into a tailspin in the winter of 2011 as a growing number of people – informed by concurrent events elsewhere in the region – began to demand constitutional reform and greater public freedoms, including the abrogation of emergency rule, the removal of the constitutional clause securing the Ba'th Party as "the leading party in state and society" and the elimination of other repressive features of the Syrian constitutional, legal and political landscape. Indeed, by the summer the Syrian regime seemed poised to roll out certain constitutional and political reforms that would defang the mobilization that was snowballing all over the country.

As of this writing, however, and more than a year later, Syrians are still struggling to win these basic demands as well as to reclaim their human dignity and some modicum of control over their political destiny. Living in Damascus with her adolescent daughter at the time, Samar Yazbek was among those brave Syrians who instinctively took action in support of the incipient uprising. *A Woman in the Crossfire* will survive as a remarkable documentation of the heady early days of the Syrian uprising, just as the "fear barrier" in Syria was crumbling and new feelings of possibility and hope sparkled in the eyes of Syrians at home and abroad. Here is a moment before it became apparent that the regime was set on exclusively pursuing a military solution that would transform any overt opposition into exogenous terrorism, a time before the conflict became irrevocably militarized. These diaries conclude just as the first defections from the Syrian armed forces started happening. It was from around that point, sometime late in the summer of 2011, that the peaceful popular uprising started to take on occasional tinges of an armed insurrection. More importantly, foreign meddling increasingly militarized the situation, from the Gulf States and Saudi Arabia to more recent attempts at intervention by the so-called "Friends of Syria."

Many now wonder whether the uprising has been stamped out. If the Syrian uprising is quelled, it will be difficult to know where to assign the blame. Disorganization, political immaturity and clashing egos among the various segments of the opposition cannot be simply written off. The skeptical if not outright sectarianist approaches to the question of Syria by many politicians, pundits and analysts certainly did not help. The unwillingness of Western governments and security services to risk coming face to face with "the devil we don't know" also played a part. Whatever the explanation, Syria has been shaken to the core by a conflict that has cost well upwards of ten thousand lives and all but ensures a continuing bloody struggle for Syria to come.

"I don't like to talk about heroic deeds," Yazbek writes. "Heroism is an illusion." Despite her appealing modesty, *A Woman in the Crossfire* indelibly chronicles simple, everyday acts through which she and thousands of other Syrians disprove her statement.

Regardless of how one wishes to characterize her – humanist, patriot, feminist, mother, Alawite – these are ultimately labels with which Yazbek would likely find fault, perhaps by arguing that they can so easily be applied, manipulated or torn off. This is precisely where there still may be some hope, though. The account of herself that Samar Yazbek gives us here as well as the dozens of tales recounted in her diaries offer some means of escape for those who seek to shake off the straitjacket of ascribed identities, be they religious, partisan, gendered, sectarian or otherwise. Despite her very real and visible human fallibility, frailty and fears, Yazbek is not cowed by the seductive dangers of clan, family or sectarian allegiance. Indeed, we do not need her or her interlocutors to claim to be heroic in order for us to honor their heroism. Amidst the rubble of almost unspeakable atrocities in Dar'a, Yazbek salvages "stories of heroism that will be told for generations." Let us hope that the day is not too far off when Syrians will benefit from real political victories as well as the freedom to revel in such legendary tales of bravery.

Translation can be a solitary enterprise; I would not have been able to bear the emotional toll of this project without the support of many people and I would like to single out a few here. Siobhan Phillips and Zaki Haidar flatter me with their generosity of friendship and critical intellectual engagement; I thank them both for reading the translation and offering tough criticism and helpful suggestions. A thousand times thank you to Jean Entine for opening Windy Hill, where I was able to hunker down and complete an early draft. I am grateful to Barbara Schwepke and Harry Hall at Haus Publishing and Yasmina Jraissati of Raya Agency for their professionalism and for offering consistent encouragement throughout this hectic process of rapid-fire translation. Lastly, and most of all, I thank Samar Yazbek for sharing her haunting personal story and for collecting these horrifying stories for posterity; she is an inspiring, courageous and virtuous asset in the nonviolent movement for change in Syria. Although nobody can predict what history has in store for the people of Syria, I dedicate my translation to all those who have given their lives and all those who continue to sacrifice in the name of building a new Syria – glimpsed in these diaries as "the Syria of the future, the free Syria that knew no fear" – where dignity, justice and happiness may flourish.

Max Weiss
Cambridge, Mass.
April 2012

SAMAR YAZBEK is a Syrian writer and journalist, born in Jableh in 1970. She is the author of several works of fiction in Arabic and her novel, *Cinnamon*, is published by Arabia Books in English. An outspoken critic of the Assad regime, Yazbek has been deeply involved in the Syrian uprising since it broke out in March 2011. Fearing for the life of her daughter, she was eventually forced to flee her country and now lives in hiding.

MAX WEISS is Assistant Professor of History and Near Eastern Studies at Princeton University, a historian of the modern Middle East and a translator of Arabic literature.

Forthcoming from Samar Yazbek

Cinnamon
A Novel
Translated by Emily Danby

In the dark of night, Hanan al-Hashimi awakens from a night-mare, confused and shaken. Roaming the house in search of some reassurance, she is drawn towards the streak of light under her husband's bedroom door. Little does she know that the beckoning glow will turn her life on its head, unsettling her fragile mind and sending her servant Aliyah tumbling back to the dusty alleyways of her childhood. Banished from her mistress's villa in the small hours of the morning, Aliyah's route back to her old neighbour-hood is paved with the memories of the family she left behind and the mistress she betrayed. Exhausted by the night's events, both maid and mistress seek refuge in sleep. In their dreams, the women's memories – of troubled childhoods, loneliness, love and their lives together – combine seamlessly to narrate the story of two Damascene women's search for security and tenderness. From the tinroofed shack of Aliyah's family home, to the isolated gran-deur of Hanan's imprisoning villa, the characters' recollections journey through Damascus, painting a portrait of the city in all of its contradictions: poverty and luxury, dormancy and change. Samar Yazbek's quick-paced narrative balances intense drama with the insightful portrayal of her characters' precarious mental states. Bizarre and darkly humorous, yet with clear emotional realism *Cinnamon* is a tale from the inner world of the women of Damascus.

Trade Paper ISBN: 978-1-906697-43-3
E-Book ISBN: 978-1-906697-44-0
November 2012
£8.99/$15.00